Economically Speaking

About the Author

Indira Rajaraman, born in 1947, holds a BA (Honours) degree from Delhi University (1966); MA from Cornell University, USA (1968); and PhD from Cornell University, USA (awarded in January 1974). Prof Rajaraman was a Member of the Thirteenth Finance Commission, whose recommendations covered the fiscal years 2010-2015. From 1976 to 1994, she was on the Economics faculty of the Indian Institute of Management, Bangalore, and from 1994 until her retirement in 2007 she held the Reserve Bank of India Chair at the National Institute of Public Finance and Policy, Delhi.

Economically Speaking

INDIRA RAJARAMAN

ACADEMIC FOUNDATION
NEW DELHI

www.academicfoundation.org

First published in 2016
by

ACADEMIC FOUNDATION
4772-73 / 23 Bharat Ram Road, (23 Ansari Road),
Darya Ganj, New Delhi - 110 002 (India).
Phones : 23245001 / 02 / 03 / 04.
Fax : +91-11-23245005.
E-mail : books@academicfoundation.com
www.academicfoundation.org

Disclaimer:
The opinions/views/findings expressed in this book are solely those of the author and do not necessarily reflect the views of the publisher.

Cataloging in Publication Data--DK
Courtesy: D.K. Agencies (P) Ltd. <docinfo@dkagencies.com>

Rajaraman, Indira, author.
Economically speaking / Indira Rajaraman.
pages cm
"This book is a collection of essays which appeared as a monthly column, with the same title, in the business standard from February 2010 to September 2014, along with those from a monthly column published in Mint, starting in December 2014 and going upto July 2015"--Preface.
Includes index.
ISBN 9789332703087

1. India--Economic policy--1991- 2. India--Economic conditions--1991- 3. Economic policy. 4. Economic history--21st century. I. Title.

HC59.3.R35 2016 DDC 330.9 23

Typeset by Italics India, New Delhi.

Printed and bound by The Book Mint, New Delhi.
www.thebookmint.in

Contents

PART II

PART III

PART IV

PART V

PART VI

If economists could manage to get themselves thought of as humble, competent people, on a level with dentists, that would be splendid!

— John Keynes

Economic Possibilities for Our Grandchildren, 1930

Preface

Economics arouses conflicting emotions in people who are not economists. Among its most die-hard critics, the subject involves a lot of algebraic mumbo-jumbo, designed to conceal the fact that its practitioners really are not competent to do anything useful at all. The very least economists could do, as they see it, is to practise good meteorology and predict the economic weather ahead. If they cannot even do that...what use are they?

And indeed, sorry to say, economists (with a few honourable exceptions) did fail spectacularly to see the coming of the great crash of September 2008. Those of us who practise, think and speak economics, nevertheless continue to think that we have something useful to contribute, even if we have not proved very useful at weather forecasting.

This book is a collection of essays which appeared as a monthly column, with the same title, in the *Business Standard* from February 2010 to September 2014, along with those from a monthly column published in *Mint*, starting in December 2014 and going upto July 2015. These are supplemented by other pieces written by invitation either in the same newspapers or in the *Hindu*. Three appeared in journals rather than newspapers – *Tax Justice Focus*, a quarterly journal of Tax Justice International, an international NGO (non-governmental organisation) in pursuit of the objective implied in its name; *Economic and Political Weekly*, an Indian journal; and *India Review*, a Routledge journal. Grateful thanks are due to all of them for permitting reproduction in this volume.

A column is a response to issues of the moment. And the five years spanned by the column were indeed momentous times. The overarching shadow over the more immediate issue addressed in each piece was the great global crash of 2008, the aftershocks of which continue to rattle us to the present day. That event informs the entire period.

The world remained in a state of shock and bewilderment. In India, after some initial euphoria over the Indian economy having initially emerged relatively unscathed, there was brewing discontent which erupted into major street demonstrations against corruption in 2011. Elsewhere in the world, there were similar large-scale street protests, against corporate greed as in the Occupy Wall Street movement, or against dictatorships in the Middle East. In India, blessed with a strong institutional structure for free and fair elections, the discontent found positive expression in the massive mandate given to the newly elected government formed by the Bharatiya Janata Party (BJP) in May 2014. The columns cover the years leading upto that watershed event, which gave Indians, including those who had not voted for the new government, renewed faith in the virtues of democracy. Subsequent columns cover the initial months of the new government in office, which have seen new policy initiatives on a number of fronts.

The book is an offering to demonstrate the uses that economic thinking can have. Like the column which it is a compendium of, the book is dedicated to the proposition that any live issue of the day, the more mundane the better, can be subordinated to economic examination and logic. Some of the issues are specific to the time at which they were written, and yet carry current consequence because of the manner in which they were resolved. Issues gather insight when looked at in hindsight. Sometimes, it is interesting to contrast the fading interest today in something which riveted attention at the time. Sadly, many warnings sounded years ago remain unattended.

The preamble to each of the six sections into which the book is divided describes the context in which the columns grouped within it were written, and carries figures illustrating the relevant series – real growth rates or inflation as the case may be. The revised value of any magnitude, and clarifications if any, are enclosed in square brackets within each essay.

Policy and legislative updates go upto the Union Budget for 2015-16, which includes accepted recommendations of the 14th Finance Commission for 2015-16. These are inserted in footnotes, or in some cases, an epilogue detailing developments subsequent to the time at which the columns were written. All insertions are necessarily limited in applicability to the time of the update. In order that readers can carry forward their understanding of the issue, weblinks are provided to the original source which carries the data or legislation in question.

In January 2015, the principal macroeconomic indicators – growth and inflation – were shifted to a new base. The GDP (gross domestic product) was shifted to base year 2011-12 from 2004-05.[1] In the past, such shifts have carried a simple linking factor permitting continuity across the break. This time however, the sharp change even in the nominal aggregate at current prices for 2011-12 (the new aggregate is actually lower by 2% than in the old series) does not carry into the nominal aggregates for 2012-13 and 2013-14, which are much closer to the earlier series. A simple linking factor becomes impossible in such circumstances. There is also a shift in the aggregate used for determining real growth rates, to GDP at (constant) market prices, from GDP at (constant) factor cost, as earlier. Until the GDP at constant 2011-12 market prices is carried forward to earlier years, a continuous growth rate series for past years cannot be put together. These technicalities would not interest non-economist readers except in so far as they affect continuity in an important metric of economic performance. Every reference to GDP levels or growth carries a reference indicating the series used.

The CPI (consumer price index) also shifted to an updated base starting January 2015. This shift, dealt with in the preamble to the section on "Inflation and Monetary Policy", does carry a linking factor to the earlier series, so that inflation rates within the old series, and levels in the index across the divide, can be spliced and rendered continuous.

The period over which this column appeared was dense with legislated enactments. A very useful source for these is the website of the Parliamentary Research Service (PRS), which during its decade of existence has filled in the void of publicly available information on the functioning and enactments of Parliament.

1. GDP, the principal metric of economic performance, is issued quarterly and annually as press releases by the Ministry of Statistics and Programme Implementation. These, and the release calendar are obtainable on its website *http://mospi.nic.in/Mospi_New/site/home.aspx*

The essays are grouped into six sections. The entries in each section are ordered not chronologically but by thematic content, with a brief description of each in the preamble.

The first section, "The World and India", groups together columns on the global policy ferment that followed the great crash, as events unfolded in 2010 and subsequent years. The remaining five sections have a purely India focus.

"Institutions and Governance" is on how the everyday processes on which we all depend for our survival require that the delivery mechanisms be well designed. It is here that economic thinking is potentially most useful. The section begins with an essay on corruption, and the centrality of inadequate attention to the issue of election funding. Subsequent essays deal with major national debates provoked by reports of the Comptroller and Auditor General (CAG).

"Centre and States" is on the fiscal relationship between the Central government and states in India. The cohesion of the Indian federation depends critically on statutory fiscal flows from Centre to states, protected from politically partisan interference. These statutory provisions are prescribed by finance commissions, independent bodies of experts required to be set up afresh every five years under Article 280 of the Constitution. The report of the 14th Finance Commission was issued in the public domain in February 2015. A summary of its recommendations is carried in the section.

Finance Commissions remain a well-kept Constitutional secret. During my membership of the 13th Finance Commission, people looked puzzled when I responded to their queries about what I did, and typically asked which finance committee I was referring to. So my early columns energetically addressed what I thought of as a lapse in public consciousness, and covered the many areas addressed by the Commission affecting all aspects of our daily lives. These included, in the case of the 13th Commission, an attempt to improve fire safety response in urban areas, where disastrous fires with high mortality rates are a sadly routine feature of living.

Following on from the fiscal links between Centre and states, "Budgets and Taxation" is on policy issues at the Centre, viewed from a number of angles. The section is updated to include measures introduced with the Union Budget presented in February 2015 for the year 2015-16. The annual presentation of the Union Budget, usually at the end of February but sometimes delayed because of elections at national or state level, are examined very closely by the media, with invitations to economists to speak and write on the event both before, in terms of their expectations, and after. The section begins with a piece advising against the practice of examining each Budget as a stand-alone fiscal statement, and in a capsule summary of fiscal history since 1996, demonstrates the need to look ahead at looming fiscal threats. Among these is the current threat in 2015 of the Seventh Pay Commission, for which no fiscal buffer has been built, despite repeated calls sounded in these essays. Other pieces look at the perverse incentives in the direct tax structure, and at compliance costs in terms of harassment and anxiety faced by the honest taxpayer. Two comments, on the Union Budgets of 2010 and 2012, are included, capturing as they do, the fiscal deterioration during that time. Fortunately, an effective course correction in 2012 put the fisc back on track. Two concluding essays deal with the continuing (in 2015) attempt to introduce a uniform non-cascading indirect tax structure that will wash away within-country tax barriers to the flow of goods and services and the attempt to move public debt issuance away from the Reserve Bank of India (RBI).

"Inflation and Monetary Policy" comments on the rising food and overall inflation during the period covered by my column, accompanied by a sudden crash starting April 2012 in the rate of GDP growth to what by the earlier GDP series was eight consecutive quarters of sub-five per cent growth (with just one exception), after nine years at an average rate of 8.3 per cent. [This was by the earlier GDP series; the new series changes the picture.][2] It was a jarring end to a spectacular growth run, and had devastating effects on asset quality in banks. The

2. These growth rates have been altered by the new series. The annual growth rate in 2012-13, the first sharp slowdown year, has gone up from 4.5 per cent in the old series (at constant factor cost) to 5.1 per cent by the new series (at constant market prices). The rate for 2013-14 stands revised sharply from 4.7 per cent in the old series, to 6.9 percent by the new series (at constant market prices). A tabular comparison of all these changes is at the end of the preamble to the section on "Budgets and Taxation", which is where the switch in GDP measurement really matters for the essays written with reference to the old series.

issues covered in this section range very widely, from the need for well-defined annuity-yielding financial instruments posing an attractive alternative to gold, or a fair income stream to surrendered agricultural land, to transmission of monetary policy through the banking system. Some of these suggestions have been heeded in the Union Budget for 2015-16, which offers a three-pronged, but unfortunately somewhat flawed, strategy to monetise gold.

The supply-side obstacles feeding into food inflation are dealt with, as are any signals of attention to the issue in official policy statements. Exploring the source of the combination of stalled growth and persistent inflation, the fundamental cause is traced back to the failure of the Indian reforms in 1991, in not having addressed structural imperfections in factor markets for land and labour.

The sixth and final section, "Reforms, Inequality and Growth", deals with the further impact of the flawed design of the Indian reform programme in terms of the unequal distribution of the gains from reform. This was an intellectual failure on the part of the fathers of Indian reform, not an implementation failure. Correct economic thinking is so very important.

There were classificatory questions surrounding which section to assign some of the essays. This was a natural consequence of each having been written to investigate structural underpinnings of the headline issue, trying to bring out connectivities across the seemingly unrelated. For example, an essay on measures in a Union Budget addressing supply side barriers propping up food inflation, will be found in "Inflation and Monetary Policy" rather than in the fiscal section. An essay in the section on "Reforms, Inequality and Growth" focuses on the damage resulting from separating elite institutions granting engineering degrees from diploma granting polytechnics.

Each piece in *Business Standard* was capped at a thousand words, a limitation I rather enjoyed. It demanded that the message be economically conveyed, and thereby justified the title of the column. The supplementary pieces added on were not constrained by so tight a word limit.

But most of all, what each column has, as its concealed objective, is to show how an economist looks at an issue and hopefully, the clarificatory value of thinking in that way. Without wishing to engage too strongly in pedagogical mode, there is a continued attempt in all the pieces to connect to economic theory and empirics. References to academic literature are kept to a minimum, since this book is not exclusively targeted at those aspiring to be academic economists. References to reports and policy documents are more liberally provided for readers wishing to follow up, and links are provided to websites for those interested in investigating further the issues raised or the numbers cited. In this way, the book should prove useful to the vast army of new entrants into the labour force, looking for economic elucidation on their journey towards skills and jobs. The essays are all embedded in the Indian institutional context, but aim at providing a link between the structures in place and the analytics of what their design is meant to do, or winds up doing. There is a continued attempt to focus on structural analysis of decisions and their consequences, rather than on personalities of the decision-makers themselves, which alas is all too common a feature of common policy discourse.

My thanks to the *Business Standard* which hosted most of the pieces in the volume, and for the cordial relationship I enjoyed with the two editors who spanned the nearly five-year period of my engagement with the newspaper – Sanjaya Baru and Ashok Bhattacharya. Shivam Saini was my immediate editor, and dealt gracefully with my protectiveness towards my prose. Grateful thanks are due to Anil Padmanabhan and R. Sukumar, editors at *Mint*, for permission to include essays first published there. During some of the time, until July 2012, I was teaching in a visiting capacity at the Indian Statistical Institute (ISI), Delhi; and starting August 2011, I was a member of the Central Board of the RBI. I benefited from professional interactions with colleagues in both settings. My daughter and husband made important suggestions from time to time as critical readers. Pooja Singh Mehta taught me the intricacies of document preparation.

It is a particular pleasure to thank Academic Foundation, founded by Dr Uma Kapila, a revered teacher of many students at Delhi University including myself. Their young and expert team of editors made preparation of the manuscript an enjoyable experience.

Policy is about laws, as enacted by the legislature, as interpreted by the judiciary, and as implemented by the executive. The essays in this collection focus on the design of policy. The recommendations in these essays have in many cases been implemented in subsequent policy initiatives; these are marked in footnote and epilogue updates. Nothing can be more gratifying for a policy analyst. If these writings make plain the analysis underlying those recommendations, they will have served their purpose.

Part I

THE WORLD AND INDIA

There are 11 essays in this section, most, though not all, reflecting on the changed world after the great crash of September 2008. It was a time when old orthodoxies in macroeconomic management were being challenged.

"Regulating Capital Flows" appeared on New Year's Day in 2011, and looks at the altered stance of the International Monetary Fund (IMF) towards capital controls, formally announced by the then Managing Director, Dominique Strauss-Kahn, towards the end of calendar year 2010. This was a major change, permitting as it did a measure of control towards resolving the impossible trinity of free capital movements, a stable exchange rate, and monetary policy autonomy, and the fact of its endorsement by the IMF gave it the legitimacy with which to confront the wrath of market fundamentalists. This position has been subsequently endorsed by Christine Lagarde, who succeeded Strauss-Kahn as managing director.

"Lessons for the G-20" was written in July 2010, at a time when the world was feared to go into a double-dip recession, a fear that was soon realised fully in Japan, in the form of a mere single quarter dip in the United States, but followed in 2011 by the Eurozone with an extended dip into negative territory. The piece deals with a world that, confused and worried by the debt implications of calls of the G-20 for a concerted fiscal stimulus, was looking for higher revenues through sanctioned routes, such as the taxation of windfall mineral profits, so as to turn the stimulus into more of a balanced budget expansion than a debt-financed one. That search for fiscal revenue, and the fear of the knife-edge alternatives between austerity-driven recession and Greek-style laxity-driven financial collapse, continues to the present day. There was also serious attention paid to those countries that had displayed greater resilience in the face of the crisis, and reorganised their financial regulatory apparatus, as in the United Kingdom for example, where the function of banking regulation was restored to the Bank of England from the Unified Financial Regulator. Some other headline fiscal initiatives taken in those early post-crisis days, such as the Resource Super Profits Tax in Australia, took their political toll and had to be reversed. The Tobin tax on international currency flows remains a distant dream.

"Reform of the International Monetary System" was a response to the 2011 report by the Palais Royale, a self-appointed group of 18 members drawn from the G-20 countries including India and China, and driven by past managing directors of the IMF, on deficiencies of the international monetary system that had led to the 2008 crisis. The new international financial architecture recommended in the report has been largely disregarded, with dissipation of the initial cohesion of the G-20.

"The Queen's Finest Hour" deals with what was surely the most prized comment on the global crisis, made on a formal royal visit to the London School of Economics (LSE). She asked why economists had failed to see the crisis coming. That question continues to hang over all of us uncomfortably in the air. Why indeed are economists so wise after the event, but rarely before?

The next essay deals with the new Financial Stability and Development Council in India, in line with the momentum of G-20 towards greater tightening of country-level financial regulatory systems, carrying in the Indian case the possible merger of banking with other financial regulation. If there is a single salutary lesson from the global crash, it is that there is no single regulatory prescription with universal validity. What works in any country is a function of its history, and institutional cultures that have developed over time. At the time that essay was written, a Financial Sector Legislative Reforms Commission was announced, which has since delivered its report in 2014. The recommendations of the Commission will not be repeated here, but there have been moves both to unify regulation to reap the efficiency advantages of synergies, and separation of regulatory authority in other spheres with, in the view of its critics, a consequent loss of synergies. The debate continues, and the recommendations are yet to be codified in legislation.

"Tax Competition" is a review of a vexed issue in this day and age of hunger for fiscal revenues – the competition between sovereign nations to attract footloose capital by a race to the bottom in terms of taxation of capital income. The debate rages on. Global co-operation is needed for any agreement to work, which has to include tax havens within its rubric. Such a possibility is not even distantly visible on the horizon so far.

"November Blues" examines the call for fiscal resources again as the single unifying factor across both the immediate growth requirement, and the longer-term environmental sustainability concern. It is connected to the next piece on the global consequences of the tsunami-induced nuclear catastrophe at Fukushima. In particular, the rise in the price of fossil fuel which followed, fed relentlessly into Indian inflation until its decline in the second half of 2014.

"Minimum Wages" comments on an event involving the expulsion of an Indian diplomat from the US. "The Economic Vision of Margaret Thatcher" was written on the ocassion of her passing, in April 2013. Although not a trained economist herself, she had deep convictions about the design of the economic system. Finally, "The Volatile Price of Oil" is on the price of a universal intermediate that, to this day, defies predictability.

1

Regulating Capital Flows

The year 2010 marked a dramatic change in the stance of the international policy establishment towards capital controls in emerging markets, where I use the term not in the sense of differences between countries in levels of restriction, but in the sense of imposition of (renewed) controls in countries which had previously liberalised their capital account regimes. The term 'regulation' is more appropriate for these reversals, but I will continue with the term capital controls, since it is still used and much of the emotion surrounding it happened when it had that name. So the term capital controls here refers to going into reverse gear on capital account liberalisation.

The change in the international stance on capital controls in 2010 was marked by the G-20 communique after the Seoul Summit in November 2010, and in the statement by Dominique Strauss-Kahn at the Shanghai meeting of International Monetary Fund (IMF) in October, both of which endorsed capital account management among permissible "carefully designed macro-prudential measures". These are big signals, even if they merely mark recognition of what countries facing the newest round of capital surge that started in mid-2009 have been doing anyway, starting with Brazil.

Prior to 2010, for a period of 12 long years, capital controls met with outright hostility and condemnation, dating back to 1 September 1998, when Malaysia imposed capital controls in what had been the most famously free capital account regime in the developing world. Malaysia gained current account convertibility status under Article 8 of the IMF as far back as November 1968, in a brazen display of export confidence. Then, in 1973, the Malaysian ringgit went into a full float, along with the dollar, pound and yen. It was a status no other developing country currency had attained, or even dared aspire to attain.

That record of early commitment to borderless capital flows was abruptly reversed in 1998. Capital controls had earlier been imposed in other countries. Colombia had unremunerated reserve requirements on capital inflows from 1993 to 2000, and even Malaysia temporarily restricted an inflow surge in 1994. The difference was that those were controls on entry, but the 1998 Malaysian move controlled exit. This was immediately condemned as an egregious abuse of sovereign power, and a violation of international trust. But what Malaysia did was not extreme. It was a carefully calibrated move designed to give Malaysia the space to lower interest rates without precipitating an outward stampede of capital. For non-resident capital, there was no ban on taking out profits and interest. It was only the principal that was incarcerated within the country. After six months, the ban was converted to an exit levy, and after another six months the levy was reduced to 10 per cent on capital gains alone; later further reduced to a levy on capital gains only on capital that had been in the country less than a year. By May 2001, all controls had been fully lifted (controls on exit of resident capital were however retained for a longer period).

This was not a story of irresponsible monetary policy at all. It enabled Malaysia to recover from the East Asian crisis with far less macroeconomic pain than other countries in the region. And it was clear that Bank Negara was continually calibrating controls to the need of the hour, removing them when no longer required.

The international reaction was swift and broad-banded so as to condemn all controls of any kind on foreign capital, at the point of entry or exit. To the basic lesson for developing countries that capital account liberalisation gave access to capital at lower cost and was therefore good for them, a corollary was appended, that such liberalisation must be monotonic at all times. The only permissible direction in which the capital account regime could go was towards liberalisation, without reversals of even a temporary kind along the way. There was no formal justification for this monotonicity requirement and no empirical support. On the contrary, Malaysia offered a clear case of a country that had worked its way out of the East Asian crisis by disregarding monotonicity.

Any country worried about its international reputation was compelled to abide by these rules. Thus it was that when capital inflows into India quadrupled over the period 2004-2008, regulating the inflow of capital was not seen as an option. The Reserve Bank of India (RBI) had to purchase the dollars surging in to prevent the rupee rate from appreciating wildly as it would otherwise have done, and to sterilise the rupee inflow from the continued dollar purchase. This task was managed well, albeit at huge fiscal cost. What also helped was use by the RBI of its role as a banking regulator to prick a potential asset bubble in its infancy.

Two other countries did dare to flout the rules at the time. Colombia re-imposed unremunerated reserve requirements on inflows during 2006-2008, and Thailand did too. In a recent paper, Kevin Gallagher[1] and David Coelho assess these actions for their effectiveness, set against the background of a panel of neighbouring countries in each case. The results of all such empirics are necessarily context-specific, since the kinds of capital control used, their timing and duration, all matter critically for success of the initiative. But the results of this and other studies show that temporary restrictions do help monetary policy autonomy, can control the composition of inflows in desired directions, do help stabilise the exchange rate, and do help to regulate the pace of inflows.

The 2010 official benediction means that countries facing a capital surge can now consider capital controls without fear of blotting their good conduct book. This augurs well for the poor in these countries, who face the brunt of macroeconomic volatility.

1. A subsequent stream of papers from Kevin Gallagher updates and expands the particular paper under reference here.

2

Lessons for the G-20

There is a dreaded spectre among the G-20 today. It is the alphabet W. Not pronounced Dubya, it stands for double-dip recession. The reach of this fear has shaped the kinder, gentler treatment given to British Petroleum[1] for what has to be one of the greatest environmental crimes of all time.

At a conference held in Ottawa at the North-South Institute in June 2010, a few weeks before the G-20 summit and leading into it, an attempt was made to gather together lessons from individual country experiences, in terms of regulatory strengths that lend resilience and reduce vulnerability to negative external shocks.

The first and most robust lesson of the deliberations was that no single institutional support system is guaranteed to work everywhere. Just a week after the conference, the new government in the United Kingdom fulfilled a campaign promise and restored the task of overseeing the regulation of banks, building societies and insurance companies to the Bank of England. The Financial Services Authority (FSA), the independent unified financial services regulator created 13 years ago, was excoriated as an experiment responsible for 'the most spectacular regulatory failure'.

In complete contrast to the UK experience, Canada ascribes its own remarkable resilience to the independent (located outside the Reserve Bank of Canada) and unified regulator, the Office of the Superintendent of Financial Institutions (OSFI). Although OSFI in its present unified form dates back only to 1987, the much longer history in Canada of independent regulation of banks and other financial

---

1. This was a reference to the marine oil spill which began in April 2010 in the Gulf of Mexico, the largest such accidental spill in history with an estimated total discharge into the sea of 4.9 million barrels.

entities might have been what made the difference between Canada and the UK. Paradoxically, the move in Canada towards independent bank regulation was the result of bank failures in the 1920s, reinforced by another round of bank failures in the 1980s. The prudential norms of OSFI as the home country regulator are among the reasons why Canadian banks, despite being heavily internationalised, remained relatively immune to practices in risky host countries like the United States. In a globalised world, a country goes blindly with global fashions only at its own peril. This was an uncomfortable lesson for some market-thumping fundamentalists, but it needs to be driven home.

The second robust lesson is that asset market regulation matters critically. The Canadian market for asset-based securities was so comprehensively regulated, that there was no scope for the kind of toxic build-up in the US. The Governor of the Bank of England now chairs a new Financial Policy Committee with a broad mandate to stop the "dangerous build-up of credit or asset bubbles". Quite a change from the days when central banks were advised to keep to their knitting, and not look at asset markets.

An asset build-up in India was expertly steered away by the Reserve Bank of India (RBI) in the years just before the great crash, at a time when it was still deeply unfashionable for central banks to meddle in asset markets. The document Guidelines on Securitisation of Standard Assets, issued by RBI on 1 February 2006, has become rightly renowned in central banking circles for its definitional clarity with respect to the various types of securitisation exposures for originating banks, and the prudential capital required in each case. The Indian asset bubble was thus contained at an early stage.

In terms of developments currently under way, there is a discernible move to appropriate rents for the exchequer to fend off W while still rolling back some of the fiscal loosening of the past two years. The leader is Australia, which unveiled a draft for a Resource Super Profits Tax (RSPT) on 2 May, a surprise move in a country that was actually relatively unscathed by the crisis. A tax on economic rent, defined as the excess of total sale value over the sum of the supply prices of all inputs going into that sale, does not distort production or investment decisions, and therefore enjoys the support of economists on efficiency grounds, quite independently of distributional considerations. Clearly, the RSPT will encounter fierce opposition from mining interests,[2] but as world growth gets underway, the price pressure on resources will increase, as will the pressure to appropriate those profits for the State exchequer.

In most countries, minerals are owned by the state, which issues a licence for their extraction. The state is thus fully justified in appropriating the rent from the activity. At the same time, rent extraction for the exchequer must not be so predatory as to deny to the mine developer a fair return on exploration and development of the mine (what Alfred Marshall termed quasi-rent).

The search is on for levies from other unearned economic rents. The British one-time windfall levy of 50 per cent on bank bonuses in excess of £25,000 enjoyed wide public support, and earned the exchequer £2.5 billion. However, the bank levy imposed by the new government on 22 June 2010 is not on windfalls. It is more designed to discourage short-term risky borrowing by banks, relative to customer deposits or longer-term debt. Levies of this kind, if successful in the behavioural change targeted, will not yield much revenue.

There remains a need for big non-distortionary revenues that will close the fiscal gap while still staving off W. It now appears likely that a financial transactions tax, at a small rate on currency transactions estimated at $3.5 trillion a day, will actually be implemented. First proposed by James Tobin in 1972, its revenue-generating and volatility-dampening properties now appear likely to win the day.[3]

2. Mining lobbies responded to the initial May draft by removing Kevin Rudd, the prime mover of the tax, as Prime Minister in June 2010, well before its scheduled rollout on 1 July 2012. The skeleton parameters suggested for the RSPT were a 40 per cent tax on super profits from all mineral resource extraction, defined as post-tax returns in excess of the yield on 10-year government bonds. This was to be accompanied by a phased reduction in the corporate tax rate to 28 per cent, along with a promise of infrastructure development by the state in the resources sector. A replacement Mineral Resource Rent Tax (MRRT) was introduced on the scheduled date of 1 July 2012 at a lower rate of 22.5 per cent, but the MRRT itself was finally repealed in September 2014.

3. The prospects of a Tobin tax have receded markedly since that optimistic forecast.

3

Reform of the International Monetary System

The Palais Royal Initiative[1]

The Palais Royal Initiative was a self-christened group of 18 formed in September 2010 to diagnose the great collapse of September 2008, and prescribe directions for reform of the international monetary system. Led by Michel Camdessus, Tommaso Padoa-Schioppa and Alexandre Lamfalussy, the group advanced a set of 18 suggestions in their final report. That report along with a selection of background materials, supplemented by papers from other invited commentators, together make up this volume.

A frank introductory sentence by the three leaders of the initiative is worth quoting in its entirety: "The crisis that engulfed the global economy in 2008 caught most experts and policy makers by surprise, bringing to light a number of 'hitherto unnoticed vulnerabilities'." All three leaders were major figures in either executive or advisory capacities in the high world of international finance before and during the crisis. Camdessus was managing director of the IMF during 1987-2000, and honorary governor of the Bank of France at the time of the crisis in 2008. Padoa-Schioppa was chairman of the Ministerial Committee of the IMF (IMFC) during 2007-08. Lamfalussy was Director General of the Bank for International Settlements during 1985-1993, and a key architect of the financial services regulatory structure adopted by the European Union (EU).

Although the report of the group does wear the abashed air of leaders caught fiddling while the world built up to the 2008

1. This review of Jack T. Boorman and Andre Icard (eds.), *Reform of the International Monetary System: The Palais Royal Initiative* (Sage: 2011) appeared in the *Hindu* newspaper.

conflagration, only one of the papers, by senior IMF staffer Jack Boorman (an editor of this volume), frontally addresses the issue of why some vulnerabilities remained unnoticed, even from key vantage points. What about the vulnerabilities they did notice? The leaders do not document their attempts to reform the system from within, and where the obstructions to reform lay. The Palais Royal initiative admittedly set for itself the brisk task of getting on with the task of reform, and was not cast in memoir mode, but in fact the latter might have served better to underscore why the reforms needed, even when clearly known, never happened.

The 18 suggestions for reform are grouped under four objectives. The first objective is stronger IMF surveillance. However, the tighter surveillance norms suggested are confined to conventional macro indicators and do not cover fresh ground. It is only one of the invited papers, by three Munich-based academics Hans-Werner Sinn, Teresa Buchen and Timo Wollmershauser, that places financial sector prudential regulation squarely at the forefront of reform.

The second objective is to foster exchange rates broadly in line with global balance and country fundamentals. The suggestion that the IMF should develop globally sustainable exchange rate norms is fraught with national sovereignty issues. Whose deviations from the norm would come up for examination in the first place, and how would correction be enforced? The power imbalance between nations underlying the global crisis comes to the fore here again.

The third objective is to ensure adequate global liquidity. The suggestions in this section do cover fresh ground. The unilateral use of capital controls by member nations to prevent disorderly exchange rate movements or financial instability is sanctioned, reflecting no doubt the influence of Dr Y.V. Reddy who was a member of the Palais Royal Initiative. It is further endorsed in an invited paper by the French academic, Michel Aglietta.

The fourth and fifth objectives, having to do with the international numeraire currency in trade and finance, and with governance of the international monetary system, are the key reform directions needed. Two papers – one by group member Xiaolian Hu, a former Deputy Governor of the People's Bank of China, and an invited paper by Pietro

Catte – chart a way by which the SDR (special drawing right) could develop into an ICU (international currency unit), usable as both a unit of account and a medium of exchange in international trade and investment. There is however a counter paper by Peter Kenen, also a member of the group, who reckons that the SDR can at best become the principal reserve asset.

The report proposes a three-tier architecture for better governance of the international monetary system. The key middle tier proposed is a Council of Finance Ministers and Central Bank Governors, which will merge functions of the present IMFC and the G-20. Implementation will be done by the third tier of Executive Directors. There are supplementary suggestions for inclusion of other individual and institutional voices.

Padoa-Schioppa tragically died in the midst of Palais Royal deliberations (the volume is dedicated to his memory). He was advisor to the prime minister of Greece at the time of his demise. Greece and the world remain mired in the search for solutions.[2]

2. The Greek connudrum continues even after January 2015 when, faced with the recessionary consequences of fiscal austerity in Greece and the consequent political developments, the European Central Bank finally took the decision to incorporate quantitative easing in the form of a Eurozone programme for the purchase of Greek bonds.

4 The Queen's Finest Hour

The final moments of the Queen's Diamond Jubilee in June 2012 have been described as her finest hour.

But her finest hour really happened some years earlier, in November 2008. She was on a visit to the London School of Economics (LSE), her first visit to that august institution and the first by any British monarch since her grandfather laid the foundation stone of the building in 1920. The London School is a 20th century institution, founded by left-leaning anti-establishment scholars, who wished to provide an alternative academic centre, more grounded in reality and less weighed down by the baggage of classical economics than the hoary old universities of Oxford and Cambridge.

On her visit, the Queen asked a question of Prof Luis Garicano of the school. It was not a televised moment, so there are varying versions of her exact wording. She either said, "Why did nobody notice it?" or "How come nobody could foresee it?" Maybe she asked both questions.

The event she was referring to was of course the great financial crash of mid-September 2008. Her clear treble rang out and found resonance in realms well beyond the cramped quarters of the London School, itself a mark of the wish of its founders to locate intellectuals in the midst of the real world rather than in more abundant and verdant acres.

In asking her question, the Queen was giving voice to the voiceless multitudes affected at the time, and it remains tragically and staggeringly relevant today. The recession in the United Kingdom, and the unsustainable debt burden of Greece, Spain and Italy, all derive their ancestry from that financial tsunami which swept the world, compounded of course by subsequent errors. Not to mention the devastating impact of that event on growth and poverty reduction in the developing world.

The immediate response by Prof Garicano sidestepped the issue. In his own words, he confesses to having said:

> I think the main answer is that people were doing what they were paid to do, and behaved according to their incentives but in many cases they were being paid to do the wrong things from society's perspective.

But that was not what the Queen had asked. Her question was not why the event happened, but why economists could not see it coming. If there was a problem of misplaced incentives, why could economists not see it and warn of its consequences, was what she wanted to know. Unlike a persistent student in the classrooms of the LSE, the Queen could not pursue the point. She is constrained by the terms of her office from saying or doing anything controversial. But her question hung uncomfortably in the air.

Eight months later, a formal response was sent in writing to the Queen, signed by her most obedient servants Profs Tim Besley and Peter Hennessy. The letter reports the conclusions of a forum convened in June 2009 by the British Academy to answer her question. As might be imagined, there are denials and prevarications in the letter. It says: "Many people did foresee the crisis." That is just plain wrong. In the years leading up to the crisis, there were only two public warnings, one by Raghuram Rajan at the annual meeting of Central Bankers at Jackson Hole in 2005, and the other by Nouriel Roubini at an International Monetary Fund seminar in 2006. That is not many people. More precisely, at both events, these two were heckled by several people. Roubini in particular was challenged to produce the model on the basis of which he predicted disaster.

However, to do it justice, the letter does make some frank confessions about what led economists astray.

> But against those who warned, most...believed that the financial wizards had found new and clever ways of managing risks....These views were abetted by financial and economic models that were good at predicting the short-term and small risks, but few were equipped to say what would happen when things went wrong as they have.

But it then goes on to wave away that inability by saying: "There was a broad consensus that it was better to deal with the aftermath of bubbles in stock markets and housing markets than to try to head them off in advance."

The word consensus is used by a minority which tries to stamp its view on the majority that is never consulted. If there was indeed such a consensus, clearly economists in their considered judgment, unlike the Queen and her subjects, saw no need to foresee the collapse of the bubble, much less head it off. The letter recovers quickly from the implications of that consensus however to make a pitch, you guessed it, for a new 'horizon-scanning capability' so that Her Majesty might never need to ask her question again.

In the old days, monarchs would have punished forecasting failures of such magnitude by cutting off grants, and perhaps a few heads as well. But we live in kinder times. And the Queen controls no grants anyway. She does not control her own grant.

Another letter to the Queen followed, from a group of economists not at the London School. It cites the report of a Commission set up by the American Economic Association, published in a 1991 volume of the *Journal of Economic Literature*, which criticised doctoral programmes for "turning out too many idiot savants skilled in technique but innocent of real economic issues".

This second letter, dated 21 September 2009, is more trenchant in its admission of culpability. It speaks of how the first letter "overlooks the part that many leading economists have had in turning economics into a discipline that is detached from the real world, and in promoting unrealistic assumptions that have helped to sustain an uncritical view of how markets operate".

Her visit to the London School was surely the Queen's finest hour.

5

The Financial Stability and Development Council[1]

The announcement in the Union Budget 2010 of a Financial Stability and Development Council (FSDC) follows suggested changes to the regulatory architecture prescribed by the Raghuram Rajan Committee on Financial Sector Reforms, which submitted its report on 12 September 2008 – just a few days before the great crash. Although the Committee prefaced its recommendations by saying that it was "premature to move fully towards a single regulator at the moment", a unified regulatory structure was clearly the goal towards which the Committee thought regulation in India must begin to move.

The principal argument advanced by the Committee in favour of unified regulation is that it is needed to combat financial conglomerates and holding companies as they begin to dominate the system across financial spheres. At the same time, the Committee adopts the contradictory stand that a unified regulator is less vulnerable to capture because it faces countervailing pressure from different segments of the regulated. Arguing from first principles, regulatory capture is actually that much easier when a single regulatory fortress is all that needs to be stormed. In developing countries with a democratic structure, and political parties in need of election funding, a unified regulator is a disturbing prospect.

In the BC (before crisis) era, unified regulation was the flavour of the time, and the United Kingdom went ahead and did precisely that. Prudential regulation was gouged out of the Bank of England, and merged into a single regulator, the Financial Services Authority (FSA). The crisis demonstrated the folly of separating prudential regulation

---

1. This was part of a debate in the *Business Standard*, with contrarian opinions appearing alongside.

of the banking sector from the central bank's role as lender of last resort. That lesson has fortunately not been lost. It is fully expected that prudential regulation of banks will soon be restored to the Bank of England.[2] Regulation in the United States, on the other hand, was not unified, and the structure there did not shine either. It collapsed more utterly than elsewhere. No single model emerges unscathed from the empirical test of the great crisis.

That leaves us with the task of thinking through the regulatory structure that will best suit us. The Raghuram Rajan Committee recommended two distinct bodies. A Financial Sector Oversight Agency (FSOA) was suggested for risk assessment and co-ordination across regulatory spheres, to be chaired by the senior-most regulator. A Working Group on Financial Sector Reforms was also suggested, with the finance minister as chairman, and regulators included in the membership. The danger is that these two quite separate recommendations will in practice be conflated into a single body, chaired by the finance minister. Political chairing of a co-ordination council is a troubling arrangement. An apolitical institutional mooring is needed for long-term financial stability, so central to the lives of all Indians whether or not they are directly linked to the formal financial structure.

Informal co-ordination and discussion across regulators is certainly a good thing, but it already existed at the time of the Raghuram Rajan Committee and is mentioned in their report. There is the High Level Co-ordination Committee on Capital Markets (HLCC), supplemented by operational coordination between regulators. All the financial regulators in place, Reserve Bank of India (RBI), Securities and Exchange Board of India (SEBI), Insurance Regulatory and Development Authority (IRDA) and Pension Fund Regulatory & Development Authority (PFRDA), have defined mandates and powers. If a further legislated layer is superimposed, a loss of accountability is foreseeable. Given the Indian penchant for ceding all power upwards, it is clearly possible that speed of response, an essential feature of

2. It was indeed so restored in June 2010, three months after this column was written.

effective regulation, will be lost as regulators seek and await approval of the highest layer.[3]

The Financial Council proposed is a solution for a non-existant problem. India during the crisis earned universal admiration for the robust shield surrounding its regulatory structure. Friends of India will watch with horror if we tamper with the very edifice that had held us up so well.

The Budget announcement of a Financial Sector Legislative Reforms Commission, on the other hand, is a good idea. There is most certainly legal untidiness that needs cleaning up, and if in the process pending cases before the clogged judicial system are also resolved, a huge source of friction hindering financial sector advancement will have been addressed.

3. The FSDC has functioned since 2010 largely as a reporting body, without impeding the functioning of the several financial regulators in place.

6 Tax Competition

Institutional Competition[1]

This collection of 10 essays from a research project of the Ratio Institute in Stockholm investigates assorted aspects of institutional competition. Going past the inevitable debates over the definitional boundaries of institutions, and the arena in which they might be said to compete, the accepted interpretation in all papers in the volume is that institutional competition denotes competition between states at national or, within nations, subnational level.

States can learn from each other. Positive advantages of this kind, from what is called yardstick competition, do not even call for elucidation, since no policy action of any kind follows thereby. These advantages are set forth in separate papers by Roland Vaubel and Michael Wolgemuth. Perhaps the only lesson that emerges, an important one, is that decentralisation of governance offers scope for wider experimentation and institutional diversity, with all the information and learning advantages that ensue. There are several related instances from all parts of the world. In India, free mid-day school meals for all children, or public employment guarantees during agricultural off-seasons, and the experimental evidence that these can be done without bankrupting the exchequer were learned from pioneering subnational governments. Learning of this kind happens naturally. It does not need prodding.

The possible negative outcomes of tax competition are however far more compelling, calling as they do for concomitant policy attention to mitigation. The paper that addresses this issue head-on is by Rolf Hoijer. In a remarkably systematic manner, he identifies three possible negatives and argues against all three. The first is that tax competition distorts investment decisions and violates capital export neutrality.

---

1. This review of Andreas Bergh and Rolf Hoijer (ed.), *Institutional Competition* (Edward Elgar, 2008), appeared in *Tax Justice Focus* 4(4), 2009.

The second is the negative impact on public revenue (and therefore on the ability to provide public goods) of a leader-follower race to the bottom on taxation of capital, in a bid to be an attractive destination to mobile capital. The third is that footloose capital can shake off the burden of taxation by roaming the world, leaving relatively immobile labour to bear the tax burden, with implications for the distribution of income.

On distortion of investment decisions and violation of capital export neutrality, the Hoijer refutation falls back on the familiar plank that tax rates are merely the price for public goods, and that mobile capital looks at tax rates and public services provided as a package. He goes even further to suggest that tax competition facilitates the pricing of public services in different destinations, thus improving the signalling properties of taxes, and therefore potentially improving welfare. This argument might possibly carry conviction in a largely homogenous universe, such as that of the European Union (EU). But the nation state in poorer destinations faced with unconstrained tax competition will try to stay afloat by ensuring public services to mobile capital, but denying them to sections of the population without recourse. Scarce water might be diverted to the corporate sector, away from the parched hinterland. Floodlit consumer malls might draw scarce electricity away from irrigation pumps. An internationally agreed corporate tax rate floor protects against this. The advantage of choice remains with mobile capital. There are still free to rank destinations by public service value for taxes paid. Meanwhile, the rate floor ensures to some degree that public goods will not be allocated within poorer destinations away from the voiceless population.

On the negative outcome of tax competition on public revenue, Hoijer falls back on Tieboutian mobility to argue that there will be eventual jurisdictional alignment of tax rates with consumer preferences for public services. Hoijer does concede that movement of people is not natural or easy across ethnic divides. Once again, this might not seem an insuperable obstacle within the EU universe, with visa-free movement. But opposition of the world community to free movement of natural persons, in World Trade Organization (WTO) terminology, illustrates the fallacy of extending the Tieboutian notion to contexts where its validity does not hold. Movement of people will become an ever more contentious issue as climate change forces people to move in the face of advancing sea levels. The 1999 empirical paper by Radaelli is cited to show no obvious fall in government revenues; but as Hoijer concedes, that merely establishes success in finding compensating revenue sourced elsewhere. If a high-rate VAT (value added tax) is the source of replacement revenue, the tax system will become more regressive. Surely that is not a happy outcome.

The third and related issue is the replacement of revenue from capital taxation with revenue from taxation of labour income. Without adopting what Hoijer labels the Marxist distinction between capital and labour, and conceding that embedded human capital is possibly as mobile as financial capital, it is difficult to accede to his argument that a burden shift is a transfer that permits no conclusions on whether tax competition introduces a Pareto change. He goes further to cite the classic Diamond-Mirrlees result of 1971 that taxes distorting production impose more deadweight costs than taxes distorting consumption, to suggest that a shifting of the tax burden from capital to labour might actually be a good thing. The leap to that conclusion is not justified. The key here is the locational distortion posed by inter-country variations in taxes on mobile capital. Even if it is argued that tax competition will occur in leader-follower rounds to successive reduced-rate equilibria *a posteriori*, a global tax treaty that imposes a uniform non-zero floor rate of taxation imposes an *a priori* equilibrium without distortionary rounds of competitive rate reduction.

The two other papers on the tax competition issue by Victoria Curzon-Price and Andreas Bergh, echo the general conclusion of Hoijer that international tax competition is beneficial rather than harmful. The argument of the former that direct tax rates have indeed fallen, but not (on average) to zero, neglects the crucial issue that some destinations have indeed come down to zero, and that the regulatory burden so placed on non-zero destinations to monitor transfer pricing is a deadweight loss that poor countries can ill afford. The case for a universal above-zero tax floor surely remains irrefutable. The Bergh paper is set squarely in the European context, where it might be possible to tie tax-benefit packages for the population saddled with a high tax burden on labour income. But in developing countries, the regulatory burden of imposing club restrictions on public services would pose an infeasibly large administrative expenditure for government to carry.

The only research paper in the book is by Lars Feld. This important contribution is the first ever to test for the impact of fiscal federalism on economic growth, using data based on an Organisation for Economic Co-operation and Development (OECD) method advanced in 1999, which differentiates even the own tax revenue of subnational governments by three degrees of autonomy with respect to rate and base decisions. The exercise conducted with panel data for 19 OECD countries from 1973 to 1998 is meticulously performed and clearly reported. Neither spending decentralisation nor subnational tax autonomy over tax rates or bases has a significant impact on economic growth. However, when subnational jurisdictions participate in joint taxation systems at the national level, the growth performance is worse. Hence, the author concludes that tax autonomy, meaning the absence of joint taxation, has had a positive influence on the economic performance of OECD countries. However, the leap from here to the conclusion that unlimited tax competition is good for efficiency is not warranted.

An excellent paper by Erich Weede, comparing the institutional features of China and India, closes the book. He executes admirably the theoretical task he sets himself, of finding a common set of institutional factors which explains both why China and India fell behind the West and eventually started to catch up, and also why China outperformed India. Weede correctly identifies the failure to protect property rights in China and India relative to Europe as a key element of the story, and correctly reaches below the surface superiority of property rights in India relative to China, to identify the distortion of incentives in India.

This book has much to commend it, because of the richness and diversity of issues addressed. However, the uniform support of many of the pieces in it for unbridled fiscal competition is not tenable. The argument in favour of placing a floor above zero on tax competition, whether between countries, or within countries, is very simple. Tax competition introduces noise into the relative attraction of investment-seeking destinations, in a manner that can seriously distort investment decisions away from efficiency. The argument that taxes are merely one side of a public services package, the whole of which goes into the location decision, is invalid in the context of developing countries, where reduced taxation of mobile capital will see a corresponding decline in services not to corporate enclaves, but to the non-corporate hinterland. Developing countries increasingly challenged by climate change and food insecurity find themselves effectively deprived of fiscal autonomy. Since at each temporary equilibrium after a round of rate reductions, relative tax advantages are evened out, settlement of a universally agreed and enforced floor will be to the revenue benefit of all, and the relative disadvantage of no partner to the agreed floor.

7 November Blues

November [2012] stormed in with Sandy in the United States and Neelam in South India and brought climate change straight to the forefront after it had been despatched to the back of public concern, chased there by the aftermath of the global crash of 2008. Very few people really have the scientific wherewithal to judge on whether these kinds of extreme weather events are a result of global warming. There have been storms of comparable severity in the past on the east coasts of both the US and India, although the frequency of such events is said to have increased the world over. What is of greater concern is the melting of ice caps, and the steady desertification in Africa and South Asia, where the latter has been worsened by violation of traditional water management practices.

But climate change as an issue has surfaced strongly with the storms, and at a time when the world wants to get growth going immediately, whatever the long-term unsustainability of it. We in India, for instance, need additional thermal power generation immediately for our own survival, regardless of climate change consequences. What complicates matters even more is that nowhere in the world does political leadership appear sufficiently in command to do what is necessary for either immediate growth or long-term sustainability.

So then, what is it that needs doing? The single unifying factor across both the immediate growth requirement and the longer environmental sustainability concern is the call for fiscal resources. The US faces a fiscal cliff within a month, when the fiscal stimulus measures introduced in the post-crash recessionary period, are due to expire. Unless the life of these is extended by legislative approval, it is feared that the automatic tax increases and public expenditure cuts amounting to an estimated 4 per cent of GDP (gross domestic product) could make the economy fall off the cliff into recession again. There is actually a ready blueprint for raising tax resources by closing avoidance loopholes rather than by necessarily raising tax rates, prepared by a bipartisan Commission on Fiscal Responsibility and Reform (called Bowles-Simpson after its co-chairs). The Commission has been criticised for suggesting rate cuts while closing loopholes, but the details are not important. What matters is that implementation will be difficult in a fractured political establishment – one section of which wants public entitlement cuts, the other section of which is fiercely opposed to such cuts. And there is not much time left.[1]

In Europe, the fiscal problem has on several occasions spilled out onto the streets. In mid-November, public sector employees facing salary cuts were on a co-ordinated strike across major member countries in addition to Greece. Actually, public sector salary cuts are a humane way of resolving the impossible Eurozone combination of high public debt, high unemployment, and rising expenditure on unemployment compensation. Salary cuts for those fortunate enough to have lifetime public sector jobs are a way to distribute the pain of expenditure cuts more equitably. But public sector employees were able to fight back in a way the unemployed could not. They simply closed down public systems. What the Eurozone needs is a carefully calibrated medium term increase in debt, allowed over an intervening period in which growth-enhancing investments are implemented, while simultaneously phasing out abuses of the entitlement blanket.[2] But tax resources will have to partly cover the net increase in expenditures over the medium term, no matter what.

Taxation is already at high levels in Europe, unlike the US. Even there, however, there is a great deal of room for taxing the rich

1. In the event, the fiscal cliff was staved off through an interim legislative sanction for public expenditure (called a "continuing resolution"). The government was eventually forced into a partial shutdown on 1 October 2013, the beginning of the US fiscal year, that lasted until 17 October, when a budget deal was reached and government employees went back to work. Fiscal arrangements of the Federal government in the US are complicated by absolute debt ceilings, independent of approved budgets, which also were in danger of being breached in 2013 and whose looming circuit-breaker forced the political cooperation needed to end the October shutdown. In December 2014, an Act provided funding until 30 September 2015. Beyond that, another bill or continuing resolution must be passed to stave off another shut down. The debt limit presently in place will be breached by early November 2015.

2. It is in fact what was forced through by the European Central Bank in January 2015, declaring a first-time willingness to a programmed purchase of Greek bonds, akin to the Quantitative Easing practised by the Federal Reserve Bank of the US.

more heavily than they are after the rate convergence that spread through the world in the 1980s. At that time, rate reductions on the rich were proposed by economists on the basis of illusory efficiency advantages, but were accepted by practitioners as a way by which to induce voluntary compliance. Since then, enforcement systems in the developed world have improved greatly, so that high rates by themselves should not pose a compliance problem. However, low taxation of the rich over a long period has bred a whole host of institutions dependent on voluntary contributions. These range from museums, broadcasting not paid for by advertisements, and private universities, all the way to charitable institutions serving the underprivileged. It will be difficult to change this network of dependence. The claim of the conservative rich who want to keep their taxes low is that they do a better job through charities of reaching the poor than the government would.

Climate change too can be fought only with fiscal resources for mitigation and adaptation. Renewable energy, for example, calls for massive public investment on transmission lines to evacuate the energy produced to consumption centres. These costs may eventually be recoverable from users, but discoms presently are unable to recover even routine charges, and need a government restructuring plan. Adaptation calls for huge investment along coasts to prevent inundation with the rise in sea levels.

In the midst of this massive need, the neglect of the Tobin tax on international financial flows is impossible to understand. It is leviable at a minuscule rate on a base amounting to several trillion dollars per trading day, and its incidence falls on global capital flows, the major beneficiary of globalisation.

Within federal nations like India, governments at all levels must have a fiscal stake for effective progress towards fiscal and climate change correction. In the coal scam, the decision not to auction licences to private sector miners was defended on the grounds that when state governments were approached for their opinion, they did not want auctions. Of course they would not, when they have no automatic share of licence fees, or of mining royalty revenues more generally, under the present fiscal structure.[3] With a fiscal stake for state and local government, their interests would be aligned with national interests, and with outcome monitoring of the use of these fiscal resources for reversal of environmental destruction, we might actually see some improvement on the ground.

3. This situation was dramatically altered with the coal ordinance introduced in October 2014, after the Supreme Court judgement which nullified allotment of coal blocks to private players. The ordinance assigns auction and royalty revenues to states, a major alteration in the fiscal outlook for the four states in which coal mines are located – West Bengal, Odisha, Jharkhand and Chhattisgarh.

8 The Economic Fallout of Fukushima

Monday after the disastrous Japanese earthquake and tsunami saw the start of a deluge of predictions and speculation over the economic impact in our connected world. Trajectories of prices were variously configured as a function of the time path of restoration of Japanese demand, and the duration of shutdowns of Japanese manufacturing facilities.

Oil prices fell in the immediate aftermath, on the expectation of a worldwide slowdown following lower Japanese imports of industrial inputs and consumer goods, but very soon started rising again. Fossil fuel demand will increase even in the short run in Japan, with demand crossing over from electricity shortages. India of course is among the countries most vulnerable to higher oil prices. And coal prices are expected to go up sharply too, as Japan attempts to replace the 5 per cent of electricity generation capacity it has lost irretrievably. Both oil and coal have undergone supply shocks, with political turbulence in North Africa and flooded coal mines in Northeast Australia.

Outward Japanese investment is expected to slow down in the short term. Infrastructure in India (the Delhi-Mumbai corridor) will certainly see some delays, if not outright cancellation. The medium term forecast is that Japanese companies might diversify into countries with lower seismic risk, but India does not feature in the list of the most attractive destinations even so.

India will not suffer a tourism loss. The ghastly experiences of some Japanese women tourists have curbed what was once a widespread desire to see the land of the Buddha. Also, Japan as a destination accounts for only around 2 per cent of Indian exports. At a more disaggregated level however, like seafood exports from Kerala and Darjeeling tea, the demand shock could be more acute.

But much the biggest issue is the impact on the nuclear power generation industry, in the world, and in India. Defenders of nuclear power generation in India are tired of pointing out that the high-level nuclear disaster just seen is a low probability event, as against the kind of grinding low level but cumulative damage to public health ever present with thermal generation. They have pointed out repeatedly that what precipitated the nuclear disaster was not the earthquake, but the tsunami. The tsunami shut down both the alternative power source from which water to cool the nuclear reactors was sourced and the back up in the event of failure of the primary source. All that is true of course.

But the nuclear incident has driven home three very sobering lessons. First, it turns out that Japan, a model of collective order, where the trains run to split second timing, was also a place where information flow to the regulator was obstructed. Stories are emerging of how employees of the Tokyo Electric Power Company, which ran the nuclear facilities, were instructed to alter inspection photographs required by the utility regulator, to conceal cracks in pipes. If this could happen in Japan, how much more possible it could be elsewhere.

Second, the world realised, for perhaps the first time, that a key ingredient for running nuclear facilities is abundant water. Clearly the water needed will be fresh water, because it was the emergency resort to use of sea water, with its corrosive salt content, which knocked out the Fukushima reactors for good. Fresh water is very scarce in India, even in coastal zones. Even with water recycling, it is not too far-fetched to visualise an eventuality where fresh water will have to be pumped out of ever deeper aquifers to keep those facilities going, while drinking water for the surrounding human population is trucked in from ever increasing distances.

Third, the world realised, also for the first time, that it is not known whether the plans for disposal of the nuclear waste from Fukushima and other such plants after orderly closure remain possible, after a disastrous closure of this kind. There is fear, and we do not know whether it is misplaced, of the slow leaching of its residual poisons into the soil and into the water sources of Japan.

None of these problems is insurmountable going into the future. A robust regulatory system should in principle be possible even in India, where the conduct of elections has been rendered largely impervious to meddling. The water problem is harder to resolve. Water is not priced in India at scarcity value. It is not even priced so as to cover the lowest cost at which it can be delivered. More even than the pricing issue, there has to be an assessment of the quantum of water requirement of a nuclear facility, and whether it can be sustainably supplied going into the future. For that matter, the water requirement of thermal generation is not insignificant either. We need a critical look at the efficiency of water use in electricity generation, both thermal and nuclear. Finally, the plans for disposal of reactor fuels at the end of their useful life, under a variety of disaster scenarios, also have to be openly discussed.

Meanwhile, we don't seem to have lent much of a helping hand to the Japanese people in their hour of need. We sent a few blankets, but could have done much more for a country that has made such major contributions to Indian infrastructure and industry. We don't know if our National Disaster Management Authority had any engagement at all with the search and rescue teams from the UK and US who arrived at the scene within 48 hours, with their equipment and dogs. We would have honed our own disaster management skills, had we sent a team from here to join in that effort.

9 Minimum Wages

The December [2013] arrest of the Indian consul general in New York City for not paying minimum wages to her Indian housemaid highlights the critical failure on the part of both countries concerned, in not having worked out the fine print of their mutual diplomatic engagement over more than 60 years.

Domestic helpers for Indian diplomats in the United States had official sanction on both sides. The US has a whole visa category for such employees of foreign missions, and on the Indian side, domestic staff are actually given an official passport and airfare. That being the case, there was failure on both sides in not having established which law the contract entered into was to be in accordance with, whether that in the particular location of the diplomat – since labour laws in the US vary by state – or with Indian law, since the contract is between two Indian nationals, performing duties in a primary or secondary capacity for the Indian state, outside the jurisdiction of India. And if the consonance required varied according to whether the officials were posted to a mission, or to a consular office, that too should have been specified in the small print.

Once the formal framework was in place, it would have been a relatively minor matter to design an enforcement mechanism, especially in the US where there is a well-developed banking system. The US could have asked for an annual report on all domestic staff, on the contracted wage in each case, and bank records of wages actually paid. Concern about enforcement of hours worked could have been met through registration with, and periodic reports to, a local social welfare officer.

Even if these details were initially seen as too minor, the Indian diplomatic establishment should have been alerted to the problem by a number of cases in the recent past, involving Indian consular officials in New York as it happens, where the validity and enforcement of these wage contracts were challenged by a succession of Indian domestic employees wanting to skip out.

More even than these individual incidents, there should have been awareness in the Ministry of External Affairs (MEA) of the priorities of the Obama administration, and the implications for immigration and minimum wage requirements in particular. Every diplomatic mission of any size has an economics counsellor. This official in the Indian mission in Washington is given the designation of economics minister. Way back after the American elections in November 2008, there should have been a report filed to the MEA by the economics minister in Washington of the areas where policy in the US was liable to change, and the implications for Indian interests. The push towards minimum wage and immigration reform and tightening of the rules on human trafficking was inevitable, given the political support base on which President Obama got elected.

As it happened, the economic slowdown following the great crash of September 2008 kept the minimum wage issue on the back-burner for a while. But at the start of calendar 2013, when there was the first faint flush of an economic turnaround, President Obama in his State of the Union message pledged to deliver on his promise to raise the minimum wage to $9 an hour. In the March 2013 Budget of New York Governor Andrew Cuomo, a Democrat, there was an announcement of a three-year phased hike in the minimum wage, to $8 an hour starting on 1 January 2014, and going up to $9 an hour by the start of 2016, the year President Obama demits office. Twelve other states announced a hike in minimum wages starting with New Year's Day 2014. These developments should have found a prominent place in reports of the economics minister to the MEA, with the implications in terms of tighter minimum wage enforcement, particularly in New York state, clearly anticipated and highlighted. A recent (January 2014) letter signed by 75 economists including some marquee names, saying there is no research evidence that a hike in the minimum wage retards the demand for labour even in a sluggish economy, adds further ballast.

The US mission in India takes the business of reporting on the Indian economic environment so seriously, that in addition to an Economics Counsellor who is a career diplomat reporting to the State Department, there has in recent years been an additional

Financial Attache, deputed from the Treasury Department, who files an independent report on economic developments in India and the region.

With that kind of feedback from our economic observers in the US, this whole unfortunate incident could have been anticipated and headed off. Now that the damage has already occurred, the opportunity to introduce systemic correctives to the diplomatic relationship between the two countries should not be lost. On the Indian side, there should be total willingness to conform to whatever conditions the US wishes to impose, as a host country. And of course, that has to go with full reciprocity, where India is the host country.

Some Indian-American commentators, acutely embarrassed by the incident, have lambasted the home country for not having minimum wages and enforcement for domestic workers. They are wrong about there being no minimum wages, but are right about the lack of enforcement of working conditions in the entire arena of informal hiring. Within this arena, domestic workers actually have an advantage over other sectors in that they get to negotiate their pay and other conditions directly with their employer. In other intermediated sectors like construction, most notoriously, what workers actually get in hand is much below what contractors make them sign for, and this disparity is very large in the case of female labour in particular. Domestic work agencies that have recently sprung up also engage in this sort of thing, with of course some honourable exceptions. But most domestic hiring is still done in a disintermediated way, with nothing going to a middle agent between employer and employee.

10 The Economic Vision of Margaret Thatcher

Margaret Thatcher lent herself easily to hatred and caricature. But she didn't care. She was an economics practitioner with unshakeable convictions about the path Britain needed to take to shake off the lassitude of the years both before and after the great oil shocks of 1970s. She chose the theories of classical economics, defiantly rejecting the Keynesian solution to the economic situation facing her, and she prevailed. But in the end, her excessive fidelity to classical economics proved to be her undoing. Hers is the only known attempt in modern times to implement the poll tax, that all-time favourite of classical orthodoxy (and to this very day the ideal tax in theory, because it does not distort relative prices, the price of leisure in particular). The people revolted, and her party removed her as their leader.

I often wonder what Margaret Thatcher's response would have been to the present fiscal conundrum in the European Union – to be or not to be austere. She was pragmatic above all, and the present situation differs from the one she faced when she had to tame a vicious inflationary spiral and bring down interest rates. It is certain she would have felt powerfully vindicated by having chosen not to yield fully to the European embrace, and to keep the British pound rather than join the Euro.

She chose fiscal austerity when she took charge as prime minister in 1979, at a time of unemployment and low growth, but also (unlike today) rampaging inflation. Reduced deficits and government borrowing did not ease interest rates adequately and it took a few years before she could achieve her ultimate objective of bringing down inflation and interest rates. She then opened up a market for small loans by enabling tenants of low-income housing owned by local government councils to buy the flats they occupied, in installments. Small businesses started at the low interest rate regime she eventually engineered have grown into medium, in some cases major, enterprises of today.

She saw opportunity in the large oil wealth from the price hikes looking for a financial home, and encouraged the use of London as the place where funds could be parked with maturities as short as overnight, no questions asked. To this day, the most widely used benchmark for floating rate loans is the London Inter Bank Offered Rate (LIBOR). The recently revealed manipulation of LIBOR was certainly enabled by the financial deregulation she set in motion, which resulted in banks and financial intermediaries becoming as arrogant and unmindful of the public good as labour unions had been in her day. She did not foresee that; but then again, there were subsequent labour governments that did not foresee it either. They could have rolled back some of the deregulation she introduced, but did not do so.

Taming inflation took a bit of time. She confronted powerful trade unions, who had built an adhesive and spiralling core into British inflation by constant work stoppages in search of wage hikes, chasing the price rise initially sparked by oil. Her victory over the unions was among the most artful of her many battles. By demanding that they take a ballot of union members before going on strike, she exposed the anti-democratic world of swagger and cigar inhabited by union bosses, and carried the public with her.

The mining unions were the fiercest holdouts, and she met their challenge with her belief in markets and free trade. Coal and inexpensive manufactured goods were imported and public subsidies for inefficient British manufacturing units withdrawn.

When she took over leadership of the Conservative Party, she was chosen for the clarity of her conviction about what needed to be done. When she set about her task, she famously inspired an open letter in 1981, signed by 364 economists in British academic institutions (including two prominent Indians). The letter condemned her fiscal austerity, and predicted that it would lead the British economy into terminal decline. She pressed on. The episode inspired a book, but economists would rather forget about the whole thing. It is said, although the story may just be a floater with no validity, that she framed the letter for her office wall, and enjoyed showing it to visitors.

The academic world had its revenge. An honorary doctorate from Oxford University was voted down. It is possible that this did not bother her. She believed in lawful protest, because she saw herself as an activist and protester against the economic policies of her predecessors. She was able in the end to hold up three fingers, for the number of times she had derived legitimacy at the polls to change those policies.

Her political stance on the international arena was not defensible. She opposed economic sanctions on the apartheid regime in South Africa (an initiative led by Rajiv Gandhi within the Commonwealth) and supported General Pinochet, when she knew perfectly well that the atrocities they committed would not be permitted by her on British soil. When a death *fatwa* was pronounced on Salman Rushdie for *Satanic Verses*, she immediately gave him comprehensive police cover at public expense, despite the fact that she herself was lampooned as Margaret Torture in that very book.

She earned epithets of that kind and worse by her adamant stance that the care of the homeless and mentally ill was not the business of the state. In this, she was limited by her upbringing in small-town England, where such matters were handled by the church and private charities. The horrific spectacle of wandering poor on the streets of London ended only in the 1990s, as the prosperity she enabled and rising tax revenue made it possible for successor governments to reactivate the old shelter homes.

Going into the next general elections, we in India need political leaders who can clearly articulate their solutions to the economic challenges we face. We require pre-poll policy commitments, not pre-poll party alliances. The electorate need to know the choices before them.

11 The Volatile Price of Oil

There were 10 reductions in the domestic price of petrol between August 2014 and January 2015, and 6 in the price of diesel over the same period. These were reductions in the price at the pump, net of 4 excise duty hikes.

These excise hikes have given rise to a general sense among consumers that they have been cheated of the benefits of the sharp crash in global crude oil prices, from $115 per barrel in June 2014, to the $45-50 range in January 2015.[1] After four years of fuel inflation at an annual average of 9.3 per cent, while being harangued the whole time about how fuel prices would have risen still more had they not been protected by the petroleum subsidy, they now demand symmetry, by being allowed the relief due from a fall in world oil prices.

This demand might be justified were there a reasonable expectation that the new lows in global oil prices are here to stay, but in fact the behaviour of the price of oil has become totally unpredictable. When the price crashed, several explanations were offered after the fact, but the important point is that no one saw it coming. If there was a prediction that the price of crude oil would go into a sudden and deep dive in the second half of calendar 2014, I for one certainly did not know of it. Even the arrival of winter, normally a season of hardening oil prices, has not arrested the fall. So the economies of several oil importers, India among them, remain in thralldom to a price that defies predictability.

If there is one thing economists are taught to revere, it is the sanctity of the unfettered market price. Shorn of distortions like uncompetitive practices, and failure to internalise environmental costs, the market price is the ideal whose discovery is the object of all economic reform. It is the signaller of scarcity, and is the parameter to

1. From that low point, oil prices rose to a little above $60 per barrel in June 2015, but fell again thereafter to below $45 by end-August 2015.

which consumption and investment decisions must be shaped. After 1973, all countries in the world were jolted into a realisation that the quadrupling of the price of oil, unpleasant though its immediate impact may have been, served as a useful reminder of the finiteness of oil. Since then, the oil market has seen new reserves come up all over, the latest being shale oil fracked out of the earth in the United States. But more malevolently, the oil market has turned into a playing ground for speculation, which has moved the price of oil far away from an orderly signaller of immediate or impending scarcity.

The G20 group, which solemnly affirmed the need for all countries to stand together after the great global crash of September 2008, has not been able to intervene at all effectively in stabilising the price of oil. Forget stabilising the price, they have not even been able to advance global understanding of what exactly is driving it. This has left individual members of the G20, along with other countries too small to belong to that august body, to fend for themselves as best they can, in the face of extreme price volatility in a key intermediate. The price of oil remains the great exogenous unknown. The best that can be said for it, in a serviceable phrase of former US Defence Secretary Rumsfeld, is that it is a known unknown.

A little over two years ago, in June of 2012, international rating agencies held a gun to the head of the then Finance Minister and threatened a credit rating downgrade, on the grounds that India suffered from fiscal obesity, and an expanding subsidy waistline that was out of control. Whatever one might think of rating agencies, and of the role they played in precipitating the great crash, this was not a threat that could be ignored. In any case, it was independently true that the fiscal structure, then as now, needed serious reform, on both expenditure and revenue sides. So a panel was formed to suggest a fiscal correction roadmap, chaired by Vijay Kelkar, of which I was a member.

Of the three major subsidies, food has held roughly steady as a per cent of GDP (gross domestic product) over the last five years (it fell a little but then rose back up again with the implementation of the Food Security Act).[2] The fertiliser subsidy actually came down very sharply in 2010-11 with the switch to a nutrient-based platform, and has continued to fall since then. As budgeted for the current year, it is only a little above half a per cent of GDP. (All these estimates straddle the changed GDP estimates for the past three years.)

It is the petroleum subsidy which grew from 0.5 per cent of GDP in 2010-11 to 0.78 per cent in 2011-12, and ended 2012-13 at nearly one per cent of GDP. Even that was achieved only by immediately following the prescriptions in the roadmap, among them a monthly hike in the price of diesel. At the time, it seemed inevitable that the price of oil would rise inexorably in response to the increasing global demand for it over time, along with the ever present upward supply side pressure on price arising from conflicts in the Middle East. In the event, the roadmap did pull down the subsidy to 0.75 per cent in 2013-14, and to slightly under 0.5 per cent in 2014-15.

So looking at the fiscal picture of the Centre, as a continuum across changes in government, what do we see? We see a fiscal response to the gyrations in the price of oil, which subsidised oil in the years when its price was high, and is now taxing it when the price is low. As a price smoothing fiscal intervention, surely this has much to recommend it. A pure economic approach, of adjusting fully and completely to the (unpredictable) volatility in the oil price would have made much less sense.

So taxing oil now when its price is low makes sense. It is also a just thing to do. The petroleum subsidy was in effect a transfer to users of petroleum in proportion to their consumption, from taxpayers, who bore the burden regardless of how much they consumed of petroleum products. A tax on petroleum when the price is low reverses that, rightfully transferring back to the taxpayer the support they earlier gave to the subsidy, a tax which is now paid in proportion to consumption. Cynics might see the opportunism of a government finding ₹20,000 crore useful at a time when the budgeted fiscal deficit is proving difficult to reach. If things were correctly done, which of course is not possible in the present fiscal situation, the tax on

2. See Figure 2.0, Part IV.

petroleum should go into a fund that will promote renewable energy. Or even into a fund that will be tapped for a smoothing subsidy in case the price of oil ratchets up sharply up again, as it well may. Certainly, sharply or not, the price of oil will eventually have to climb up again.

But whether or not the tax is used for approved ends, formal price smoothing with an upward trend over time carries justification in itself. Smoothing of deficits over an economic cycle is part of the arsenal of approved policy recommendations from economists, and in fact was widely followed as a concerted G20 action after the global crash of 2008. Following from that, price smoothing over oil price cycles, which have so far defied predictability, is also justifiable. A smoothed price offers a stable benchmark against which the alternative of renewable energy can be reliably worked out, and funded. A jerky benchmark leaves renewable investment proposals in disarray.

Not all volatility calls for direct price intervention. The increasing seasonal volatility in the price of fruits and vegetables is an example. Farmers respond to the high off-season price spike by increasing acreage, which then leads to a sharp on-season slump, in the absence of adequate preservation chains. The proper policy response to that is to increase investment in cold chains and warehousing, which were a part of both the railway and finance budgets for the current year. If those provisions have been compressed because of the fiscal crunch, that would be a most unfortunate delay in something that is needed sooner rather than later.

When the nirvana of a fully renewable energy supply dawns, we will finally be released from the scourge of volatile energy prices. That nirvana is a long way off. Off-grid solar is probably the best alternative, but it carries seasonality issues. Big solar is besieged by problems of land availability. Covering irrigation canals with solar panels, as Gujarat did, was a great idea, but the land mass will have to be tapped big time, if we want seriously to go the solar way.

Part II

INSTITUTIONS AND GOVERNANCE

Many of the essays in this section were written in 2011, when there was a mounting crescendo of civil society agitation against corruption, led by Anna Hazare, a senior moral crusader. There were resemblances to Occupy Wall Street – that spontaneous and contagious eruption in industrial countries of public disgust at the corporate greed that had led to the crash of 2008.

The first essay in this section, "Tackling Corruption", makes the point that corruption has to be addressed as a systemic rather than a moral issue – arising as it does from the failure to set up transparent funding mechanisms for political parties in a democratic form of governance, rather than from the mere presence of morally deficient holders of public office.

In response to the Anna Hazare movement, there was a public clamour to appoint a Lok Pal, a 'caretaker of the people', whereby ordinary people could directly carry their grievances to a body which would investigate them. It was a form of disintermediation, bypassing the Comptroller and Auditor General (CAG) and giving ordinary people direct access for financial redressal. There were titanic struggles rocking Parliament on whether the prime minister of India would be brought within the purview of the Lok Pal. "The Lok Pal and Deterrence" urges focus on the issue of deterrence and prevention, and away from a catch-the-thief mentality.

The next two essays focus on CAG reports on the losses suffered by the public exchequer from the manner of allocation of spectrum to telecommunication companies (popularly known as the 2G case), and coal mining rights to private companies. "Scams and the Media" criticises media sensationalisation of the reports of the CAG, with selective quoting of numbers from what were balanced and responsible documents into flashy allegations. "Coal and the CAG" looks at the report on allotment of coal mining rights. The essays defend the CAG for having attempted to quantify the losses implicit in the manner of allocating vital national resources, at a time when the office was under attack for having ventured out of its musty role of rapping knuckles for departures from received procedure. These issues have been settled by Supreme Court judgements, described in updates to these pieces written when the reports first came out.

"A Checklist of Waste" deals with the paradox of needless waste of electricity in a country that is chronically short of electric power. Following the excellent injunction of Atul Gawande in his book, *A Checklist Manifesto,* the essay deals with the kinds of simple changes that can be made to the way we do things, such that human and machine error are reduced to a minimum.

"Voting for Governance", written in the context of state elections being held at the time of writing, urges a shift of attention away from the issues of party alliances which were the stuff of newspaper headlines, and towards demands for prior commitments from electoral candidates that they could be held to if voted into power. "Governance and Information" deals with the need to provide the voter with the information required for responsible voting. "Improving Financial Governance" was in response to the scandalous revelations of financial misappropriation of funds for the Commonwealth Games, held in New Delhi in October 2010. That episode was indeed the trigger for the Anna Hazare movement, highlighting as it did the monstrous misuse of the generous funding provided in order to ensure that the Games brought credit to the country. The essay deals with the larger issue of financial misgovernance at all levels rather than with the specific scandal of the Commonwealth Games, and the need to further empower Constitutional bodies like the CAG so as to help them better perform their mandated functions of watching public expenditure – and better still, tighten structures for preventing misuse rather than locating it after the fact.

"Whose Triumph?" breaks the litany on failed institutions by highlighting an enormously successful Indian institution – the Election Commission. At the time the column was written, the Commission had become an international dispenser of advice on the proper conduct of elections to countries newly having to start the election process after the Arab Spring.

"The Power Grid Knockout" was prompted by the massive failure of the power grid in much of North India in July 2012, which grabbed international headlines (and possibly even a place in the Guinness Book) for its reach and the millions that descended into powerlessness. Power breakdowns and load shedding are routine occurrences in the lives of all but a privileged few in India, but this breakdown was on a hitherto unparalleled scale. The essay deals with the systems failure which precipitated it.

"Look Past 100 Days" was written immediately after the historic majority verdict obtained by the Narendra Modi government in May 2014, and advises against impatience with speed of implementation of the government newly voted in, so as to give it room to go about the massive task of structural reform it faced, at a speed and manner of its choosing.

Finally the last essay, "Replacing the Planning Commission", was written after the abolition of that body in the form in which it had existed for 65 years. The essay makes the point that, as an institution without Constitutional legitimacy, it had usurped functions assigned to other bodies under the Constitution that were more aligned to the federal fabric of India.

12 Tackling Corruption

In a party-based electoral democracy like ours, there can be no getting away from the central link between corruption and the need to fund political parties. Until this issue is confronted head-on, any control devised in one part of the system will merely push corruption to some other part. There has to be some process like that which moved the drafting of the Constitution, which looks into this central cause, and devises some way by which to contain if not quite eliminate it.

In the United States, political funding is legal and declared by both giver and receiver, but other problems have arisen in its wake. Policy is susceptible to capture by large funders, and has therefore loosened the regulatory apparatus that alone can prevent large corruption. The legal cap on any single contribution can easily be evaded by a concerted lobby, each member of which is below the cap. In a bid to shake free of this, President Obama famously collected substantial campaign funds through small online contributions, and even now, has begun his bid for a second term with an early start to a second online call.

In India too, political contributions are legal, and even carry an income tax deduction under sections 80GGB and 80GGC of the present Act.[1] But estimates made in the Union Budget documents [for 2011-12] show the tax foregone as a result of this deduction at a paltry ₹42 crore in 2009-10 from corporates, and ₹2 crore from small firms.[2] At statutory rates of taxation then prevalent, that works out to a total contribution of around ₹130 crore. The deductions claimed by individuals under section 80GGC were a bit larger, at ₹170 crore.

1. A replacement Direct Tax Code (DTC) was presented but not passed during the tenure of the United Progressive Alliance (UPA) government which ended in May 2014, and thereby lapsed. The new government in Union Budget 2015 has announced that with the adoption of some of its major recommendations, the DTC itself is to be dropped.

2. The "Statement of Revenue Foregone" is part of the documentary responsibilities assumed under the Financial Responsibility and Budget Management legislation, enacted in 2003-04, and notified in July 2004. The financial year 2004-05 was thus the first year for which presentation of revenue foregone fell due. The latest figures, for 2013-14 were not much higher at ₹51 crore from corporates, ₹8.4 crore from small firms, and far lower for individuals, at ₹32 crore.

Applying the top marginal rate of taxation on these, we get a total contribution from individuals of around ₹500 crore. Adding together coporates, firms and individuals, we get ₹630 crore. Over five years, if initial collections are well invested by party treasurers in the interim, it could amount to nearly ₹4,000 crore.

How many Parliamentary campaigns would that fund? One candidate each in 400 constituencies, maybe? There are 550 Parliamentary constituencies, and at least three other major contenders in each race who would need equivalent funding. Then there are state elections. These in some cases are more serious business in terms of funding required. In the current campaign in Tamil Nadu, small refrigerators have replaced colour TV sets as the electoral inducement of choice.

You see why political parties have to look elsewhere for funding. The Indian diaspora provides some of it. The rest has to be domestically raised through organised corruption. There is also unorganised corruption, where the demand is placed by an unsupported individual, which takes inspiration from the organised variety and runs along the same channels.

As illustration, some years ago I was travelling by autorickshaw in Bangalore, when at a traffic stoplight, a cop came over to my driver and demanded ₹100. The driver pleaded poverty. The cop described himself as a kind-hearted man, trying to save the driver the penalty for the traffic offence he had committed, which was ₹500. The driver furiously disputed the charge, and the cop eventually let him off.

No move to legalise bribe-giving could have headed off the incident.[3] The cop was anonymous. If traced, he could have turned the tables on the auto driver and accused him of trying to wriggle out of a traffic offence. Even if bribe-giving becomes legal, an allegation of obstruction of justice will always carry the day. No witness could have testified against that accusation.

Later, the driver said the only reason he was let off was because this was an individual without the department behind him. He said

3. The reference here was to a paper by Kaushik Basu titled "Why, for a Class of Bribes, the Act of Giving a Bribe should be Treated as Legal", issued in March 2011 as a working paper from the Ministry of Finance, where he was Chief Economic Adviser at the time.

in cases of organised collection by the police department in response to demands from above, the demander gets to keep none of what he collects, and even gets the sympathy of the bribe-giver.

In the old import control days, the banned and restricted lists were a steady source of income for political coffers. Defence deals are another perennial standby. The pattern of collection evolves continually. The only people who have an understanding of the pattern of organised collection as it stands today are the treasurers of various political parties. They are deeply knowledgeable and have gained their very important posts as fundraisers by virtue of the trust the party places in them. As people in stressful jobs, they might extend their cooperation towards devising a more open system of political funding.

But what might such a system be? Maybe a political cess, to add to all the others now in place? But that will surely bring upon us cess fatigue, particularly since we do not know what happens to all the other cesses that we pay.

At a recent conference on renewable energy, questions were raised about the cess on coal that feeds into a Clean Energy Fund. One of the speakers estimated that accumulated collections from the cess should have amounted to ₹3,332 crore by the end of 2010-11. But the Fund has become a black hole from which nothing emerges.[4] Renewable energy, which is characterised by the natural regional imbalance in generation capacity, critically needs transmission lines to evacuate the energy generated. It was to fund those transmission lines, along with other facilitative investments towards replacing thermal with renewable energy, that the cess on coal was introduced.

Against this background, yet another cess will not at all be welcomed. There are even huge issues that will go with it, such as ways to distribute the fund between political parties. But some such mechanism has to be devised if we are serious about tackling corruption in the Indian system.

4. Subsequently, some funding did emerge from the Fund, amounting by 2014 to around half of the collections from the coal cess.

13 The Lok Pal and Deterrence[1]

When it is notified, the Lok Pal structure will, in the first instance, focus on calibrating penalties to errant acts performed in the past, but if it does not reduce the number of such acts, it will have failed utterly. For the deterrence effect to work, there has to be a short time interval between the lodging of a complaint and action taken. Hence, there has to be enough manpower so that allegations received can be investigated quickly and fairly.

But when the Bill is enacted and notified, unless some admissibility limits are placed, the tsunami of grievances will overwhelm whatever pace of processing the manpower strength of the appointed bodies will allow. A flood of cases is inevitable, because of the unreasonable expectations that the movement has generated. If the time limits prescribed in the bill are crossed as a result, perpetrators will know that a large volume of cases is their best protection against any specific case ever being brought to justice.

So the first few months are very critical. An initial delimitation could be that only cases within the preceding 12 months will be accepted for processing in the first year. In each such case, deterrence will call for focus not just on the individual wrong-doer, but on the corruption enabling feature of the transaction, and on how this can be disabled going forward. So cases will have to be clustered by type of office or functionary, and by the type of transaction.

One of the critical demands of the Anna Hazare team, acceptance of which paved the way for the final agreement with the government,

1. This piece was written after introduction on 4 August 2011 of the first Lok Pal Bill in Parliament, subsequently withdrawn. A replacement Lok Pal and Lok Ayuktas Bill, introduced on 22 December 2011, was eventually passed in amended form two years later in December 2013, and notified on 1 January 2014. Details on the amended Bill as passed, with commentary, are available on the website of Parliamentary Research Service (PRS), at *http://www.prsindia.org/pages/all-about-the-lok-pal-bill-137/*. Lok Ayuktas under the Act as passed are state-level bodies subject to consent by state legislatures. An Amendment to the 2013 Act was introduced in December 2014, and awaits passage through Parliament.

was that the ambit should extend to the lower bureaucracy. Although the 2G scam and the CWG (Commonwealth Games) scam were the headline events that drove the mass movement, and pulled in sections of society that do not normally encounter corruption on a daily basis, the larger support drawn by the movement is entirely because of extortion at the points where the average citizen must interact with government. These are the gateways to caste certificates, death and marriage certificates, passports, ration cards and such, manned by the lower bureaucracy.

Complaints will have to clustered by the type of office of the accused, taluk offices, or customs depots, or police stations, so that the deterrence wing of the Lok Pal can then demand a reform plan for each within a short period of time. Thereafter, the reform plan will get implemented only if the entire staff of an office on which a reform notice is served will be penalised for any further complaints lodged against any individual member of it.

Clustering will also be needed by the type of complaint. The Indira Awaas Yojana (IAY), a Central Plan scheme which gives housing grants to selected beneficiaries below the poverty line (BPL), is one of many schemes involving cash payments, where payments made to the gatekeeper are routine. Similarly, payments to contractors and suppliers are subject to the same malaise. The only variation over the country lies in the fraction deducted.

The basic source of corruption in payments to BPL beneficiaries is uncertainty about timing, which is why beneficiaries are forced to make several trips before finally settling for a discounted sum. The remedy should be simple enough. If there is an announcement made at the start of the financial year, regarding the dates on which IAY payments will be made in various states, the problem should in principle be nipped in the bud. This kind of timetable will also help tighten the process of selecting beneficiaries at the local end.

The call for reform of Plan schemes, as distinct from particular types of offices, can therefore precede enactment and notification of the Lok Pal considerably. If this homework for all schemes involving payments to selected beneficiaries, whether in the Central or State sector, is fully worked out and payment dates are duly announced, then complaints admitted can be confined to failure to adhere to the announced dates going forward. Past grievances can be shunted out with no damage to deterrence.

This might seem totally unfair. After all, if the Lok Pal is supposed to address corruption, should it not admit grievances of every kind that have happened in the past? The only possible justification is the need to keep the Lok Pal process sustainable, since IAY complaints alone could drown a Lok Pal in no time. The overriding importance of deterrence is served not by handling large numbers of cases all stemming from the same systemic cause, but by correcting that cause itself.

A public information campaign has to accompany the setting up of the Lok Pal, whereby the new machinery is not perceived as an instrument for the settling of individual scores. Corruption at the lower levels is often organised and directed from above, so that the person collecting the bribe does not necessarily keep the bribe, or not all of it. I have written on this before ("Tackling Corruption"). Penalties served on past acts must not unjustly target small cogs in a larger wheel.

As for bribes for obtaining routine certificates, several states like Chhattisgarh have already outsourced the process to authorised personnel operating computer kiosks, subject to verification through a central server. These experiments could be recorded in a central database, perhaps the Inter-State Council, which the Lok Pal can access for its reform directives to states.

The primary intent of the Lok Pal has to be correction of enabling features of corruption presently in place. The correctives needed are simple and well-known; so the Lok Pal has to function as an enforcer of those correctives, as a macro-prudential body, rather than as a dispenser of micro-penalties. The rewards, in terms of growth with social justice, could be huge.

14 Scams and the Media

November 2010 was loud with the roar of scams. Tumbling out of political closets at such a pace that the average citizen is left with no sense of the magnitude of damage inflicted by each. Some, like the 2008 2G spectrum allotment, affect the Central exchequer alone since state governments do not get a statutory share of Central non-tax revenue. (The scam itself might not have happened if states did have a share of non-tax revenue; there is nothing quite as effective as monitoring by diverse stakeholders with something to lose.) The land scams are typically confined in their revenue impact to the state where they occur, and some, like the diversion by the Delhi government of scheduled caste welfare funds towards the Commonwealth Games, affect particular classes of beneficiaries.

Media reporting tends to distort rather than inform. Take for example the 2008 telecom scam. Chapter five of the CAG report was very careful not to provide just one estimate of revenue loss to the Central exchequer. It specified a range, with the methodological underpinning to each number in the range clearly spelled out. The media seized the estimate at the high end, and flogged it to the point where the figure of ₹1.76 lakh crore is now firmly lodged in the consciousness of the public as the measure of revenue lost. That was the most fanciful of estimates provided by the CAG, based on the bonanza from the 3G auction in 2010 of ₹1.03 lakh crore, three times what was expected.

Economists are fond of the term counterfactual, standing for what might have been. The 3G auction could be used as a benchmark if it were in no way influenced by consequences of the underpriced 2008 allotment. I have seen a persuasive unpublished argument by Abheek and Debdatta Saha, that the price war following the 2008 allotment in the 2G space made 3G more enticing and led to an unexpectedly high realisation. That rules out the 3G auction as a basis on which to quantify the loss in 2008.[1] The numbers at the low end of the CAG range are far more plausible as the revenue counterfactual, based on what some of the primary allottees realised upon immediately offloading their allotment. These show an exchequer loss of around 1 per cent of current GDP (gross domestic product). A big enough loss, not in need of further exaggeration.

Media slant was similarly responsible for generating a public sense that the Obama visit in November 2010 prised a $10 billion import commitment out of India in order to generate jobs in the US. Those import deals would have happened anyway, but were bunched together for the Presidential visit. The reporting that followed made it look as though we had capitulated to a charming commercial salesman.

Likewise, a flap is periodically raised over Obama's threats to remove the tax breaks under US law that favour firms transferring jobs 'from Buffalo to Bangalore'. So widespread was the conviction of the potential damage to India, that the Republican victories in the November US elections were hailed as a stop to that threat.

Those tax breaks are irrelevant to the Indian IT sector anyway. When business processes in the US are outsourced to an independent IT provider in India, the move is driven by cost advantages, not fiscal advantages. The US tax break impacts only US firms with foreign subsidiaries, and refers (principally) to the provision whereby profits earned outside the US get a tax deferral until actually brought back to the US. This has clearly fueled expansion of US multinational subsidiaries, especially in destinations where the corporate tax rate is lower than in the US. India does not offer a corporate tax rate advantage, but the 10-year tax holiday for units located in Software Technology Parks (STPI) has driven the expansion of captive centres belonging to IBM, HP, Oracle and Microsoft.

1. In a landmark judgement on 2 February 2012, the Supreme Court declared the 2008 allotment unconstitutional and arbitrary, and cancelled the 122 licenses so issued. Auctions held in March 2015 before expiry of these licences fetched ₹86,000 crore after 24 rounds of competitive bidding for 380.75 MHz of 2G spectrum in three bands (along with 5 Mhz in the 3G spectrum band). This is a little under half of the amount at the upper end of the three loss estimates supplied by the CAG.

The US tax deferral may not be ended altogether (although that would make the US tax regime more location-neutral).[2] Instead, there may be a more targeted amendment, whereby payments by US multinationals to foreign subsidiaries for services rendered may disallow the profit margin of the foreign subsidiary (in effect, taxing external profits at the full American corporate tax rate). A more extreme move may make payments for services to foreign subsidiaries entirely non-deductible. If these make subsidiaries in low cost destinations unprofitable, the subsidiaries may just be spun off into host country (Indian) ownership. Ending of the tax break is not a fearsome prospect, in short.

It is time that a responsible official assessment of prospective external fiscal developments of this kind, and of the fiscal impact of scams, is routinely made available by the Ministry of Finance at the Centre in order to temper some of the wilder flights in the media. Central budget documents in recent years include a listing of tax revenue lost on account of concessions in both direct and indirect taxes. Scam impact assessment could be an appendix to this document, with a revenue component and an expenditure component (for rotting foodgrain, NREGA scams, and such).

Every scam is enabled by a system failure. A permanent scam impact and prevention cell in the Ministry could issue periodic notifications on procedural correctives needed to prevent each type of episode, and a status report on these correctives should be a required component of annual budget documentation. An official website, inviting suggestions from academics and practitioners, would be a useful supplement.

The media have played a vital role in the uncovering of scams. Thereafter, governments at the Centre and states need to take ownership and responsibility for damage assessment and correction. This will reduce the amount of Parliamentary and executive time spent on scams rather than on matters of governance. Also, it will give less room for media spin.

2. It remains in place as of 2015.

15 Coal and the CAG

The macroeconomic situation in the Indian economy today[1] is so dire, that the only desperate need of the moment is getting the coal to flow from those blocks. That is the real scam – the failure to scoop out the coal even after an allotment procedure apparently chosen to hasten production. Any ham-handed attempt at restoring revenue to the exchequer, which further retards coal production, will only impose yet another cost on the long-suffering Indian population, over and above what they have already lost through selective allotment in place of auction of rights to mine coal. Power generation and growth are not the only concerns. At stake is the health of the banking sector, which is exposed to the allottees and will get payback only when the coal begins to roll.

On the Comptroller and Auditor General (CAG), there are three strands to the public debate about the report, which need to be separated out. First, there is an allegation that the CAG exceeded his remit by addressing a policy issue. Second, there is that estimate of ₹1.86 lakh crore, of how it was calculated and what it represents. Third, there is the issue of whether the report is politically neutral.

On the first, the problem arises because the word policy is loosely used to cover both public policy choices, and the procedures and processes through which those choices are pursued. The CAG was not questioning the decision to issue coal blocks to private players. He was only investigating the manner in which that decision was

1. This was written in September 2012. The background to the coal scam was the 1972-73 nationalisation of coal, and the selected and discretionary departures from that legislation starting in 1993, whereby private players were granted the right to mine from allotted coal blocks. The burden of this piece was to defend the role of the CAG in having questioned use of an allotment process, in place of an earlier decision to auction rather than allot coal blocks. Subsequent to that report and this essay, a Supreme Court judgement in 2014 rendered void all such allotments, including those where mining was under way. A coal ordinance was issued by the new government in October 2014 setting out the sequence and process by which the coal blocks would be auctioned and very importantly, assigning revenues from auctions and revenue to the states where the coal mines are located. The ordinance was legislatively enshrined in the form of the Coal Mines (Special Provisions) Act, 2015.

implemented, as he is Constitutionally required to do. In this case, the issue was even more tightly circumscribed. It had to do with why the government did not adhere to its very own statement of intent, as set out in a note from the coal secretary in June 2004, to auction the right to mine coal. This intent, aside from making powerful sense in itself, is entirely in line with global trends. Although the Labour government in Australia fell in 2010 for daring to introduce a super tax on mining profits, the worldwide move to tax windfall gains from mining has gathered political strength in the context of the global fiscal crunch and buoyant commodity prices (and incidentally, carries the support of economic theory).

Now to that vexatious estimate of ₹1.86 lakh crore. As the report makes clear, this is a rough measure of the potential profit accruing to the lucky few who got the licence. Readers have to go no farther than the Executive Summary to get the following sentence:

> Audit has estimated financial gains to the tune of ₹1.86 lakh crore likely to accrue to private coal block allottees...*A part of this financial gain* could have accrued to the national exchequer by operationalising the decision taken years earlier to introduce competitive bidding for allocation of coal blocks. [Emphasis added].

If the entire sum continues to be wrongly played up by the media as the loss to the exchequer, the fault does not lie with the CAG.

I have written on media misreporting before ("Scams and the Media") in connection with the CAG's estimate of losses from the 2G spectrum allotment. The figure of ₹1.76 lakh crore from 2G has been flown from so many media pennants that it can no longer be dislodged from the minds of the public as the true estimate of the exchequer loss. In chapter 5 of the 2G report, the CAG was very careful to present three estimates, of which the figure 1.76 was at the far end, and the most contestable, because it was based on the 3G auction that followed much later. But the media seized it for its sensation value, and ran with it.

In the current coal case, the figure of ₹1.86 lakh crore, as the measure of potential profit over the lifetime of the mine, has been criticised for being an undiscounted sum, and for the price figures used. No one is prevented from constructing a time stream and discounting at any rate of their choice, or trying other price and cost configurations. The issue survives any correction of the sum.

Finally, any reader of the CAG report cannot possibly see it as politically partisan. Details of policy in place are fully presented going back to coal nationalisation in 1972-73, along with numbers on coal blocks allotted right from 1993, when captive mining was opened up to private players in power, and iron and steel. The (net) number of blocks allotted after 2004 stands at 142. Between 1993 and 2004, it was either 39 (para 4.2) or 52 (para 5.1).[2] These small internal inconsistencies were avoidable, but they do not detract from the objectivity of the report. The office of the CAG, underpinned by the Indian Audit and Accounts Service, is among the prominent provisions in Constitution for economic protection of the Indian population. Over time, it got reduced to insignificance because of a narrow interpretation of its mandate. But when those shackles are thrown off, it becomes particularly important to keep the focus on the output of the office, not the person occupying it.

The fiscal history of the country is replete with similar instances of lost revenue. The most egregious of these happened not in the last two buccaneering decades, but way back in the fifties, sixties and seventies when licences to import goods on the restricted list were given away to selected allottees. The switch to a tariff equivalent finally happened only in the mid-1980s, and garnered huge tax revenues for the exchequer. Those revenues evaporated again with tariff reduction in the 1990s. The point is that we have repeatedly failed to gain revenue advantage from such policy configurations as were in place at any time, because of poorly designed procedures. The political motivation for design failure lives in the system, regardless of the party in power. It can be removed only with deep structural reform of public institutions.

---

2. Yielding total figures for mines allotted after 1993 of either 181 or 194. Both these numbers are at odds with those in the bill following the ordinance issued in response to the Supreme Court judgement referred to in the previous footnote, where the total number of blocks allotted after 1993 is quantified at 204.

16 A Checklist of Waste

The multiple road bypass outside the All India Institute of Medical Sciences (AIIMS) in Delhi is grandly laid out, with a landscaped lawn decorated with metal art forms, its whole sweep floodlit by night. During the day, the sun takes over the task of illumination, but the floodlights sometimes remain on right through. Looking at this profligacy, you would never guess that India suffers from an acute power shortage. Is there an employee of the Municipal Corporation of Delhi (MCD) to whom the task is exclusively assigned, so that when he is on leave, the lights stay on during the day? Or is there an automatic switch, with no one assigned the task of checking whether it switches off at dawn the way it is supposed to?

Is the MCD not bothered about these lights because it does not pay its power bills anyway? Power distribution companies borrow to keep themselves afloat in the face of non-paying consumers. The latest Financial Stability Report, number 11 in the series (June 2015), shows the share of the power sector at 18.3 per cent of total loans, but at 16.1 per cent of stressed loans.[1] The health of the financial system is at risk.

India has a chronic water shortage. In most urban residential areas, continuous all-day water supply is a fond but distant memory. Ground level sumps function as private catchment buffers between the irregular supply and the domestic need for a continuous supply. Residents form their expectations of the hours of water supply on the basis of what economists call an adaptive expectations model, expecting for tomorrow the pattern established in the most recent days and weeks. But all of a sudden there can be a flood of water, supplied well beyond the usual time, bubbling uncontrollably out of sumps, and forming lakes that can provide sustenance for at least one larval cycle of mosquitoes. Then there can be a drought for some days,

---

1. Financial Stability Reports issued twice a year, can be accessed on the RBI website *http://www.rbi.org.in*

when no water comes through at all, and people anxiously await water tankers to provide an emergency minimum for those empty sumps.

In a country that leads the road accident mortality league tables, we continue to have malfunctioning automated traffic lights. Traffic lights don't necessarily switch off when they fail; they remain permanently on the last colour. When motorists facing an unending red light decide to move on, they pose grave risks to those favoured with an unending green light.

At toll booths on highways, the sum asked for can be an awkward figure like ₹21, where the toll collector carries no change. It takes only a single motorist without the exact sum, and refusing to forgo his change, to cause a car hold up stretching for a kilometre or more, adding pointlessly to the oil import bill, and thereby to the weakness of the rupee.

These instances are taken only from the kinds of public mismanagement confronted by the privileged citizens of India. When it comes to the underprivileged, their survival is more directly threatened. The most horrific are the recent cases in public hospitals, where lethal liquids were served to patients entrusted to their care.

As public systems, or any systems for that matter, have become larger and more complex – in the sense of multiple components all needing to be sequenced in a particular order for effective functioning of the whole – something as simple as a formal checklist may be all that is needed. Atul Gawande, a distinguished surgeon of Indian origin in the US who is as renowned for his writing as his surgical skills, has a recent book (*The Checklist Manifesto*), in which he documents cases where the checklist as a formal prior procedure has saved lives in diverse settings ranging from surgical theatres to aircraft preparation for flights, or improved the speed of completion of buildings and public infrastructure.

The checklist cannot be easily accepted in his country of origin however. In our culture, excellence is measured by contempt for externally-imposed discipline. We rely on the unwritten rather the written, the informal rather than the formal. We are proud of our ability to improvise in the moment, the desperate dash by the orderly from the surgical theatre to the blood bank if an operation goes awry and lets loose a torrent of blood. And if the blood bank is temporarily shut because the keeper is out to tea – well, the orderly just continues his dash to the canteen. Everyone cooperates to find the man with the key, but the patient may need the blood no longer when it finally reaches him.

Checklists lower the risk from human failure and failings. They are a way by which routine safety nets in the form of contingency personnel can be brought into play for staff failing to report to duty. In India, more than elsewhere, effective service delivery requires contingencies in place for pervasive public failure. Traffic, VIP movements and a host of external shocks are more likely here than elsewhere to make for staff absences and delays.

Even large and formal systems neglect the need for contingency replacements. As a result, available staff are made to perform multiple tasks or to work excessively long hours without a break. Raja Parasuraman, a distinguished cognitive neuroscientist of Indian origin in the US, has a number of recently published papers on performance by military personnel tested through high-fidelity simulations of soldier tasks, showing that collateral damage in warfare results from avoidable multitasking at the front line. Likewise, when people are pushed to work for long hours without a break, such as drivers of freight trucks, our highway mortality rates go up.

Complex systems require engineering to protect against risk from human failure. The damage done through inattention to the structure of public systems extends far beyond the delivered outcomes of those systems themselves.

17 Voting for Governance

There is an astonishing lack of debate on economic issues in states going to the polls[1] at a time when the economy faces a deadly combination of low growth, raging food inflation,[2] rising interest rates, and recurrent wobbles in the external value of the currency. Instead there is a focus on personalities and on the groups they would favour and disfavour. Anti-incumbency features in discussion but without demands for granularity in promises of change.

There have over the years been state elections in which parties with a good governance record won successive terms. But conversations between candidates and electorate are still not about the details of what contenders would do to raise the productivity of agriculture, or vest employable skills in school-leaving cohorts, or facilitate industrial production and employment, or reform the power sector, or improve the quality and quantity of water supply, or combat climate change, or improve sanitation. Electoral strategy lapses into particular forms of segmentation of the electorate. Election warfare then degenerates into schoolyard group formation, where scare tactics are used to prevent the formation of party coalitions that can forge alliances across these partitions.

On 26 October 2013, the *New York Times* (NYT) joined the Indian election fray in scare mode. (Subsequent external electoral assessments for India such as that by Goldman Sachs had a more sensible focus on economic issues and expectations.) In an editorial, the newspaper warned that one among the prime ministerial candidates in the general elections slated for May 2014 inspires fear among India's minorities. It did not mention that the entire electorate fears the continuance of misgovernance at all levels.

1. Five states went to the polls between 11 November and 4 December 2013: Delhi, Chhattisgarh, Madhya Pradesh, Rajasthan and Mizoram.
2. Food inflation climbed above 10 per cent in April 2012, and remained there until December 2013.

By coincidence, the newspaper carried an op-ed that very same day by Frank Bruni on another country, the identity of which is an unfortunate red herring in the current Indian context:

> Italy is what happens when a country knows full well what its problems are but can't summon the discipline and will to fix them. It's what happens when political dysfunction grinds on and on and good governance becomes a mirage, a myth, a joke....Italy's current way of doing business... [is] based on personal allegiances, debts owed and time served instead of merit.

Sounds familiar. The difference of course is that India is a far poorer country, with much less room for waste or error.

A current example of misgovernance is the epidemic of dengue fever that took grip post-monsoon [2013], a classical public health failure, which ran riot through rich and poor alike. A popular movie director, Yash Chopra, succumbed to dengue some months ago. There is no political party exclusively culpable for this, in Delhi at any rate, where the municipal level at which responsibility for public health principally lies is controlled by the Bharatiya Janata Party (BJP), and the state government by the Congress party. The general credibility of government is at such an all-time low that when incidence in Delhi was reported (most recently) at 4784 cases, and deaths at 15, the public routinely applied a factor of as much 10 to those numbers.

Even 48,000 cases might be thought of as a low probability affliction in Delhi with a population of 17 million. The absolute numbers were nevertheless large enough to cause an acute shortage of hospital beds for routine surgeries. India now has the proud distinction of having the largest number of dengue cases in the world. Since the dengue mosquito breeds in any collection of water, including those inside homes, controlling their numbers might be thought to lie beyond the reach of the country's governance capabilities. It was not always so. In the 1950s, there was a systematic effort to stamp out malaria in Delhi through home visits by field staff of the public health department. Supervisors later did sample checks to see if their investigators had actually visited. Before the worldwide eradication of small pox by a remarkable international effort, when there was an outbreak in Delhi in 1958, every home was visited and every resident inoculated. Delhi was a smaller city in those days of course, but available channels for outreach were also much more limited.

Voter memory is short. When a public programme succeeds, there is no reminder of what it was like before. People forget the ravages of malaria, of what it was like to be reduced to a shivering wreck. Slowly over time, the focus of elected governments shifted from the universal benefits of good governance to identifiable beneficiaries. The advantage there is that the larger problem can be neglected, and bailouts given to selected groups. The governance solution to food inflation would be to steady the price level in order to benefit all. The votebank solution is to give subsidies to selected identities.

Aadhaar just by itself drives home the decisive shift in the practice of governance in India towards identifiability as the basis for receipt of governance benefits. Aadhaar undoubtedly has huge potential for eliminating ghosts from lists of pensioners, or for enabling financial inclusion. But the core driver of the scheme, which has cost around ₹5,500 crore so far, was its promise of being able to differentiate the entitled from the unentitled. And the failure to secure legal opinion prior to spending all those crores is in itself a massive instance of misgovernance.[3]

Governance is about systems and procedures. It is if anything more relevant in the state context than in that of the general election, which is in any case too far away in time. Any promise or performance of governance has to descend from grand abstractions to specifics, so that voters know what is on offer. Not just chief ministerial candidates, but plain ordinary representatives have to declare what they think are the problems facing the country, and the constituency they are running for. What will they do to fix those problems? What do they think of food inflation, food adulteration, ensuring hygiene in public places? What will they do to enable economic activity and overall betterment?

3. A Supreme Court judgement on 25 March 2014 ruled that Aadhar could not legally be used as a basis for denying entitlements. At the time this piece was written, a ruling of this kind was expected.

18 Governance and Information

No improvement in governance is possible unless information is freely and publicly available on fund flows and the outcomes targeted. Not every citizen has the time to use the Right to Information channel, and in any case they need prior knowledge of what government is attempting in the first place.

The routine business of governance at local rather than at state level is what mostly determines the quality of our daily lives. Whether we wake up to the aroma of blocked sewage, or get our daily quota of potable water, or have police protection, or have to navigate our way through footpaths strewn with food remnants squashed into plastic bags, is all a function of fund flows and expenditure efficiency at our very own local level.

Local governments have received a statutory fund flow from the Centre every year since 1995, in amounts set for five-yearly periods by a succession of nationally appointed finance commissions. This funding must be routed through state governments, as per the Constitution. State governments become pass-through agents for this flow, and have no incentive to transmit quickly what they receive. If failure to provide certification of onward transmission blocks release of subsequent installments, state governments are not the immediate losers, and have no incentive to comply.

Faced with the clear need to restructure incentives, the 13th Finance Commission, which addressed the period 2010-2015, broke the local grant into a two-part flow. A basic flow in two tranches (July and January) was made payable each year by the Centre to local governments, designed as a wholly unconditional entitlement. A performance grant was added on, also due each year in two tranches, but subject to nine platform conditionalities. One of them requires that states supply certified evidence of a mechanism for electronic onward transmission of funds to local governments within five days of receipt. Another was certification by the state of the institution of a property tax board, to assist all urban municipalities in the state with expertise in property tax assessment and collection.

The performance grant was designed to flow only from 2011-12, with 2010-11 left as a gap year in which states could put together the necessary procedures that would qualify them for the grant.

The administrative guidelines sent to states, through which these provisions were formally notified, added on the transmission requirement for the basic grant as well, with penal interest for any delay beyond five days. Another add-on was that the state should hold local elections on time. These conditions apply only after the first tranche in July 2010, which went to all states without exception, but needed to be satisfied for all tranches starting with the one due in January 2011.

So then, are all states getting the basic grant? Citizens have a right to know what has actually been received by local bodies of the state in which they happen to be located, from a statutory provision which must either flow, or if not, the conditionality which was not fulfilled.

The natural place to look for such information would be websites of the relevant Central ministries. The Panchayati Raj Ministry website does display the finance commission guidelines, but provides no clue to its implementation.[1] The Urban Development Ministry website has no information on the basic grant, but displays a list of 13 states qualifying for the performance grant for 2011-12, without any pointer however as to which conditionalities remained unmet in states not on the list. Without that, the interested citizen does not know what must be done, going forward.

There is however a remote link in the Ministry of Finance website, which lists all releases to states from the Centre in excruciating detail. From there it is possible in principle, though extremely tedious, to stitch together those states which got the basic grant, and residually those which did not for whatever reason.

---

1. The situation stands dramatically improved as of 2014. Information on the yearly grant flow in both tiers of the award, basic and performance, are displayed on the website of the Ministry of Panchayati Raj, upto 9 September 2014. *http://www.panchayat.gov.in/panchayat-finances*. However, no underlying information is provided on the sources from where state compliance in respect of conditionalities underlying the performance grant may be verified.

So here is what seems to have happened with the basic grant in 2010-11 (the first year of the 13th Finance Commission horion, when only the basic grant was due). Five states failed to get the full basic *panchayat* grant due in 2011-12, and seven states failed to get the basic urban grant. In 2011-12, these numbers grew to 9 and 14 respectively. This is just the basic grant, for which the requirements are minimal.

The performance grant became payable in 2011-12. The Urban Ministry website list of 13 states recommended for the performance grant for 2011-12 has some surprise inclusions. Andhra Pradesh makes it, despite its reputation for impeding decentralisation, as does Uttar Pradesh, not a state known for good governance. West Bengal is not among the 13 states listed for the urban performance grant for 2011-12, nor was Tamil Nadu, a state which normally leads the governance league tables.

Some of the conditionalities are not easy to fulfill. One of them for example is that all million-plus cities in the state publish in the state gazette a fire response and mitigation plan. Difficult to push through, but after the horrific hospital fire in Kolkata, surely something worth installing for its own sake, independently of the grant riding on it. The qualifying condition is just that the fire plan should be published, not that it should be followed through. Inserting that would have placed too onerous a monitoring requirement at the Central end. But when information of this kind is made accessible to ordinary citizens, they in turn can do the monitoring needed, and the incentive system becomes enabled.

[The Ministry of Urban Development website *http://moud.gov.in/local governance* did not subsequently improve its display. There continued to be no information on the flow in respect of the basic grant to municipalities. On the performance grant, there was merely the report of a meeting convened in November 2014 to review the flow, listing 5 states deemed eligible for the performance grant for 2014-15. This is lower than the 13 states listed as eligible in early 2012. This is something of a mystery, since once a state satisfies the basic platform requirements, there can be no roll-back in terms of eligibility. The functioning of the local grant provides a textbook example of how conditionalities designed to incentivise better governence can be subverted by bureaucratic indifference at the Centre].

Any funding incentive works only if the amount promised is worth the effort required to earn it. The basic grant was around ₹70 per capita in 2010-11, surely enough for the minimal conditionalities involved, and structured to grow in absolute amounts upto 2014-15. The performance grant amounting to two-third of the basic grant, was harder to reach for, but still well worth the effort.

19 Improving Financial Governance

The scandalous squandering of taxpayer money over the Commonwealth Games[1] highlights the sad lack of financial governance at the highest levels. This particular episode showcases our inability to ensure prudence about expenditure which of its very nature can brook no delay.

There is an internal mechanism for financial approvals, which is perceived as rigid and dilatory, and therefore needing to be bypassed where speed is of the essence. There is no fast-track protocol that will preserve time-bound expenditures from flagrant violation of benchmarked norms, to the point where equipment can apparently be leased for amounts far exceeding the purchase value.

But even on the slow track, audit of the Food Corporation of India (FCI), which has presided over large-scale grain losses several times in the past, has apparently had no impact. The FCI after many audit reports is still under tarpaulin sheets.

The need for improved financial governance is most acute at the level of local government. With urban bodies, the problem is not incapacity so much as political capture, but in rural India, there is plain lack of capacity. Well before recent enhancements in statutory fund flows to local government, the Ministry of Panchayati Raj estimated funds released directly to Panchayati Raj Institutions (PRIs) in 2009-10 under an assortment of schemes at ₹95,000 crore, an average receipt per PRI of ₹38 lakh. These are large sums to handle for the financially uninitiated.

In the rural local context, governance capacity has to be created at the most basic levels of physical structures, staff, and honoraria and expenses for elected representatives. The approach taken by the 10th Finance Commission (covering 1995-2000, the first after local government formally came into being), and endorsed by subsequent

1. Held in Delhi in October 2010.

commissions, is that these basics are the responsibility of state governments, since local bodies are brought into being by state legislation. The 10th and 11th Commissions, therefore, explicitly directed that their funding provisions for local bodies should not go towards establishment costs on structures and salaries, so as to carry additionality.

These commissions sought further protection from misuse by earmarking their local grants for specified functions, like water or sanitation or solid waste management. The 11th Commission also dedicated a sum for account keeping and building up a database, key capacity needs. But earmarking led to obstructions in fund flow. The certification needed to ensure that utilisation matched the purposes intended led to procedural delays within the system, to the point where some fraction of the funds intended for local bodies never reached them at all. The 12th Commission therefore earmarked only the funding for urban local governments, at 50 per cent, for solid waste management. The result was that 10.6 per cent of urban funding never reached its destination, as against 7.4 per cent for *panchayats* where funding was functionally untied (but hedged by other requirements).

Finance Commission funds for local government must be routed through states, under the present Constitutional provisions. The state thus becomes a pass-through agent, with no incentive whatever for monitoring usage. The response to conditionalities is very different for grants where the state is the ultimate recipient. This has to be factored in when funding for local government is designed.

The 13th Commission, therefore, consciously eschewed earmarking of grants for local bodies, whether for capacity building or specified functions, since delay and obstructions in fund flow achieve no purpose at all.

There remains the need to train local government functionaries and elected representatives in effective governance. The network of State Institutes of Rural Development (SIRDs) set up for this purpose presently bear the full cost of training, funded by state governments. The Rashtriya Gram Swaraj Yojana (RGSY), a CSS (centrally sponsored scheme), provides supplementary support for training and capacity building, but has been poorly funded.[2]

This model, whereby training is funded at the supply end, is a recipe for ineffectiveness. Training works best when it is bought into by the organisations from where the trainees originate. Organisations depute personnel and pay towards the cost of the programme. Funding from the demand end makes for a more rational match of trainee and training.

The large untied grant provision made by the 13th Finance Commission for 2010-15 now makes this possible. The prescribed flow to local bodies is set in two-track mode, with a basic grant, which amounts to roughly two-third of the total provision, completely untied in respect of usage. For PRIs, this basic grant alone amounts to ₹8,245 crore per year. Taking the total number of PRIs at all levels at 2.5 lakh, this is an average fund flow per PRI per year of ₹3.3 lakh. The sum disbursed could be even higher, since the grant has been configured to a stipulated share of Central tax revenues, which could turn out to be more buoyant than projected. But even the minimum assured sum is a large provision, and it is completely untied. Even if just one-third of this is used by PRIs to buy training for functionaries and elected representatives, it amounts to ₹2,750 crore in annual potential demand for training.

While the purposes for which the funds are used remain entirely at the discretion of the recipient PRI, the need to ensure that reported expenditure actually goes towards the stated purpose remains. The second track of the Commission's provision therefore, supplementing the basic grant, is a performance grant conditional upon a number of institutional reforms, including financial audit under the supervision of the Comptroller and Auditor General (CAG).

There is the larger need to enhance the powers of the CAG itself. Financial governance can only be as good as the agent that secures it. Part of the reason for ineffectiveness of the CAG is the delay in release of audit reports. A CAG bill is on the anvil, which empowers the CAG

2. There has also been a programme for the distribution of printed and pictorial training material to local bodies, undertaken by the nationally funded Indira Gandhi National Open University.

to demand time-bound responses to its documentation requirements for scrutiny. CAG reports on local bodies must then be placed on websites accessible to the general public in order to enable comparison and correction.

20 Whose Triumph?

The Election Commission has emerged as a robust feature of the institutional landscape in modern India. It has achieved that ultimate nirvana of collective achievement whereby the names of individuals directing operations are not as well known as the Commission itself. It has moved seamlessly through controversies over a few appointments here and there, and has become a lighthouse for other countries in the developing world looking to hold free and fair elections under equivalently rough conditions. Co-ordination with the law and order machinery has been remarkable. Booth capturing, which inspired terror among voters who had the misfortune to confront it over the years, has a quaint ring today.

The success of the Commission has had a great deal to do with its early embrace of modern technology. Electronic machines were used for the first time on an experimental basis in the elections of 1982. Between 1999 and 2002, electronic voting moved quickly from partial to full coverage of general and state elections.

At the same time, the Commission did not discard some features of the old technology package used in elections. To supplement voter identity cards, it chose to retain the indelible ink marker, as a physical safeguard against duplicate voting. This has acquired an international following. Countries in the Middle East, in their post-revolutionary task of actually having to elect public officials, are interested in buying that same indelible ink from Mysore Paints and Varnish (MPVL), a state-government owned PSU (public sector undertaking).

A company like MPVL manufacturing decorative and industrial paints, polishes, varnishes and sealing wax should have been privatised long ago, by all tenets of reform. Its owner, the state government of Karnataka, should have vacated that space for the private sector. But in one of those delicious bits of resistance one finds only in India, it remained stubbornly under government ownership. And it has earned profits for its owner, due in no small part of course to its monopoly status as a provider of indelible ink, granted by exclusive licence in

1962. Critics of Indian resistance to total reform will say that MPVL thrived on that monopoly status. But it is unlikely that a national body could have been motivated in its decision to stay with the indelible ink marker by the need to keep a state-government PSU going. At the end of the day, MPVL survived on the quality of its indelible ink. They guaranteed three weeks and, by gum, it does last that long. MPVL delivered.

Those electronic voting machines also come out of two (centrally-owned) PSUs, Bharat Electronics (BEL) and Electronics Corporation of India (ECIL). They work pretty well too, although the one in my booth in the 2009 elections did look a bit rickety.

The recommendation to privatise ownership of PSUs is based on a number of assumptions, which equate ownership to destiny. Perhaps the most recent and lucid statement of the downsides to public ownership is in the 2009 report of an official Committee set up to design liberalisation of the financial sector in India. The chairman was Raghuram Rajan, subsequently appointed economic advisor to the prime minister.[1] Making a case for bank privatisation, the report says (p.78):

> Public sector entities do exactly what private sector entities do, though less well because they have more constraints, a poorer skill pool, and poorer incentives...the skill deficit will make public sector firms less effective at pricing risk. And the costs will partially have to be borne by the government when the under-priced risk eventually hits public sector balance sheets.

There is a string of assumptions there, of which the weakest is about public sector entities having a skill deficit. That is not uniformly true. New private sector entrants in most fields in India are able to survive only by poaching on the rich skill pool within the public sector. It should not be surprising that talented young people gravitated, and still do, to the public sector. Its trump card is the offer of tenured employment, in a country where employment risk is a huge turn-off. The talent that the public sector in India has attracted and nurtured over the years is huge. Ravi Shankar was a salaried employee of the

1. And since September 2013, Governor of the Reserve Bank of India.

Delhi station of All India Radio in the 1950s, as a conductor of one of its two orchestras. The work was light because they mostly did signature tunes for various programmes. The income was not spectacular, but it was steady. The job freed Ravi Shankar to put in long hours on his sitar, but could not retain him when George Harrison beckoned.

So yes, there is a retention problem, but incentives are a matter as much of the work environment as of compensation packages. These things can improve automatically when there is competition, and it really does not matter if the competition is from public or private players. There are 29 public sector banks out of a total of 92 scheduled commercial banks in India.[2] Even within the publicly owned subset of the Indian banking sector, there is keen competition. In an empirical exercise I did 10 years ago with Garima Vasishtha, we found that while public sector banks performed worse on average than private sector banks,[3] individual banks in the PSU category handily outperformed individual banks in the private sector. In the private sector as well, as the global crisis has shown, incentives can be seriously distorted when employee remuneration is tied to short-term enhancement in shareholder value.

A few years ago, three PSU vaccine manufacturing units were closed down. After several cases came to light of children paying the cost for poor quality vaccine sourced from private manufacturers, that decision has now been reversed. Policy must never be predicated on untested assumptions.

2. With the licensing of two more private banks in 2015, and the proposed induction of payments banks and small finance banks, the banking landscape is set to change.

3. These relative group positions can vary over time. In the immediate aftermath of the global crisis in 2008, PSU banks carried a lower per cent of non-performing assets to total liabilities than private sector banks until 2011-12, when the two groups crossed over again.

21 The Power Grid Knockout

Of the multiple deficits plaguing the Indian economy today, the electricity deficit is the most damaging from the perspectives of both growth and equity. Small manufacturing units cannot afford back-up generators. For plumbers and such itinerant service providers, the mobile phones which are their lifeline need to be charged. For women doing electric-powered job sewing, their children can eat only if they are able to deliver their daily quota. If we did not already know this, it was brought home by the big bang knockouts of the northern and eastern power grids at the close of July.

The immediate cause was inability of the Regional Load Despatch Centre (RLDC) to control overdrawal of power by states connected to the grid. The RLDC was not empowered to operate circuit breakers, and could only warn erring states. The erring states were too powerful politically for the RLDC to do anything other than sound repeated warnings.

Why should politics have anything whatever to do with something as routine as drawing electricity from a grid? Clearly, if technical systems of this type have not been ring-fenced from political pressures, a regional chieftain could hold the entire country to ransom, pulling down the country if he or she is displeased. Something is seriously wrong with structuring of the Indian federation.

I have written repeatedly about the desperate need for an inter-state platform where states could meet regularly on their interconnectedness on a number of issues. The Constitution actually provides for such a platform in the form of an Inter State Council (ISC) under Article 263, but the Council came into being only in 1990. The ISC provides in principle a forum where states could meet on issues, and decide in concert on ceding to technical bodies, like the RLDC, the right to operate traffic signals in a purely rule-bound manner.

This kind of process, whereby members of a group cede to an external authority the right to enforce discipline among the group, in a way that cannot be legally challenged by a displeased member, is very common. In academic departments in American universities, for instance, where yearly salary fixation based on productivity involves contentious and unpleasant decisions, it is not uncommon for faculty to agree to an externally appointed Head, who functions in effect as a constitutional dictator.

In practice, the ISC has atrophied through disuse into a somnolent institution tucked away somewhere in the folds of the Vigyan Bhavan office complex. Every once in a while, the ISC acts as the local partner of the Canada-based Forum of Federations for conferences on what are sometimes quite topical issues. The conference is held, but there is no follow up.

Around 10 years ago when I lobbied strenuously for a revival of the rightful role of the ISC, I got two responses. One was that the National Development Council (NDC) provides the platform I was looking for. The second was that when an issue involving state co-operation comes to the fore, temporary platforms spring up to deal with it.

The NDC is a large unwieldy body that meets sparingly, with a set agenda typically centred around approval of national five-year plans. Meetings of the NDC have ritual value like those of the United Nations General Assembly, but lead to no systematic resolution of problems.[1]

Temporary platforms do indeed get formed when there is a pressing issue calling for co-operation and consensus between states. The most recent and successful of these is the Empowered Group of State Finance Ministers, which shepherded the coming on board of all states on the VAT (value added tax), and is presently carrying forward – with many a hiccup – the further move to a dual-track Centre-state GST (goods and services tax). And of course, river water disputes are governed under a separate Constitutional provision (Article 262).

Even so, there are many issues that arise from time to time, each one possibly a problem confined to just a few affected states, that does not by itself justify a separate temporary platform. But these could if ignored, snowball into a general sense of isolation and

1. After August 2014, the NDC has been replaced by the Governing Council of the National Institution for Transforming India (NITI) Aayog, with the same membership as the NDC, but what seem to have been more meaningful meetings focused on selected issues.

disempowerment, which could severely hamper the co-operation needed for any federation to endure. The number of states affected by any single issue could be small, but the problem itself could be large and of overwhelming importance to them.

My earlier battle for restoration of the ISC as a dispute settlement platform arose out of documented instances of the Central government not implementing the recommendations of the 11th and 12th Finance Commissions in full conformity with the intent of those bodies. Aggrieved states had no platform to which they could take their case, from where they could carry a shared grievance to the Centre along with other states similarly affected.

A permanent empowered inter-state body is needed not just to resolve issues of state *versus* Centre, but as a solutions exchange where states can be exposed to best practices. Most of all, a politically-neutral platform is needed from which the Centre can shepherd reforms in critical areas which, if left unaddressed, will bring growth to a shuddering halt. Power, land and labour – the three big inputs into the production process – are all on the concurrent list of the Constitution, with shared responsibility between Centre and states. Transfer of agricultural land is on the state list. States need to reform these markets, a difficult process that will be rendered easier if they do it with a support group of other states facing similar challenges.

Going forward, the India growth story can be revived only on a platform that recognises the mutual dependence between Centre and states.

22 Look Past 100 Days

The fevered focus on the first 100 days of any new government in office most likely originated in the United States, where the newly elected have a transition period of 10 weeks between election day and assumption of office. In the Indian system, the government takes oath within a week or so of declaration of election results. Therefore much of what needs to be done of a purely transitional nature happens after the government assumes office. At such a time, for a new government to be hounded for whether it is leaping to fulfil its campaign promises is a form of harassment it can do without.

The immediate task any new government at the Centre faces, given the timing of the last few general elections, is to frame a budget for a fiscal year already under way. It has six weeks to execute this. The interim budget passed by the outgoing government covers only the first three months of the fiscal year, going up to the end of June. Budget preparation is a massive operation, and although there is in place a serving bureaucracy, ready to present a set of options, six weeks is very little time to complete a process that calls in the normal course for at least three months.

The further problem in India at the present juncture is that the term governance itself has become so subverted over years of neglect, that there is no common understanding of what it means. In the rest of the world, good governance is held to mean efficient functioning of public services. In India, by contrast, the appeasement of particular groups through budget provisions and legislated entitlements of various kinds has become so deeply ingrained in the system, that governance is regarded as a term inherently defined by the ideology of the party or faction advancing it. Underlying this is a sense that there is no such thing as the common good. For any particular governance initiative, even of the textbook variety carrying universal benefits, a search is launched for people not served by that initiative.

On May Day 2014, the Lieutenant Governor of Delhi ordered five key departments of the Delhi government charged with regulatory functions to perform field checks on service delivery points. Half of 26 fair price shops were found to be either closed outright, or engaged in diversion of food items. Touts selling drivers' licenses, key enablers of horrific road accidents in the city, were located in five zonal offices of the transport department. Thirteen out of 16 petrol pumps were found to be cheating buyers by fixing their meters to deliver less than the stated volume. Several private schools were found to be not paying their staff. Most nightmarishly of all, in two major wholesale markets for drugs and medicines, insulin and tetanus injections were found lying in the open in the May heat of Delhi, when they are required to be kept within 2°-8° Celsius. Needless to say, medicines meant for public hospitals were found on sale in these markets.

This is the level of governance found in Delhi, the capital city. To most people, faced with the binary choice between letting these practices continue, and correcting them, the choice will be clear. Yet, there are critics who will point to how the focus on these types of misgovernance is an elitist concern. As they see it, fair price shops cheat those lucky enough to have ration cards, but there are poor people who cannot even get ration cards. Touts help people too poor to pay for driving lessons, but with enough ability to pick up the skill on the job. Petrol pumps cheat customers rich enough to have a vehicle needing petrol. Staff on school payrolls are better off than contractual employees. Ineffective injections only affect people lucky enough to access some kind of medical care.

Misgovernance has gone on for so long, and has become so comprehensive a feature of our lives, that any correction is treated with a cynical search for a hidden ideological or political agenda. The measured correction begun on orders by the Lieutenant Governor, an unelected former bureaucrat, is a welcome change from the theatrics of the short-lived Aam Aadmi Party (AAP) government, even though the latter was actually elected on a platform that promised better governance to the ordinary citizen.[1]

---

1. The AAP was elected back to power when elections were called after a long period of direct rule by the Lieutenant Governor.

The AAP government suffered from a particularly virulent form of 100-day fever, wanting to display fireworks and turn cartwheels while the focus of the media was still on them. In their case, the period for which they intended to stay in office was even shorter, and the pressure to display speed correspondingly greater. In the process, they weakened important public institutions that (are supposed to) serve the common public.

It can be no one's case that the Delhi Jal Board serves its public well. However, its institutional functioning is not helped when senior officials are summarily transferred out, which is what the AAP government did when they encountered bureaucratic resistance to their free water programme. The office of the Comptroller and Auditor General (CAG) is unable to obtain the co-operation of the power distribution companies for the audit begun under an AAP *fatwa*. This weakens the authority of the only constitutionally appointed guardian of public funds. The dramatic confrontation between AAP ministers and the police was not designed to improve functioning of the only institution to which the common citizen can turn for protection in public spaces.

At the end of the day, the best the citizen can do is to vote into power a government, which then takes over the task of strengthening institutions provided for in the Constitution to guard the public interest.

The first 100 days of any government should be a period when it is allowed to get its act together, with no media pressure for faster or higher. Slower is fine if it is directionally good, and places us irreversibly on a better governance platform.

23 Replacing the Planning Commission[1]

The Planning Commission became a powerful centre of extra-constitutional authority, but not because the Constitution overlooked the need for the roles that it played. The prescription of fiscal flows from Centre to states was assigned under Article 280 to finance commissions, set up every five years with what by convention has been a two-year term. The need for co-ordinated policy between Centre and states was likewise foreseen and assigned. Article 263 provides for an Inter-State Council (ISC), for "investigating and discussing subjects in which some or all of the States, or the Union and one or more of the States, have a common interest; or making recommendations upon any such subject and, in particular, recommendations for the better co-ordination of policy and action with respect to that subject." How much more explicit could our Constitution have been? The Planning Commission in that sense was not merely extra-constitutional but actually anti-constitutional, since its existence effectively blocked the appointment of ISC for nearly four decades.

The ISC was eventually born in 1990, but it has existed wanly and apologetically in the shadows as a poor cousin of the Planning Commission. Both bodies were headed by the prime minister who had no time for either, but the Planning Commission had a full-time deputy chairman with Cabinet rank, where the Council had none. Appointment to the ISC as secretary was regarded by bureaucrats as a punishment posting.

Many of the schemes for which the Planning Commission assumed authorship actually originated in the states. The Employment Guarantee Scheme in Maharashtra and the mid-day meal scheme in Tamil Nadu were the pioneers that led to national adoption. Their

---

1. This article was written soon after the disbanding of the Planning Commission, announced on 15 August 2014.

spread to other parts of the country, voluntarily rather than by fiat, could easily have happened through exchange of ideas in the ISC.

The Planning Commission itself became widely seen as an Employment Guarantee Scheme for bureaucrats and economists. Appointment to that Valhalla as Member guaranteed that erstwhile colleagues became supplicants for funded projects, membership of committees, and just plain boondoggles of various kinds. Whole institutions were seriously dependent on the job of evaluating outcomes of Plan schemes in the region where they were located, where it was understood that they would not bite the hand that fed them by conducting an objective evaluation.

The actual damage done by the Planning Commission extended to both the small and the big. Small damage, to give one example, might be a handout towards the corpus of a social science institution of a crore, say, where this amount was actually deducted from the Plan flow due to the state (in which it was located) as support to the State Plan. So the state was done out of its due by this diversion towards an institution, a decision in which it had no say. But these were mere nibbles at the margin.

There was bigger damage. The constitutional channel for Central assistance to states is through finance commissions. The statutory flows prescribed by these bodies are formulaic, and admit of no discretion. These are the flows that have held the Indian federation together. The governments at the Centre and states might be bitter enemies, but the latter could not be denied funds that were its statutory right, as prescribed by the Finance Commission.

Planning Commission flows, on the other hand, for its first 18 years, were entirely discretionary. The first prime minister is not held guilty of institutional destruction, unlike his dynastic descendants, but he did sideline finance commissions while elevating the Planning Commission, as the discretionary arbiter of which state was to get what for its development. If development funding was not amenable to statutory apportionment between states, how else was fairness to be ensured? Gosplan, his role model, was responsible in no small measure for the break-up of the former Soviet Union.

It was only after the 1967 elections, when states elected governments not politically aligned with the Centre, that Planning Commission assistance to State Plans became subordinated to a formula (Gadgil-Mukherjee). In a 2007 research paper, I show that the formulaic share of total flows from Centre to states over a 55-year period from 1951, aggregating across statutory and Plan flows, rose (or fell) systematically for every rise (fall) in political diversity among states, with a two-period lag.

In time, new schemes pushed assistance to State Plans, the original rationale for existence of the Planning Commission, into insignificance. Some schemes did carry apportionment formulae of their own, but because of administrative requirements like utilisation certificates and more recently, co-funding, states with poor administrative capacity and not enough revenues (the two go together) were unable to access the new Plan schemes.

In the end, more even than the inequality of access to funding which it fuelled, the Planning Commission destabilised the federation by the manner in which state governments were made to engage with it. The ISC, as Constitutionally conceived, is a multilateral body where Centre and states were meant to sit around a table together, on an equal platform. The Planning Commission, on the other hand, engaged with state governments serially, one by one. Elected heads of state governments were made to appear before the Planning Commission singly, and justify the outcomes of Plan funds. Its eight or nine members sat before them in judgement, while not being electorally or otherwise accountable themselves.

In the interests of full disclosure, I must reveal that I was a Member of a Finance Commission (the 13th), and in prior years a willing participant in several committees of the Planning Commission. During my episodic association, the power wielded by the Planning Commission was effectively concealed by the ramshackle socialist era interiors of Yojana Bhavan. But in recent years, the Indian taxpayer has done up the interiors too. The ISC could use both the premises and the expertise of the staff,[2] and start the task of convening issue-

2. In the event the Planning Commission premises, and many of its functions, have been inherited by the National Institution for Transforming India, the NITI Aayog.

specific meetings with departmental representatives from states, so as to remove the procedural obstacles that have landed us in the present combination of high inflation and low growth.

Part III

CENTRE AND STATES

The prescription of statutory flows from the national government of India (called the Union government in the Constitution, but in common parlance the Centre) to the constituent states is a major feature of its federal structure that has held the country together. Every five years, by Article 280 of the Constitution, the President of India is mandated to appoint a five-member body called the Finance Commission, which is charged with the task of looking at the tax revenues of Centre and states, and prescribing flows from the Centre that will cover expenditure needs of the states. As the language of the Constitution also demands that the manner of calculation of states' shares be laid bare by the Finance Commission, there has been a commendable degree of transparency with respect to the allocation of these flows between states. Most of all, once the recommendations are accepted in Parliament, which has been the case at least in respect of all 14 commissions so far, there can be no departure in practice from what is due to each state, regardless of the nature of the political relationship between the state and the Centre. This has been the statutory strength of the Indian federation, underpinned as it is by a Constitutional guarantee, and a legal system that stands ready to enforce it.

The first three essays in this section are about the 13th Finance Commission of which I was a member. Its report was submitted at the end of December 2009, in time for the start of its award period, from April 2010 to March 2015. The first essay is on the contents and approach of the report. It is a useful summary of the constitutional task faced by all finance commissions. A number of assumptions underpinned the projections for its award period. An epilogue juxtaposes these against realised actuals. More details on fiscal deficits during the award period are in the next section on budgets and taxation. The second essay is a response to an article by Mihir Rakshit in the *Economic and Political Weekly* commenting on the report. It summarises the points made by Rakshit and therefore stands alone. It is included here for the opportunity it provides to understand the alternative ways of thinking that could underpin the prescription of fiscal flows to states. Being cast in the mould of a debate, it provides a clear opportunity for defence of the need for fiscal discipline, and the compulsion to control the growth of public debt even in a country desperate for expansion of physical and human capital.

"Barriers to Equalisation" is about the limitations posed by data availability to the task of finance commissions, which among other things try to equalise access to public goods across the country by compensating for the revenue raising potential of states in a manner inversely related to that potential. Potential is of course different from observed revenue, which is a product of tax effort and the potential to which it is applied.

The fourth essay, "From Outlays to Outcomes", was published in *India Review* and is on ways to embed incentives in the design of flows of funds, such that expenditures actually result in fruitful outcomes. The three principal initiatives needed to propel public expenditure towards better outcomes remain substantially neglected, four years after this essay was written.

The next two essays are about additional grants prescribed by the 13th Finance Commission for the period 2010-2015 in order to address the need for structural reform in the Indian system. "The Supply of Justice" is on the blocked Indian legal system, where pendency and delays turn all but the most hardy away from seeking legal redress. This piece deals with the funding provisions made by the 13th Finance Commission to unblock courts and increase the supply of judicial personnel. "Tribes, Forests and Mines" deals with the vexed conflict between development and environmental concerns.

The two essays that follow are on eleven states with cost disabilities arising on account of hilly terrain, which were separately notified as belonging to a special category deserving of affirmative action in fund flows for developmental purposes. The 14th Commission abandoned the distinction. "Special Category States" deals with how poverty is routinely taken on board by finance commissions, and is not a relevant criterion for inclusion of any other state for special treatment, although as I have suggested, there are other ways by which hilly terrain can more directly be taken on board in the formulae. The piece was written in response to a powerful political demand made by Bihar as the poorest state in India, to be included in that list.

"Funding States" reviews a report commissioned by the Planning Commission to prescribe a formulaic way by which to rank states and thus quantify their entitlement to development funding. The Planning Commission, until its abolition in August 2014, was an additional source of funding to states, over and above the statutory flow prescribed by finance commissions. The essay makes a nuanced argument for why pooled outcome deficits cannot be the basis for prescribing state shares in an unconditional fund flow. This is an important issue – the need to keep out perverse outcome incentives from the structuring of fund flows.

The final piece is on the Report of the 14th Finance Commission, written on the day of its placement in Parliament on 23 February 2015.

24 The Report of the Thirteenth Finance Commission[1,2]

The core task before all FCs (finance commissions) is to ensure the capability for roughly equivalent levels of public services to all Indian citizens, regardless of state of location. The equalisation sought is citizen-centric, and calls for compensation across states for differences in fiscal need, modified by cost disabilities. There can be no pretence that this by itself, even if fully and correctly done, will guarantee equalisation of delivery on the ground, but statutory transfers to states are clearly a necessary enabling pre-requisite.

Finance commissions make provisions corresponding to this core task. They also make an assortment of other recommendations, if asked to do so. Chief among the additional tasks imposed on the 13th Commission was that of prescribing a fiscal roadmap for the Central government, with oil bonds and other off-budget financing pulled into the mainstream fiscal accounts.[3] Among the other assigned tasks was a review of the first round of state fiscal legislation, incentivised by the 12th Commission through conditional concessions on state debt owed to the Centre, with the implicit charge of recommending a second round.

The 13th Commission has set the aggregate annual share of states at 32 per cent of the divisible tax pool of the Centre for the horizon

1. Finance Commission (2009). *Report of the Thirteenth Finance Commission 2010-15*. New Delhi.

2. This column appeared in *Mint* newspaper by invitation in my capacity as a member of the 13th FC, just preceding the Union Budget 2010, the first of the five years for which the provisions of the Commission in terms of statutory flows from the Union Government to states applied.

3. This was a practice previously in place, by which subsidies promised to oil marketing companies to compensate for administered prices below their supply cost were repaid not through explicit expenditure provisions in the annual budget of the Centre, but through interest-bearing bonds. This was in effect a borrowing by the Centre from these companies, but neither the expenditure due nor the bonds given in exchange, with accumulating interest, entered into the formal fiscal accounts.

2010-2015, up slightly from 30.5 set by the 12th FC.[4] The shares of individual states in the total are set, as always, through a transparent formula. The formula is newly configured. The report demonstrates that even states whose per cent share has fallen will nevertheless get a higher transfer as a per cent of their respective domestic product, owing to the larger aggregate provided for.

Tax shares are supplemented by absolute grants in FCs' provisions. With grants added on, transfers to states ramp up to 39 per cent of the divisible pool. There are 10 grant categories, some with multiple components. The third largest grant, for ₹50,000 crore, is to compensate states for revenue losses following introduction of the GST (goods and services tax), but heavily conditional on conformity with a nationally uniform single flat-rate model, as well as a comprehensive tax base that includes real estate transactions. If this is adopted, the GST will replace the stamp duty levied by states. Despite the three-year interval allowed for implementation and a few permitted relaxations, the requirements are sufficiently exacting that the grant may not become payable.[5] Minus the GST grant, total transfers come down to 38 per cent of the divisible pool.[6]

The nominal growth projections in the FC report are likely to be greatly exceeded in the event. Data which became available a month after submission of the FC report at the end of December 2009, project a real rate of growth of 7.2 per cent for 2009-10, and thus nominal growth at around 13 per cent. This is far above the 10.5 per cent nominal growth rate assumed in the budget exercises for 2009-10.[7]

---

4. The 14th FC raised the tax share substantially to 42 per cent of Central tax revenue.

5. It did not, in the event. Even the Constitution Amendment Bill, tabled in 2010, was not passed by the United Progressive Alliance (UPA) government whose term ended in May 2014, and had to be tabled afresh in December 2014 as the 122nd Constitution Amendment bill. In any case, the tax base in the earlier Amendment tabled did not include real estate transactions, which was the key feature of the 'ideal' GST proposed in the 13th FC report.

6. These percentages are based on tax revenue of the Centre as projected in the report, as an aggregate across the entire five-year period. The corresponding projected estimate in the report of the 14th FC is 47.72 per cent over the period 2015-2020. Actual estimates of tax shares plus grants would be lower if realised tax revenues exceed projections, and vice-versa.

7. Higher still was the real growth eventually realised of 8.6 per cent in 2009-10, and nominal GDP (gross domestic product) growth of 15.1 per cent. Projected and nominal GDP for the award period of the FC (2010-2015) are shown in the epilogue.

What therefore becomes a matter of critical importance is whether there are enough incentives for fiscal discipline built into the 13th FC provisions and recommendations, so that the good growth prospects are turned into a fiscal correction opportunity.

A very large number of methodological innovations in the report aim at sharpening incentives for fiscal discipline; better outcomes and spatially dispersed growth; strengthening monitoring and accountability in the system; and restructuring the measure of fiscal need in pursuit of the core task. This is done through design alterations in the formulae underlying transfers to both states and local bodies, the grant conditionalities, and the operational and other features of the fiscal roadmap recommended for Centre and states.

The fiscal roadmap is approached not as a matter of targets and paths alone. There are heavy disclosure obligations placed on the Centre. The recommended measures include giving the Medium Term Fiscal Plan (MTFP) primacy as a statement of commitment rather than a statement of intent, with a detailed breakup by budget head of plan and non-plan transfers to states three years into the future. This will render flows to states predictable, and in turn enable medium-term commitments by states. The revenue consequences of new capital expenditures are also to be quantified, so as to factor in the cost of adequate asset maintenance, going forward. Structural shocks such as Pay Commission arrears are to be avoided by making the pay award commence from the date of acceptance, not with retrospective effect from a past date. The arrears from backdated dues consequent upon the Sixth Pay Commission award were a major cause of fiscal uncertainty among states during 2008-2010, as much as the revenue shock resulting from the global slowdown. Additional disclosure requirements from 2013-14 include the listing of all vacant land and buildings, valued at market prices by all departments and PSUs (public sector undertakings).[8]

The FC has no instruments with which to either incentivise or enforce the fiscal roadmap recommended for the Centre. However, since the roadmap was an added term of reference from the Centre,

8. None of these additional recommendations was implemented in the event.

it is hoped that it will be legislated, with the recommended provision for an independent review mechanism, to enable ongoing monitoring. Disinvestment proceeds are recommended for inclusion in the fiscal accounts as non-debt capital receipts, and have been conservatively estimated to rise from half a per cent of GDP in 2010-11 to 1 per cent in 2014-15.

The projected correction path for the Centre turns the revenue deficit into a surplus of half a per cent of GDP by 2014-15, winds down the fiscal deficit to 3 per cent for that year, and in conjunction with disinvestment proceeds of 1 per cent, makes possible capital expenditure at the Centre of 4.5 per cent of GDP.[9] States are expected in aggregate to achieve a zero revenue deficit (or surplus) by 2014-15, and a fiscal deficit of 2.4 per cent of GDP. For both Centre and states, the year 2010-11 is treated as an adjustment year, with options left open for a moderate pace of fiscal exit. Indeed, the permissible deficit limits for 2010-11 for the Centre are higher than those projected in the MTFP accompanying the 2009 Union Budget. The consolidated debt of Centre and states together is expected to come down to 68 per cent of GDP by 2014-15.[10] The paths for individual states are tailored to their initial conditions in a base period before onset of the global meltdown.

States are incentivised to enact legislated commitments to the roadmap as prescribed in the report, with three inducements. These are interest concessions on debt owed to the National Social Security Fund (NSSF), waiver of debt owed to Central Ministries other than Finance, and withholding of state-specific grants for failure to enact. They are given a year to do this, so that their fiscal correction horizon starts only in 2011-12.

Enactment carries these incentives, but enforcement of state paths is left to the Centre through state borrowing caps. A new formula for determining borrowing entitlements uses actual growth (with data

---

9. The Commission essentially envisioned a return by 2014-15 to the targets of the original Central Fiscal Responsibility and Budget Management (FRBM) Act (as amended in 2004), which required the revenue deficit to be reduced to zero, with the accompanying rules targeting an FD reduction 3 per cent of GDP, both by end-March 2009.

10. This and other fiscal projections are examined for their realisation in an epilogue to this essay.

availability lags) in place of projected growth rates, which was the earlier practice. High growth states will thereby benefit from their performance, and this will also avoid the phenomenon observed in the past, of these states being confined to borrowing limits well below their deficit per cent entitlements, by virtue of using (lower) projected rather than actual growth.

The Central subsidies on food, fertiliser and petroleum are examined in great detail, and a feasible correction path for each is prescribed. The total subsidy bill is projected to be lower by 10 per cent in nominal terms in the terminal year, relative to the budget projections for 2009-10 of around ₹111,000 crore.[11] The fertiliser subsidy is to be reduced in 2014-15 to one-fifth in nominal terms of its budgeted sum in 2009-10. The oil subsidy is brought on-budget, confined to families below the poverty line for LPG (liquefied petroleum gas), and for kerosene, with a further reduction by 40 per cent through better targeting. The food subsidy however is allowed to rise by 40 per cent in nominal terms, given the expected passage of legislated right to food.

The Non-Plan Revenue Deficit (NPRD) Grant is a most unfortunate vestigial remnant of the inherited transfer structure, an embedded invitation to fiscal profligacy by states. Owing in part to restructuring of the transfer formula, the number of states qualifying has been reduced to eight from the special category.

The provisions for transfers to local bodies mimic tax shares of states, but are prescribed in absolutes as Constitutionally required, with reference to the divisible pool of the previous year. There is a basic grant of 1 per cent, and a performance grant that ramps up the total provision to 2 per cent of the (current) divisible pool. The performance conditionalities strengthen accountability and monitoring at the third tier, improve the efficiency of the state as a pass-through agent, and call for full disclosure of state-local transfers. The urban share, hitherto roughly half the rural provision in per capita

11. This target was laughably beyond reach in the event. Subsidy containment was the greatest challenge faced by the outgoing UPA government, voted out in May 2014 and therefore in power for four of the five fiscal years of the 2010-2015 award period of the 13th Finance Commission. The subsidy story is detailed in the next section on Budgets and Taxation, which focuses on fiscal developments at the Centre.

terms, has been raised to parity with the urban population share by the 2001 Census. With this, and in conjunction with the three-part environmental grant, it is hoped that the grave water and sanitation conditions faced in urban cities, no less than in rural habitations, across the country will be somewhat mitigated.

Epilogue

The website *http://indiabudget.nic.in* has year-wise budgets of the Central government going back to 1996-97. The story of what happened in realised actuals as against what was projected or hoped for by the 13th FC is summarised below in respect of four key issues.

- Oil bonds have already been referred to in a footnote above. Moving that off-budget item to the on-budget petroleum subsidy was certainly one of the reasons why the subsidy shown in the budget declined as slowly as it did.[12] In addition to the subsidy during each budget year, there is also the outstanding stock of oil bonds that has to be redeemed. These issues are before the Expenditure Commission appointed in the first budget of the new Bharatiya Janata Party (BJP) government in July 2014.
- The fiscal correction programme designed by the Commission for the Central government required an FD at 3 per cent and RD at (-)0.5 per cent (a revenue surplus) for 2014-15. The Commission also asked for an amendment of the earlier FRBM legislating fiscal correction along these lines. This was finally enacted with the Finance Bill accompanying the 2012 Union Budget. The new legislated target capped the RD at 2 per cent for 2014-15, corresponding to an effective RD (after removing capital expenditure content of current account expenditures) at zero. Other targets delegated to the rules, which were issued as late as May 2013, targeted reduction of the FD to 3 per cent of GDP by 2016-17 through an annual reduction path of 0.5 per cent of GDP. The annual budget for 2014-15 targeted the FD at 4.1 per cent and RD at 2.9 per cent, where the latter clearly

---

12. See Figure 2.0, Part IV.

violates the provisions even of the amended act, let alone the Commission's targets, which required a current account surplus by 2014-15. However, the FD target at 4.1 per cent could be considered to lie along the path of the FRBM rules as amended in 2013. The provisional final figures for 2014-15 place the FD at 4.0 per cent, and the RD at 2.8 per cent.

- A further amendment to the FRBM act moved with the Finance Bill accompanying the Union Budget for 2015-16, has re-set the target years for both revenue and fiscal deficits to 2017-18, pushing back the earlier target year for the FD by one year, and for the RD by three years. The targets themselves remain at 3 per cent, and 2 per cent as before. There is also a path set for reduction of the FD from the level of 4.0 per cent achieved in 2014-15 (slightly below the budgeted target), to 3.9, 3.5 and 3.0 per cent for the three years that follow.
- Notwithstanding the poor performance in terms of fiscal targets achieved, the debt trajectory over 2010-2015 remained substantially on target. Figure 24.1 illustrates this. This paradoxical achievement was on account of nominal growth rates of GDP having been substantially above nominal interest rates on government debt, especially in 2010-11 and 2011-12. The GDP nominal growth rates were projected by the Commission at 12.5 per cent and 13 per cent in the first two years 2010-11 and 2011-12, followed by 13.5 per cent in the last three years, working out to an expected yearly compound growth rate of 13.2 per cent over the period 2010-2015. The realised nominal growth rates (by the old series) were 20.3 and 15.6 in the first two years, and 12.2, 12.3 and 13.4 in the last three, working out to a realised compound yearly rate of 14.7 per cent. These are shown in Figure 24.2 below. The small stretch of the new series shows higher nominal growth rates for 2012-13 and 2013-14, but lower for 2014-15 than that projected in the old series.
- A recommendation by the 13th FC, for transparency in budgetary documentation, has gone substantially unheeded. That segment of the report, therefore remains a plan for action going forward.

Figure 24.1

Debt as a Per cent of GDP 2010-2015

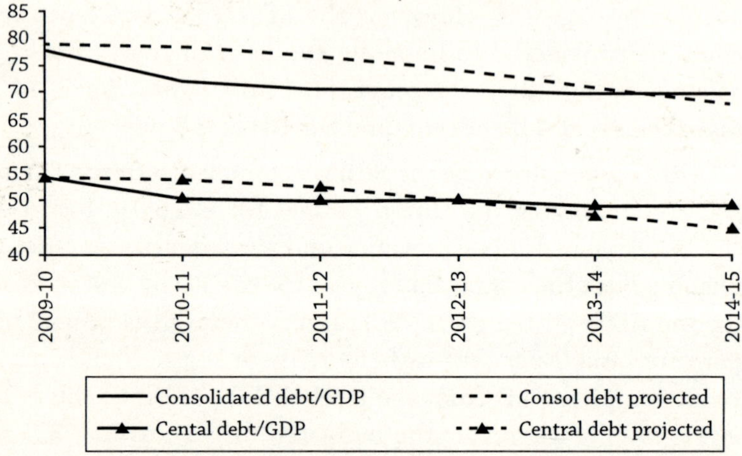

Source: All consolidated debt from *Indian Public Finance Statistics 2013-14*, generated for 2014-15 using *Union Budget 2014-15*. For 2013-14. Projections are from the *Report of the 13th Finance Commission, 2009*. The GDP estimates used are from the earlier series, since the new series introduced in January 2015 provides data only starting 2011-12, and does not carry a uniform linking factor that can be applied to past years to enable splicing of the two series.

Figure 24.2

Nominal GDP Growth Rates Achieved and Projected by the Thirteenth Finance Commission, 2010-2015

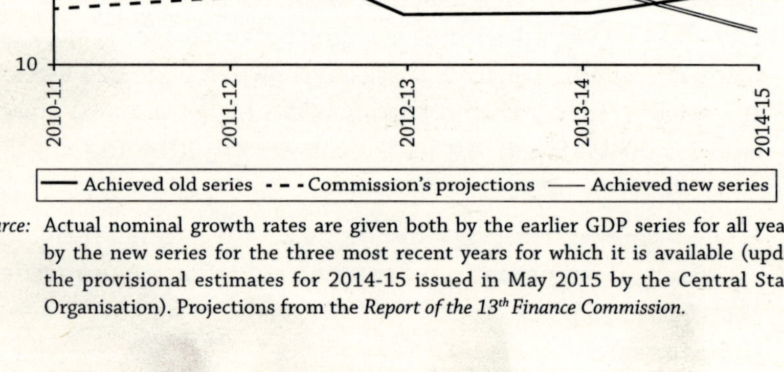

Source: Actual nominal growth rates are given both by the earlier GDP series for all years, and by the new series for the three most recent years for which it is available (updated to the provisional estimates for 2014-15 issued in May 2015 by the Central Statistical Organisation). Projections from the *Report of the 13th Finance Commission.*

25 Response to Rakshit on the Report of the Thirteenth Finance Commission[1]

Following a succinct summary of the principal recommendations of the Thirteenth Finance Commission (THFC) for fiscal consolidation, Rakshit raises several issues.[2] They are listed below, followed by my response to each. In all quotes from his paper, any additions are shown in box parentheses.

The Targets of the Fiscal Adjustment Programme (FAP)

Rakshit's principal criticism is: "The overarching goal of FAP, we have noted, is to bring down the debt-GDP (gross domestic product) ratio to 68 per cent by 2014-15. Yet it is not explained why this constitutes the primary target or how its magnitude is estimated." Debt reduction was a goal of our, as of any, fiscal consolidation exercise, but the actual numerical level of 68 per cent by 2014-15 was a projected outcome, not the primary target. The primary targets were to bring the revenue deficit down to a balance of zero consistent with feasible projections of revenue and expenditure; and to protect public investment upto a permissible limit of 3 per cent of GDP (for the Centre, and separately for states in aggregate). Pursuit of fiscal correction along these lines over five years led to debt reduction to 68 per cent of GDP, as an outcome.

The following extended quote from para 9.5 states the approach adopted quite clearly:

---

1. This appeared in the *Economic and Political Weekly* 46(13): 137-39.
2. Rakshit, Mihir (2010). "Fiscal Consolidation and Inclusive Growth: The Finance Commission Approach", *Economic and Political Weekly* 45(48): 38-45, 27 November.

> In our view, it should be possible to reduce the combined debt of Centre and states to around 68 per cent of GDP by 2014-15. This target has been arrived at as the feasible and desirable correction, based on our projections of the medium term macroeconomic situation during the award period and our assessment of the resource position of the Centre and states over this horizon.

The correction was what was deemed possible and consistent with protection of public investment at 3 per cent of GDP at each level of government.

It is most certainly true that debt sustainability, or the lack thereof, is a function of a large number of factors, including the growth potential of the economy. But in so far as that potential itself is a function of the availability of capital for private investment at reasonable cost, we believed that reduction of public debt was a necessary condition for its realisation. We saw the growth potential of the country as endogenous, and inversely related, to the level of public debt. Rakshit's subsequent statements follow from that initial misreading of our exercise:

> Given the initial situation, fixing the terminal year debt target first and then constructing the debt-deficit time-path over the award period are in violation of economic logic...

I am sure he will be happy to know that we were not in violation of economic logic, and that our terminal target was an outcome of the feasible debt-deficit time-path constructed by us. The watchword in our construction of this time-path was feasibility, for both Centre and states. We did not want to prescribe a correction path that would be sure to be violated. Besides that, developments subsequent to our report have confirmed our belief that the recommended path is indeed feasible and attainable.[3]

We were well aware that prescription of state limits at 3 per cent of GSDP (gross state domestic product), which is available only at factor cost, scales down to an aggregate limit of 2.4 per cent of GDP at market prices (Table 9.7 in the report). Our retention of 3 per cent of GSDP for states was a concession to continuity.

---

3. Although written a mere year after the publication of the report, the public debt trajectory was indeed close to full realisation, as shown in Figure 24.1.

The Projected GDP Growth Path

Rakshit believes that the (nominal) growth path underlying our fiscal prescriptions, 12.5 per cent and 13 per cent in the first two years, followed by 13.5 per cent in the last three years, did not factor in the output gap in the pre-award year 2009-10. "With underutilised resources and weak private demand, not only is a relatively large public investment required for closing the output gap, but such expenditures involve little opportunity cost or crowding out."[4] An excellent point, but consider the implications. If we had prescribed a large public investment in the very first year, 2010-11, the governments at the Centre and states would have had a lead-time of less than two months between issue of the report and formulation of their budgets for 2010-11. Capital expenditure that is productive, and not of the make-work variety, requires considerably more lead time. The difficulty with prescribing a jump-start, as happened also with the US response to the crisis of 2008, was that shovel-ready capital projects are not always conveniently at hand. By phasing capital expenditure evenly over the five years, we believe we recognise this important practical limitation. In this, as in our fiscal correction programme, we chose the feasible, over the optimal but infeasible.

Crowding Out

No one would disagree with Rakshit when he says: "...even in the worst-case scenario of one-for-one crowding out, compared with private capital formation, public investment could be both growth and equity-promoting." The key word there is "could". Yes, it could. But alas, given the vast scope for corruption in public capital expenditure, which for political economy reasons will remain in place until political parties find other ways to fund themselves, there has to be a limit even on public investment, desperate as our need for such investment might be. The hope is that, when public investment is limited by fiscal

4. In the event, as shown in Figure 23.2 in the previous chapter, nominal growth rates in the first two years of 2010-2015 far exceeded that projected by the Commission, even without a deliberate Keynesian push to public investment, and dramatically slowed down in the last two years, for reasons related to procedural delays to official approvals for private investments rather than insufficiency of public investment (see essay 43, "Transparency as Cure").

rules, the productive fraction may well be higher than in an uncapped situation, since some physical outcomes have to be shown against the limited expenditure. Uncapped public investment could unleash a terrifying lack of both public infrastructure and private investment.

Disinvestment

Rakshit argues: "In fact, given the prospective profile of returns on PSUs and the fact that the borrowing costs of the government are significantly less than private sector discount rates, disinvestment, contrary to popular belief, constitutes a costlier means of financing public investment." The natural corollary is that all investment should be funded publicly as long as borrowing costs of government are significantly below private sector discount rates. Clearly, market assessment of the sovereign appeal of public debt can reach the tipping point, as happened [in 2010] in Greece. The issue really is one of the level and projected trajectory of public debt, and how close governments wish to skate to the tipping point. Disinvestment has finite limits, but offers a supplementary alternative to borrowing in the present case where (in the judgement of the Commission) the debt/GDP ratio was already at a level high enough to ramp up the cost of government borrowing. The recommendation of the THFC (para 6.46) is that the proceeds from disinvestment be utilised to finance the changing requirements of the public capital portfolio. Thus, one class of assets in the form of government equity is to be replaced by another form of assets, either social infrastructure such as school buildings and hospitals, or urban transport systems or infrastructure for environmental protection.

Financial Inclusion

Raskhit recommends that direct budgetary support to financial institutions like public sector banks, National Bank for Agriculture and Rural Development (NABARD) and Small Industries Development Bank of India (SIDBI), for on-lending to Small and Medium-sized Enterprises (SMEs), could actually strengthen rather than impair fiscal viability. He recognises that administrative costs of lending to SMEs will be high, and does not recommend an interest subsidy, but considers direct deployment of public funds for removal of the credit constraint facing unorganised enterprises as profitable even so, because the government's borrowing cost is lower than the return on private investment.[5] He concedes that this support will have to be phased in only after the front-loaded expenditure on public infrastructure that he earlier argues for. Thus, the whole argument for publicly-funded financial inclusion presupposes an earlier successful corruption-free front-loaded thrust on public investment. Since the fiscal programme of the THFC did not, for reasons spelled out above ("Crowding Out"), either front-load public investment or leave it uncapped, the issue of a backloaded publicly funded thrust towards financial inclusion simply did not arise. Summing together both the Rakshit reasons, it would appear that he thought a starting public debt to GDP ratio of a little under 80 per cent in 2009-10 was a good jumping off point for such a further unbridled expansion of public debt. We fundamentally disagreed there. At present levels of efficiency of public expenditure, such an expansion would have (rightly) frightened prospective private investors. And to have assumed a radical overnight improvement in government efficiency would have been irresponsible. We believe our prescription for a steady accumulation of public investment in infrastructure, at an average of 6 per cent of GDP each year over 2010-15, provides the potential for a widely-flung net of public infrastructure that will naturally attract private initiative and private funding.

Human Capital Formation

Rakshit argues, as many have done, that expenditure on human capital is as much an addition to productive capacity as expenditure on physical capital. He sees a problem with the THFC having accepted the conventional budgetary (and national accounts) classification

---

5. This recommendation has been heeded in the Union Budget for 2015-16, which proposes the setting up of a Micro Units Development Refinance Agency (MUDRA) Bank, with a corpus of ₹20,000 crore, and a credit guarantee corpus of ₹3,000 crore. The risk-sharing model of this initiative has to be worked out in such a way that there is no perverse incentive propelling the primary lender towards lower due diligence.

of expenditure on human capital formation as current, not capital, expenditure. To quote him:

> Clearly, the entire expenditure on education and a major part of health care cost constitute investment (as do expenditures on R&D, including payments to researchers)... What is worse, given the overarching requirement of non-negative revenue balance, clubbing HRD expenditures with current ones not only leaves little scope for enlarging investment in human capital, but the stipulated FRBM targets might in all probability be met through a slowdown in HRD spending.

The Sixth Pay Commission, like all earlier Pay Commissions, ramped up expenditure on education and health care, relative to other state-level functions because these are the most salary-intensive in nature. A matrix for any state of functional by economic classification would show that the education and health care functions are ranked at the top in terms of salary content. There is no established link between salary levels and performance indicators like student achievement levels or teacher presence (teacher absenteeism in India is commonly estimated at 25%). On the contrary, states that have improved delivery of these functions have been those that tried to stretch a given budgetary allocation by hiring of contract teachers. Several recent econometric studies show that contract teachers, paid between one-seventh to one-ninth of tenured teachers, perform as well or better. Some states such as Madhya Pradesh and Chattisgarh have allowed Panchayati Raj Institutions (PRIs) to recruit teachers at pay scales different from that of the government. The state government continues to bear the cost of the teachers' salaries; but since they are now appointed by *panchayats*, they are more accountable at the grass-roots. The *panchayats* too are more empowered.

It is precisely because education expenditure was curbed by limits on revenue deficits that effectiveness of delivery was looked to. Had the fiscal curb not existed, we would have seen skyrocketing expenditure on health and education, sanctified by being equated to physical capital, with no commensurate impact on outcomes. Expenditure on physical capital, even though anchored to physical outcomes, has a high corruption element. The slack in expenditure on human capital is considerably harder to measure. This measurement difficulty must necessarily inform prescriptions for public expenditure far more than the conceptual similarity between physical and human capital formation, which surely does exist. There can be no denying Rakshit's point that "a fiscal road map for securing rapid and inclusive growth has to ensure speedy removal of the human capital constraint." This is not secured however by transferring these expenditures out of the current expenditure limit. It will be most effectively removed when the curbs on current expenditure force an examination (as it already has done to some degree) on how best to secure better outcomes (which is what we all want), rather than by merely lifting the lid on public expenditures. Given the pressure from the population for education (see Mahal and Rajaraman, 2010),[6] it is unlikely that HRD expenditures will be reduced in either nominal or real terms. And if the fiscal pressure leads to better modes of public delivery, perhaps we will have better human capital formation, which is the ultimate objective.

Reducing Input Subsidies

Rakshit commends our attention to reducing subsidies, but says we do not go far enough. We totally agree there. Ideally, we should have reduced all input subsidies to zero, as he suggests. In this, as in all our deliberations, we debated on whether to prescribe the ideal target, knowing well its infeasibility from a political economy perspective, or to opt for the feasible. We chose the second option, in order to underline that the FAP (Fiscal Adjustment Programme) we prescribed was achievable in our considered judgement.

Seignorage

Rakshit sees the complete disregard of seignorage by the THFC as glaring. A glaring example of our wisdom, I would have thought. The Reserve Bank of India (RBI) is in any case no longer compelled to accept primary securities issued by the government, and is free to set its own limits of absorption on the secondary market. Yes, the

6. Mahal, Ajay and Indira Rajaraman (2010). "Decentralisation, Preference Diversity and Public Spending: Health and Education in India", *Economic and Political Weekly* 45(43): 57-63, 23 October.

negative seignorage of the pre-crisis era carried heavy fiscal costs, but the alternative combination of letting the capital inflow lead to rupee appreciation, in conjunction with heavy direct borrowing by the government from the RBI (were that for argument's sake an option), would surely not have been a happy alternative.

Rewarding Performing States

Rakshit says: "...allocative efficiency of public investment will improve if better performing states are permitted (within limits) to borrow more, taking advantage of their higher credit worthiness." We did precisely that. The major change in our equation determining state entitlements to borrow over 2010-2015 (para 9.85) will be that borrowing entitlements, set in year (t-1) for year t, will be determined, not on the basis of GSDP for year t as projected by the Commission, but on a continually revised projection re-set to the growth performance of the state, as revealed by the most recent GSDP estimates. A growth performer like Gujarat will thus indeed reap the rewards of its better growth by setting its borrowing entitlement as a percentage of a GSDP projection informed by its growth achievement.

Setting projections on the basis of current GSDP estimates is a major departure from convention for another reason. Anyone familiar with finance commissions knows that they are compelled to use not the GSDP estimates of states, as reported on the Central Statistical Organisation (CSO) website, but a set of 'comparable' estimates issued by the CSO on the grounds that states are said not to be using comparable methodology for their estimates (although why that should be so when the estimates are issued after discussions with the CSO remains unclear). State borrowing entitlements over 2005-2010 were based on projections of the 12th Commission from the comparable estimates, but states were actually judged by their achievements in fiscal consolidation with respect to the website numbers. Thus, Haryana, for which the comparable estimate was systematically below the website figure by an average of 8.5 per cent, ranging upto 13 per cent in some years, looks like an unduly fiscally conservative state when its fiscal deficit is normalised by the higher website figure. The reverse would be true for other states for which the comparable estimate was systematically above the website number.

Fiscal Adjustment for Macro Stabilisation

Rakshit seems to agree with the provisions of the Commission for building stabilisation flexibility into the FAP. Specifically, we asked that the range in the values of key parameters underpinning the projections, like the international price of oil, the exchange rate and the interest rate, be specified.

Rakshit says the elimination of petrol and fertiliser subsidies would insulate the budget from petroleum price volatility. As explained above, that happy nirvana of subsidy elimination[7] was not seen by us as achievable over the horizon 2010-2015. As for the interest rate and exchange rate, he sees them as policy variables, not parameters. Policy variables, yes, but they do parametrically underpin fiscal projections nevertheless.

His principal point on this is the possible need for expansion due to an output gap, "which, barring the recent crisis, has generally been driven by volatility of private investment – a factor totally missing in the THFC list." It was the very need to fortify the outlook for private investment that we prescribed our fiscal consolidation path.

Finally, Rakshit advises:

> clear signals of demand deficiency should be enough to permit departure from FRBM targets...While countering recessions the government, our analysis suggests, should rely more on investment in critical areas than on tax concession, and on seignorage rather [than] borrowing from the public or external sources.

This pre-supposes an earlier era of forced absorption of primary securities by the central bank, an era now irreversibly behind us. A Financial Responsibility and Budgetary Management (FRBM) is a signalling of the intent of a government to abide by a projected path of fiscal discipline. Financial markets are reassured if there is legislated evidence of commitment to fiscal governance. Clearly, in any crisis like the one in 2008, the need for an immediate fiscal and monetary

7. This and other fiscal projections are examined for their realisation in the epilogue to Chapter 24; for subsidies in particular see Figure 2.0, Part IV.

response will be widely understood. In asking that the three price parameters be specified, we did not imagine that the whole gamut of possibilities was thereby covered. In an uncertain world, cognisance of the parameter dependence of the projections adds transparency and credibility to fiscal projections and adds further reassurance to that very same private investor, whose centrality in preventing an output gap is conceded by Rakshit.

26 Barriers to Equalisation

Finance commissions are the only statutory instrument through which equalisation in access to public services is sought to be achieved in the Indian federal structure. Parallel state-level commissions exist for third-tier local services within each state. Couched in legalese, the terms of reference of national finance commissions have an arcane ring for those unfamiliar with articles and clauses in the Constitution, but the core burden of their task is to ensure the capability for roughly equivalent levels of public services to any Indian citizen, regardless of state of location. Finance commissions attempt compensation for differences in fiscal need, modified by cost disabilities, across this vast and varied country. This is necessary, but not sufficient, to ensure equality of access.

By convention, every commission seeks to familiarise itself with the needs of states by making a formal visit to each state. But no visuals can substitute for comparable numbers on fiscal capacity, on the basis of which alone any objectively equitable allocation of fiscal resources across states becomes possible.

For some reason, this is not an act we have managed to get together in 60 years. We do not know the relative income of states on an accrual basis; we only have estimates of domestic product originating within each state. Expenditures taxable by the state, whether in the pre- or post-GST (goods and services tax) era, are financed from income, regardless of its source. Income may accrue from (net) inward remittances into the state, or from activity originating within the state. And this is where we live in a vast ocean of ignorance.

Remittances accruing to a state could alter very substantially the relative ranking of states by fiscal capacity. Kerala is informally estimated to receive inward remittances from other countries amounting to a quarter, at least, of income originating within the state. In recent years, it has also become a source of outward domestic remittances to eastern states. The net balance is anyone's guess.

Although external remittances flowing into the country are known, their distribution across states is not tracked. Periodic eruptions of turbulence alert us to the phenomenon of labour movements within the country, but there is no systematic record of the corresponding domestic remittance flows.

This is by no means to disparage the hard work done by the national income unit of the Central Statistical Organisation (CSO). Perhaps the pressure to issue country-level estimates, in full view of the world, with quarterly frequency and greater accuracy than was the case as recently as 10 years ago, has come in the way of looking at the subnational situation. But a minimal degree of co-ordination between national and state statistical authorities could have ensured the generation of subnational estimates simultaneously with the national effort. A mutually cooperative process could actually reduce the burden of estimation at each level.

Presently, states generate their own estimates of domestic product originating, and these are reported on the CSO website. However, official bodies, like the finance and planning commissions, cannot use them because they are said to lack methodological uniformity. But why is this so? Every state finalises its domestic product estimates only after bilateral discussions with the CSO. The entire country follows a standard methodology laid down by the United Nations Statistical Office (UNSO). Indeed, many distinguished Indian statisticians were among those who drafted that manual. Why then should there be departures within the country for a process which, though arduous, should have a uniform information gathering mechanism in place?

The CSO, therefore, supplies official bodies with 'comparable' estimates of state domestic product. Fortunately, finance commissions by convention publish these in their reports, so as to facilitate a comparison with the website numbers. If the margin of disparity between the two is not wide, there should be no need for estimates on two tracks. And if it is, as indeed is the case for some though not all states, the need for methodological convergence to a single set, publicly available, is paramount.

A few possible reasons for the disparity are dimly visible in what remains a dense fog. Agricultural estimates are revised several times for the reported (website) estimates, often substantially, but frozen at the first estimate in the comparable estimates which are never revised. If agriculture was the only cause of disparity between the two estimates, the margin should in principle alternate in sign between years, which it does only in the case of some states (Bihar, for example).

There are other states where the margin is systematically positive or negative (and large) across the years. One possible reason could be that they use their own index of industrial production, in place of what the national index assigns to them. Instead of incorporating state-level estimates of industrial production into the national index, which should ideally be so built-up, the comparable estimate imposes the national index on all states.

For both reasons, the (final) reported estimate on the website is likely to be the truer estimate. But official bodies are compelled to use the 'comparable' number. Quite aside from this functioning in effect as a data barrier to equalisation, we need to clean up our act on state income estimates for other reasons.

The GDP (gross domestic product) series introduced in 2010 carries some methodological changes along with the switch in base year to 2004-05.[1] One of these is the shift to the Annual Survey of Industries in place of the Index of Industrial Production as the base for estimating industrial production. That is a good start. If state estimates are also shifted to this platform, the national and state estimates will be aligned, at least for this sector. And if we are serious about agricultural productivity, as indeed we should be if we do not want food price inflation to get hard-wired into the Indian system, we need to sharpen our measurement instruments there as well.

1. Hopefully, the new series issued in January 2015 with 2011-12 as base will be congruent with state-level estimates, going forward.

27 From Outlays to Outcomes[1]

In the terms of the reference of the 13th Finance Commission, item 6 reads: "In making its recommendations, the Commission shall have regard, among other considerations, to......(vii) the need to improve the quality of public expenditure to obtain better output and outcomes..."

For this to have been inserted into the terms of reference of a Commission 60 years after formation of the Indian republic, it is clear that a focus on outcomes has not in practice become hard-wired into political processes and institutions. Public expenditure outcomes should in principle have been routinely monitored by oversight committees of legislative bodies, such as the Public Accounts Committee. These do exist, but clearly their investigations have not looped back into the system in such a way as to achieve a sustained improvement in the quality of public expenditure.

The single biggest provision embedded within the system, which could form the nucleus of a move towards better monitoring of outcomes, is the office of the Comptroller and Auditor General of India (CAG). Fortunately, this institution continues to command respect for the integrity of its functioning. So far, the routine scope of this agency covers outlays, processes and objectives. Outcomes lie beyond its purview, by and large, but could easily be assigned to the CAG, with any required research elements of outcome assessment outsourced if necessary to institutions with the relevant competence.

The auditing function, as conventionally performed by the office of the CAG, suffers from excessive delay and consequent irrelevance, although these delays are a result of inadequate powers by which to enforce supply of documents from any government agency under audit within a reasonable period of time. In that respect, the office of the CAG is more enfeebled than the ordinary citizen of India under the

1. This was published in *India Review* 9(2): 275-79, April-June 2010.

Right to Information (RTI) Act. The provisions of the 1971 legislation under which the office performs its functions need to be amended so as to enable timely audit, and expansion of the ambit of the CAG to include the very large number of decentralised entities that have come into being as a result of many Central schemes carrying final expenditure points at district or sub-district level. These agencies, such as school management committees, the last point of expenditure under the national Sarva Shiksha Abhiyan (SSA) scheme, slip outside the audit net. Adding the National Rural Employment Guarantee (MGNREGS), and the Indira Awaas Yojana (IAY) for improved rural housing, also expended through decentralised points of disbursement, these three major flagship national schemes alone are budgeted at a little over 1 per cent of GDP (gross domestic product). Decentralisation of the point of expenditure in these schemes is itself the result of an attempt to improve outcomes. The paradox is that the potential for improved performance through better access to local requirements carries the trade-off of reduced coverage by the national auditor.

Public expenditure targeting social outcomes is segmented into schemes, each carrying monitorable (and to some extent monitored) objectives, where the further progress beyond the instrumental objectives of each scheme towards the ultimate outcome is lost sight of. The SSA has multiple instrumental objectives such as filling of teacher vacancies in primary schools so as to raise teacher-pupil ratios to national standards; improvement in school infrastructure; and reduction of pupil dropout rates. These objectives are monitored within the system. The final outcome targeted by the SSA initiative, however, is to produce a stream of children with embedded literacy and numeracy skills upto an acceptable standard at the conclusion of the primary school process. This is much harder to monitor, and has for that reason not become the focus of attention.

Several schemes bear on the same outcome. Thus for example, reduction in infant or maternal mortality rates will be the outcome of several schemes, some with a direct bearing, such as rural health and nutrition schemes, and some that may seem unrelated, such as schemes to improve access to and quality of drinking water. In such a situation, the incremental contribution of any one of these schemes to the desired outcome is difficult to disentangle.

Therefore, a focus on outcomes calls for a radical restructuring of the partitioning of public expenditure as we presently have it. The only exceptions to outcome neglect have been those schemes cast in mission mode like the oilseeds mission, for example, which target a single desired outcome. But more complex outcome targets like reducing child malnutrition and mortality call for the synthesis of several schemes as we presently have them, into a mission mode package of expenditures with a quantified target outcome at the field end. This calls, as a necessary pre-requisite, to benchmark surveys against which to measure progress.

The problem is further exacerbated by the fact that several levels of government play in the same functional space. Even where this functional overlap is entirely consistent with the Constitution, for example education, which was moved to the concurrent list in 1976, it becomes difficult to map from the outlays of, say, a state government, onto an outcome impacted upon by national schemes.

The Finance Commission is mainly in the business of prescribing unconditional transfers to states. Tax shares to states are in the nature of an entitlement without any conditions. The component of their prescriptions prescribed in the form of absolute grants is the only one permitting any kind of conditionality. Absolute grants account, even with the enhancement of the 12th Commission for the period 2005-2010, to around one-fifth of the total transfer prescribed. So the Finance Commission is in general not in a position to enforce a focus on outcome conditionalities.

The Planning Commission, on the other hand, which is the point of origin of several very substantially funded CSS (centrally sponsored schemes), is clearly the place to start the process of outcome-based monitoring. If the ambit of powers of the CAG is expanded to include decentralised entities at the final point of expenditure, there will be in place a more comprehensive framework in place for conventional auditing of outlays, processes and instrumental objectives.

Even for such a limited focus, not extending to outcomes, there is a problem posed by new demand-driven schemes such as the NREG.

These represent a major improvement over earlier schemes which targeted person-days of employment generation from above. But by the same token, the demand-driven configuration makes it difficult to monitor objectives without surveys on the extent to which demand for work was not responded to. A small number of person-days of employment does not in and of itself indicate failure in terms of the objectives of the programme. As for the ultimate outcome, which is mitigation of rural poverty in a manner that has a positive impact also on rural infrastructure, surveys are required again to calibrate the wage and labour supply response to the scheme, and on the quality of infrastructure created. What does remain possible even for demand-driven schemes like this, however, is detection of process irregularities, and that is always useful and carries within it possible identifiers of factors making for outcome failure. There is also need for continued focus on design deficiencies, such as inflexibilities which make the programme unresponsive to local need, or incapable of producing local assets of any durable worth. A new Rajiv Gandhi Seva Centre for monitoring of this scheme is proposed, and can become the mechanism through which process and design deficiencies are continually corrected over time.

Large areas of expenditure are carried forward from year to year with no stated expectations in terms of outcomes. These include tax expenditures and subsidies, whose magnitude is staggeringly large. For example, tax expenditure in the budget documents of the Central government is estimated for the year 2008-09 at ₹4.18 lakh crore, around 7.4 per cent of GDP.[2] Even if the customs component is excluded because of ambiguities surrounding the notified rate from which distance to the effective rate is computed, the direct tax component of this alone amounts to ₹1.09 lakh crore, nearly 2.0 per cent of GDP. The outcomes sought to be achieved with the provisions enabling reduction of tax liability of this magnitude are varied and nowhere stated, and therefore not measurable. However,

2. By the year 2014-15, although tax expenditure had ramped up in absolute terms to ₹6.25 lakh crore, it was a lower per cent of GDP (4.85, new series). The direct tax component stood at ₹1.39 lakh crore, just 1.1 per cent of GDP. These numbers reflect commendably on attempts to tighten tax loopholes between 2008-09 and 2014-15.

the new direct tax bill[3] seeks to place a streamlined tax code, which can if implemented, result in considerable reduction of direct tax expenditure.

Another major component of public expenditure is the subsidy bill, which is budgeted for 2008-09 at ₹1.29 lakh crore, well over 2 per cent of GDP.[4] The major components are the food and fertiliser subsidies (other than petroleum), where the immediate objectives in terms of enhancing access are known, but where the larger outcomes sought – improved caloric intake, or improved agricultural productivity – are not monitored in a manner related to the pattern of uptake of these subsidies. Even within the limited sphere of known objectives, there is no mechanism whereby the configuration of these subsidies is subjected to continued examination and improvement.

Perhaps the most egregious instance of auditing failure is in respect of state-level public sector undertakings. As of the end of September 2008, out of 853 working companies in this category, 607 had accounts pending for anywhere from 1 to 26 years. This underlines once again the need for strengthening legal powers of the CAG. Loss cover for loss-making public sector undertakings can lie buried within state budgets under the head of capital expenditure, in the form of loans or equity contributions.

To summarise, there are three principal initiatives needed to enable progress towards better public expenditure outcomes in India.

First, in order to progress beyond the instrumental objectives of single schemes towards complex outcome targets like reducing child malnutrition and mortality, all similar schemes need to be bundled into a mission mode package of expenditures with a quantified target outcome at the field end, regardless of the point of origin in terms of scheme or level of government. Ideally, these bundled expenditures should be the responsibility of local government, which can be held to account for outcome failure.

Second, good initial benchmark surveys followed by periodic surveys are needed to measure progress towards the notified outcome.

---

3. See the essay titled "Tax Policy".

4. In the years since, despite an almighty effort, the subsidy bill has proved difficult to reign in at 2 per cent of GDP.

Finally, a focus on outcomes should not diminish the need to monitor utilisation of outlays, process deficiencies and achievement of instrumental objectives of each scheme. Such monitoring is best performed by the office of the CAG, which has an exemplary record in terms of its reputation for integrity, but whose powers need to be considerably enhanced to enable more timely performance of its present monitoring functions. Amendment of the CAG Act of 1971 is urgently needed for such enhancement of powers to be legislatively enabled.

28 The Supply of Justice

The replacement of indigenous systems of justice by the colonial British system of jurisprudence radically re-shaped the structure of property and other rights in the country. The implications of this implant in the legal landscape continue to be explored in a large literature by historians and economists.

Painstaking surveys of the topography of the land were a necessary underpinning of the new legal system. The initial cadastral surveys performed more than 100 years ago remain the basis for land rights to this very day. The new legal structure spawned a class of Indian lawyers who functioned as its gatekeepers for a bewildered population, and consequently earned fabulous wealth. Ironically, some members of this class, Motilal Nehru prominent among them, ploughed their wealth into the movement for eviction of the colonial government, the very means of their enrichment.

The pre-existing legal systems varied widely across the country. Marc Galanter, a renowned scholar of legal systems in South Asia, has documented the changes wrought by the new system in great detail. In some parts of the country, the new system was perceived as less capricious and more squarely based on factual evidence, but in many others, it was seriously at odds with received notions of justice and community rights.

Whatever the regional variations in the indigenous systems earlier in place, one feature that they all had in common was the short duration of time between initiation of a case and the final verdict. Legal examination was less complicated procedurally, and a final decision was soon reached. The demands of the new system, on the other hand, introduced delay between case and verdict that by itself was seen as unjust. What the new system did do uniformly across the country was to lengthen pendency.

Given this history, it might be thought that independent India would move to reduce legal pendency, but sadly that has not happened. The constraints on the supply of justice in India have congested the judicial system to the point where what is nominally a public good has become sadly excludable and rivalrous. Every new case jostles along with existing cases for the limited attention of courts. The stock of pending cases in the country today [2010] is estimated at 30 million. The situation has reached crisis proportions.

The 13th Finance Commission, in a departure from tradition, makes provision for an absolute grant to states in order to improve the supply of justice, a concurrent subject in the Indian constitution. The total provision of ₹5,000 crore for the period 2010-2015 is broken down into nine monitorable components, so as to drive the system towards correcting specific deficiencies identified in the action plan of the Central Ministry of Justice. It is useful to run down this list for an understanding of the multiple disabilities that plague the judicial system.

The single biggest problem is that the existing physical infrastructure is not fully used. Accordingly, half the total provision is earmarked for the operation of morning/evening shifts in sanctioned courts. Serving officers can man these extra shifts with additional compensation, and the pool of retired officers can be tapped if required. The distribution across states of this segment of the grant is calibrated to the number of sanctioned courts in each.

The Alternate Dispute Resolution (ADR) mechanism, a fast-track option for settlement of civil disputes, is presently available only at High Court level in state capitals. An infrastructure grant for the creation of one ADR centre in every judicial district of the country is provided, allotted to states in proportion to the number of their judicial districts. The grant will also cover the cost of training mediators and conciliators needed to staff the new centres. There is an independent grant for Lok Adalats for mass resolution of cases, at 10 per year at High Court level, and 5 per year for lower courts. Legal aid for under-trials (those in litigation) lacking the wherewithal to pay for their defence has a separate grant provision. These three grants for enhancing the pace of case flow together receive ₹1,050 crore.

Then there is an unavailability of trained judges to fill vacancies in the system, currently estimated at 18 per cent. The proposal to establish 5000 new village level courts under the Grama Nyayalaya

Act notified in October 2009 will add further vacancies to be filled. The Finance Commission, therefore provides each of the 20 High Courts in the country with two grants for the training of judges. One is meant for additional infrastructure in presently operating judicial academies, or for the creation of new judicial academies where none presently exist. The second is for bolstering the training capability of these institutions. Another closely related grant is for creation of the post of Court Manager, which will free the time of trained judges for performance of their judicial functions, without the distraction of administrative claims on their time. There is a separate grant provision for the training of public prosecutors, since the government aggregating across all levels is the single largest litigant in the country. These four programmes together receive ₹1,000 crore. A small remaining grant of ₹450 crore goes towards restoration of heritage court buildings.

The provision for improved justice delivery is available for the current year, 2010-11, without any conditionalities. However, a state will qualify for receipt of the grant for 2011-12 only if a State Litigation Policy is in place before close of the current fiscal year.[1] Otherwise, the grant can begin to flow to a state only prospectively from the time at which such a policy is framed. The budget head structure currently in place does not permit quantification of the total expenditure on the legal entanglements of government; but if a portion of that had been spent on enhancing the supply side of the judicial system instead of imposing further demands upon it, the pendency situation might not have been what it is today.

1. This article lays out the judicial grant as provided by the 13th Finance Commission over the horizon 2010-2015. The outcome of the grant will be known only if there is an official paper issued on the usage of the grant.

29 Tribes, Forests and Mines

Among the prominent depictions in Buddhist iconography is Buddha the teacher, unravelling the knot of life with the thumb and forefinger of both hands. It will take quite some unravelling to undo the knot underlying the violence unleashed on Indian security forces in April 2010.

As is well known, the maps of tribal occupancy, forest cover and underground mineral wealth in India, can be overlaid on one another with a good degree of concordance. Tribal populations live on the strength of renewable forest produce, and the forests in turn have rendered inaccessible the mineral wealth underneath them.

The first line of battle is between the imperative to protect forest cover in India for preservation of our water resources, agricultural productivity and food security, and the fevered push by the mining lobby to get at the mineral wealth underneath. Conversion of forested land to non-forest uses is actually permissible under the law, following a Supreme Court judgement in 2002. Such conversion is subject to compensatory payments calibrated to cover the expenditure required for equivalent afforestation, in addition to the net present value of forest land lost. The exact method by which these payments have been arrived at need not detain us here, although the numbers do matter a great deal. The more serious issue is that the fund into which these payments were to flow was to be managed by a Compensatory Afforestation Fund Management and Planning Authority (CAMPA) at state-level, the rules governing which were to be formally notified at Central level. The rules were not notified, and payments meant for afforestation and compensation were accumulated with an ad hoc CAMPA at the national level. Following protests from states,[1] a recent

1. Fortified by a Supreme Court judgement of 10 July 2009, which directed interim ad hoc payments. The CAMPA lies in a legal limbo since a bill to give it legislative underpinning was defeated in Parliament.

decision was taken to release ₹100 crore annually to the respective states' CAMPA, over the next five years, in proportion to the area diverted in each state to non-forest uses.

What the states do with these funds will be a function of the monitoring system in place, and the penalties if any for diversion to other uses. In a bid to give states an incentive to direct CAMPA funding towards afforestation, among other compelling reasons, the 13th Finance Commission provides for a forest grant of ₹5000 crore to states for the period 2010-2015. To quote the Finance Commission report, the provision will provide states "with the wherewithal for preservation going forward, so as to halt and hopefully reverse past declines in the quantum and quality of area under forests." The formula for allocation of the grant between states is calibrated to the standing stock of forest cover, and therefore rewards those states that have not in the past fallen victim to the lure of (promised, but not yet realised) compensating CAMPA payments. The conditionalities attached to the forest grant require states to draw up working plans for forest zones within their jurisdictions, within the first two years of the award period, 2010-2012. Working plans carry a 10-year horizon, and prescribe the pattern and limits of sustainable forest harvesting. The baseline documentation provided by working plans serves as a valuable measurement benchmark on the basis of which progress over time, or the lack thereof, can be assessed. Ground level surveys of this kind are the only possible basis on which biodiversity, the key dimension of conservation, can be reliably marked and measured.

Working plans clearly need funding. Accordingly, one-fourth of the forest grant prescribed by the Finance Commission will flow over the first two years and is unconditional, designed to cover survey costs. For the following three years, the remaining three-fourth of the total grant entitlement will be disbursed, conditional on well-documented working plans. This provision for the three years is earmarked for state forest departments only to the extent of 25 per cent. The remainder may be used by states for any developmental purpose. The idea is to signal that forest cover will entitle states to generalised compensation for the economic disability posed by it.

None of this resolves the problems of tribals displaced by past diversion of forest land, unless they are actively involved in the afforestation programmes of state forest departments, which will now have funding from two streams – the statutory Finance Commission flow, as well as the much smaller flow from delayed CAMPA entitlements. Forest departments would be well advised to involve tribal populations in the preparatory work for putting together the working plans required as conditionality for release of the Finance Commission grants, and indeed to give them a measure of control over the process. The present relationship between state forest departments and forest dwellers is badly fractured. Involving tribal populations in the preparation of working plans will provide immediate employment in a field where their expertise is unmatched, and can pave the way for mainstreaming and re-settlement in newly afforested areas, admittedly not their original homes that are lost forever, but in a milieu that will be familiar. The untied portion of the forest grant can be directed towards the welfare of displaced tribal populations.

Too much however cannot be expected from the forest grant. The inducement of ₹5,000 crore over five years for all states may be a feeble counter to what mining lobbies can promise.

Before any new mining is sanctioned, the first imperative is to enforce pollution control laws on pre-existing mines, and on downstream smelting and processing units. A visual sweep of mining areas in these states, even where the activity is legally sanctioned, exposes the ravages wrought on the land and on water bodies. It does not have to be that way. There are states in the country, Goa being an example, where iron ore mining has been accompanied by successful ongoing restoration of the original density of vegetation. State Pollution Control Boards (SPCBs) hold the key to environmental monitoring and enforcement. Until these bodies function in a manner protective of the public interest, we cannot begin to address one of the many factors that feed the sense of betrayal among forest populations.

30 Special Category States

The plea of Bihar to be designated a special category state has been gaining ground over the last year. In April [2012], Anil Pathak, general secretary of the Bihar State Citizens' Council, marked the start of the fiscal year by saying the Centre should end its discriminatory policy towards Bihar and accord it special category status.

The special category was so nominated at the time of the Gadgil formula in 1969, as a group of states with distinct problems of hilly terrain, turbulent international borders and resulting poor infrastructure. Three states were named initially: Assam, Nagaland, and Jammu & Kashmir. There are now 11, with new states contiguous to the initial threesome added on, as a result of state partitioning and conversion of former union territories to states.

The Bihar claim seems to draw sustenance from the contiguity criterion, from its international border with Nepal, and from the fact that it is poorer in per capita GSDP (gross state domestic product) than many states within the special category. There is also anger over the share of Bihar in Central taxes having fallen from 11.028 per cent as prescribed by the 12th Finance Commission, to 10.917 by the 13th Finance Commission.[1]

Statutory flows from the national government in any federation are designed to compensate for variations in fiscal capacity across subnational states. Typically, a uniform tax effort is (implicitly) applied to the estimated fiscal capacity of each state. A particular state may choose a level of taxation at a level below (or above) that of others. This does not affect the basis of the transfer, which is what they could potentially collect in taxes at uniform effort.

1. It fell further, to 9.665 per cent by the 14th Finance Commission. All of these are shares in Central taxes other than the service tax. The service tax is not levied in Jammu and Kashmir. Shares of all other states in total service tax collections are therefore slightly higher than their shares in other taxes.

Poverty translates into low fiscal capacity, which is routinely taken care of by the formulae used for state shares in statutory transfers. The fact of Bihar being poor is indeed why they get a higher share in both statutory and Plan transfers than their share in population.

What justifies the separate consideration given to special category states is their hilly terrain, which imparts a cost disability in public service provision. For example, if the construction cost of a district road is ₹15 lakh per kilometre in flat terrain, rising to ₹30 lakh per kilometre in hilly terrain, and if two habitations separated by 1 kilometre on a 2D map require 2 kilometres of connecting road length in hilly terrain, then both together will make a road link between two habitations, separated by 1 kilometre as the crow flies, higher in hilly terrain by a factor of 4.

In the Canadian federation, the principles governing fiscal transfers from the national government to subnational provinces are Constitutionally enshrined, but all areas north of 60° latitude are territories directly administered by the Government of Canada, and therefore outside the scope of the formulae governing transfers. These constitute a contiguous arc across the north of Canada, and clearly carry cost disabilities defined by their location and consequent extreme climatic conditions.

The special category states likewise define an arc across the north and northeast of India, separate from the mainland by virtue of both a more difficult terrain, and/or difficult climatic conditions. But there may now be a case to re-examine the routine inclusion in the group of the residual state of Assam which, after the partitioning out of Meghalaya and Mizoram, is not substantially different in terrain or climate from general category states.

So why did the Bihar share of Central taxes fall somewhat with the 13th Finance Commission? Finance commissions upto the 12th Commission assessed the fiscal capacity of states with reference to per capita GSDP alone. The 13th Finance Commission for the first time took formal cognizance of the fact that the special category states, in addition to their expenditure disability, suffered also from a revealed revenue disability. The average ratio of tax revenue to GSDP for special category states is lower than the average for general category states. So it adjusted for this.

As a result, special category states got a higher share of Central taxes from the 13th Commission, with a corresponding reduction in the share of all other states, not just Bihar. But the 12th and all earlier finance commissions gave special category states an additional ad hoc statutory grant anyway, beyond their tax share, to cover routine expenditures. So, the move to the new procedure was a more objective and transparent way of dealing with the greater fiscal difficulty of Special Category states. When aggregated across tax shares and grants, the share of general category states in total statutory transfers did not fall by as much as their decline in tax share alone.

The low income and social indicators of Bihar give the state high entitlements not just in statutory Finance Commission flows, but also in Plan flows through Central schemes like the Sarva Shiksha Abhiyan (SSA), but do not justify special category status. The international border is no justification either, since Rajasthan and Gujarat are border states too.

One of the reasons for the variation across states in the tax to GSDP ratio could be differences in the sectoral composition of GSDP, since sectors are not uniform in their taxability. Even after adjusting for varying sectoral composition, however, the tax effort of the Special Category states is low (as estimated in a study I did with Rajan Goyal, published in a 2012 memorial volume for Raja Chelliah). Bihar gets a score of 0.81 out of a maximum of 1, well above the 0.20-0.67 range in which the special category states lie. The low tax effort of Special Category states is clearly a matter of concern, but can only be addressed in conjunction with the law and order problem faced by many, whereby residents are compelled to pay into parallel revenue streams collected by insurgents.

Bihar should view it as a matter of pride not to be in need of special fiscal accommodation.

31 Funding States

The report of the committee for a CDI (composite development index) for states, released in late September [2013], has attracted criticism for having been politically motivated to give a larger share to Bihar in fiscal flows from the Centre (non-statutory flows, directed not by the Finance Commission but by the Planning Commission until August 2014, and by an assortment of Central government ministries thereafter). Of greater interest than the motivation is how the committee addressed its task, and what its collective effort led it to.

The report has two aspects. In the first and most harmless, it is an exercise along the lines of the HDI (Human Development Index), using an assortment of outcome indicators to quantify and rank states on a scale. Indeed, the report plots a scatter of its CDI against the HDI and finds a very high negative correlation of 0.9. Negative, because the HDI assigns high scores to high achievers, like any academic test. The CDI on the other hand, assigns high scores to low achievers. That gets us to the second (and main) task of the report, which is to quantify the relative entitlement of states in development funding from the Centre, grounded in their low achievement.

This aspect of the report is more problematic. Even the dissenting member agrees with the committee's use of outcome variables for the ranking, rather than what they call background or process variables. He merely disagrees with inclusion of per cent scheduled caste/tribes in the population as it is not an outcome variable, and with the use of per capita consumption rather than income.

Outcome variables have in the past been used in Plan schemes floated by the Centre, such as the Sarva Shiksha Abhiyan (SSA) whose objective was to even out the primary education deficit in deprived regions; or the Pradhan Mantri Gram Sadak Yojana (PMGSY), which provides last mile connectivity for villages not so linked, thereby favouring states with a large number of marooned villages. There can be no legal challenge to such schemes because the Centre is autonomous within the federation and therefore free to address particular outcome deficits across the country.

But when a whole bunch of these deficits are pooled together as a basis for determining overall state shares in development funding, that becomes an approach subject to legal challenge. Why does pooling become a problem, when funding a specific outcome deficit is not? Simply because this then becomes an unconditional fund flow, and thus mimics the statutory tax share prescribed by finance commissions, which similarly quantify unconditional relative state entitlements. When that happens, the formula must necessarily begin from a neutral construction of the relative needs of states. What the Constitution most certainly permits is adjustment of this neutrally obtained entitlement for the relative fiscal capacity of states to meet these needs themselves. Any measure of relative prosperity like per capita income applies here not as a measure of poor outcomes and hence higher entitlement, but as a measure of fiscal self-sufficiency (or lack thereof).

Per capita income is not the best indicator of fiscal capacity. I have written on how better measures of fiscal capacity are possible,[1] and on the poor quality of the per capita income estimates used.[2] Once the GST (goods and services tax) comes into being, we will have a readily available measure of relative tax capacity in place, and can then perhaps approach the Canadian ideal in respect of adjusting for fiscal capacity. The point here is that a poor state's claim to higher shares in Central flows can only rest on its low fiscal capability to meet its needs itself. But the basic building blocks of need have to be neutral across states. The report acknowledges the perverse incentive properties of the CDI, and prescribes a one-quarter share in the final formula for improvements in performance (i.e., reductions in the CDI). Yet, the CDI clearly overrides the performance component.

The very 'background' variables that the committee rejects for arriving at relative entitlement are in fact the only bases acceptable to states. It also accepts adjustment for the cost disability posed by

1. Referred to in "Special Category States".

2. Covered in "Barriers to Equalisation" in this section.

hilly terrain, although placing 11 states in a Special Category may have been a ham-handed way of dealing with it. I have written on better measures of cost disability that are possible for application ("Is Bihar a Special Category State?"). The committee does use the basic cross-state neutral indicators of need – population and area – but merely as 80:20 weights to the CDI, which is constructed from outcome disparities on 10 indicators.

The requirement of neutrality and the rejection of perverse outcome incentives is taken so seriously in our country, that the very terms of reference of finance commissions over the last 40 years have mandated the use of frozen population shares by the 1971 census, in order to not reward states that went easy on population control. This feature, just by itself, has reduced the share of Bihar relative to what it would have been with the use of current population. Only the 14th Finance Commission has been given some leeway by being allowed to consider 'demographic changes subsequent to 1971'.

The CDI gives Bihar a 12.04 per cent share, as against what the report says was a 10.06 per cent share across tax shares and grants awarded by the Thirteenth Finance Commission (TFC). The TFC tax share, the more appropriate comparison, was 10.92 per cent. If the TFC share were reworked with current population, and with fiscal capacity more carefully assessed, it would easily cross 11 per cent.

The excess of the CDI over this revised tax share yields a rough and ready measure of the (accumulated) governance deficit in Bihar. The people of Bihar undeniably suffer from acute outcome deficits, which call for redressal, in mission mode. The first and most urgent must surely be the eradication of Japanese encephalitis, an annual visitor after the monsoon, which leaves dead and disabled children in its wake in several districts of Bihar and Uttar Pradesh. Targeted interventions with measurable outcomes are a better way to confront these horrific consequences of accumulated governance deficits, rather than more unconditional funding poured into those deficits.

32 The Report of the Fourteenth Finance Commission

The standout feature of the report of the Fourteenth Finance Commisssion (FFC) is its recommendation that the share of states in the tax revenues of the Central government (net of collection costs as always), be raised from 32 to 42 per cent. I personally find this a most refreshing change from the risk averse approach adopted by FCs (finance commissions) in the past, whereby they balked at making any radical changes to the historically trodden path.

Aversion of FCs to recommending any dramatic change results from what otherwise is a most laudable convention – of governments of the day at the Centre accepting the core recommendations of finance commissions without any alteration whatever. This then has made every FC fearful that too radical a departure from the past might give them the dubious distinction of being the first to have their recommendations partially rather than fully accepted.

Room for the 10 percentage point increase has been purchased by not prescribing as many grants as previously. Some grant provisions have however been retained, such as to local governments for example, and also for revenue deficit grants. These are absolutes, and so will have to be summed to the absolute equivalent of the 42 per cent tax share provision to obtain the overall percentage provision, for comparison with previous FC provisions. When that is done, the increase in the overall statutory provision will ramp up from 38[1] to 48 per cent.

That is still a big increase, and clearly can be accommodated only by folding in other non-statutory transfers that have hitherto gone

1. Minus the grant of ₹50,000 crore provided by the 13th Commission for implementation of an ideal GST (goods and services tax), which did not come to pass during its horizon 2010-2015.

to states as a part of Plan flows. The issue of which of these will be folded in has been left to the Centre's discretion, but from the expressed discomfort of the dissenting Member in his note, he fears that Normal Central Assistance (which is subordinated to the Gadgil-Mukherjee formula), the Backward Region Grants Fund (BRGF), and the Rashtriya Kisan Vikas Yojana (RKVY), will be among those folded into the 42 per cent.

Until we know the full extent of the fold-in, the net impact of the increase in statutory flows to any individual state cannot be determined from its formulaic share within the FFC provisions, since what each has lost from the fold-in will have to be factored in. In general, I am in favour of streamlining flows so that there is greater coherence at the level of the receiving state in terms of what it is to receive, and when. But I do agree with the dissent note that there could be huge problems transiting from segmented transfer channels being consolidated into a single flow. The way governments in India work, it is entirely possible that promising state-level agriculture programmes funded under the RKVY might wither and die unless equivalent allocations are quickly made within the state from the single statutory flow.

States at the end of the day are interested in their share of the total, and the formula determining that share. Two changes have been made in this. One is that the problem of staying with the 1971 population census, a vexed resolution of the population control incentive problem, has been ameliorated by bringing in the 2011 census figures in addition, with a weight of 10 per cent, as against 17.5 per cent for the 1971 figures. The other is that the income distance formula used, with a 50 per cent weight, has reverted back to what was used by the 12th FC. I regret to say that the report exhibits a failure to understand what the 13th FC did in this regard (para 8.28). Average taxable capacity at a common average tax to GDP ratio underlies all formulae using income distance; all that the 13th FC did was to differentiate between the average tax to GDP (gross domestic product) ratios of general and special category states. That shift was done to accommodate the fiscal disadvantage of special category states so that their entitlements would be worked into the devolution formula, rather than be discretionarily dealt with through deficit grants. Now the FFC has had to retain deficit grants to special category states (although the designation of 'special category' has been dispensed with), along with some other general category states with legacy problems, which is an unfortunate vestigial remnant of an earlier and faultier way of dealing with the problem.

States have been held to a targeted fiscal deficit of 3 per cent of their respective GSDP (gross state domestic product), with flexibility to go up to a maximum of 3.5 per cent, if their debt profile permits it. The flexibility is a good feature. Fortunately, the growth rates to be used to determine the borrowing entitlements of states from year to year are to be determined in the manner prescribed by the 13th FC, with respect to achieved past actuals rather than a projected rate, so the growth incentive remains preserved within the system.

Table 14.1 of the report sets out the fiscal roadmap for the federation over the 2015-2020 horizon. The amended revenue deficit target for the Central government, requiring 2.0 per cent by 31 March 2015, has been given a happy go-by, and the Centre has been permitted to bring down the revenue deficit slowly to 0.93 per cent over five years. Probably a reasonable recognition of that which is feasible, over that which is desirable. The juxtaposition of Central fiscal and revenue deficit targets does not leave a lot of room for capital expenditure by the Centre, which will cross 2 per cent of GDP only in 2019-20. But then again, the Centre can always generate supplementary funding for capital expenditure from disinvestment. The report says nothing at all about that possibility.

There are many things left unaddressed by the report, such as issues of transparency in budgetary documentation of the kind addressed by the 13th FC. At a time when land is at the forefront of public debate, surely the 13th FC recommendation that unutilised landholdings (acquired but unused) of governmental bodies (such as the Food Corporation of India) be made public as part of fiscal documentation, needed to be sounded again. Perhaps the FFC considered the matter and thought it lay beyond their remit. Yet, documentary transparency of that kind can lead to resolution of a lot of problems that bedevil growth and development in this country, in a systematic and orderly fashion.

Part IV

BUDGETS AND TAXATION

The previous section on "Centre and States" was about the fiscal links between these two levels of government, as informed by the statutory provisions of Finance Commissions. The limits on states are enforceable and duly enforced by the inbuilt mechanism of Central approval for state borrowing from financial markets. But the Centre itself is under no such enforcement authority.

This section is about the fiscal behaviour of the Centre, from a number of angles. "The Fiscal Middle Distance" was written in the month just prior to the first Modi administration Union Budget in July 2014. The purpose of this piece was to deflect attention from the stand-alone approach to annual budgets, and to look at the fiscal threats looming up ahead, principally arising from the premature setting up of a new Pay Commission by the outgoing government, to revise civil servant salaries and pensions. As anyone with even no knowledge of economics or budgets knows, civil servant salaries, pensions and interest are payable from tax revenues before the government can spend on anything else. Those constitute a prior statutory claim on the revenues of government. This essay provides a useful review of the fiscal impact of past Pay Commissions, and in that sense is a capsule summary of the fiscal history of India at the level of both Centre and states since 1996.

"Tax Policy" was a comment on the new Direct Taxes Code, which was readied for presentation for the monsoon session of Parliament in 2010. The bill presenting it lapsed in 2014 with the outgoing government. The new Finance Minister has chosen to retire the bill, with the promise that the principal recommendations will be adopted with a one-year lag.

"Tedious TDS" is about the practice of tax deduction at source, which has been a most useful tool in the arsenal of the revenue collection machinery, in providing a tax trail on incomes paid. But the process of collecting evidence on TDS paid and reporting it in income tax returns had become so tedious, that compliance costs in terms of harassment and anxiety for the honest taxpayer had become unbearably burdensome. Since that piece was written, in early 2011, the electronic recording of TDS has relieved some but by no means all of the burden. New problems arise when the electronic record is incomplete, and the taxpayer has to obtain not merely paper certification as before, but in addition upload it to the electronic database where the TDS forwarding agency (a bank, or employing institution) is at fault.

"Fiscally Induced Investment" looks at the perverse incentives embedded in the structure of direct taxation. This is one of the many running themes in the book, about how outcomes, such as low growth despite reasonably high investment, are directly traceable to perversity in the structure of policy.

"Financing Urban Infrastructure" looks at the pervasive failure all across the country to exploit the property tax base, which is the tax handle assigned all over the world to local governments. Without that, it is inconceivable that India's urban areas will get the infrastructure they need.

The next two essays are comments following the Union Budgets of 2010 and 2012, detailing the disastrous fiscal slide during that time. The problem resulted from failure to roll back the sanctioned fiscal stimulus that came immediately after the post-crisis call from G20. Inflation rose, the Reserve Bank of India (RBI) starting monetary tightening in response, the GDP (gross domestic product) growth rate fell, the current account deficit widened, and international rating agencies began in mid-2012 to look askance at the macro management of the Indian economy. In defence, it must be said that the problem of pushing back the fiscal stimulus was not unique to India by any means. To take just one prominent example, the United States experienced extreme problems getting even routine government expenditures approved by a legislature that disapproved of runaway deficits and public debt, resulting in a Federal shutdown of inessential operations over a 17-day period in October 2013.

Matters came to a head in July 2012, when international rating agencies threatened a downgrade, and a Committee (the Kelkar Panel) was constituted to draw up a roadmap for fiscal consolidation, of which I was a member. Figure 1.0 presents the fiscal deficit over the period 2010-2015 against the projected correction path set by the Finance Commission, and the mid-term correction course set by the Kelkar Panel in August 2012.

Key to the problem of deficit control has been the political difficulty of reigning in subsidies. Figure 2.0 shows the time path (as percentages of GDP by the old series) of the three major subsidies, and the overall subsidy bill.

Since the new GDP series introduced with effect from 2014-15, starting from the new base year 2011-12, has posed problems of discontinuity for comparisons over time, Table 1.0 presents the growth rates for the three most recent years by the new series juxtaposed against growth rates from the old series. The percentages by the new and old series for each of those GDP aggregates shows the change in the estimation of growth with each. There has been a simultaneous shift away from basing real growth on GDP at constant factor cost, as was the case with the old series (shown in bold face), to basing real growth on GDP at constant market prices (bold face).

"Make GST" was about the 122nd Constitution Amendment Bill, introduced in Parliament in December 2014, to enable the GST (goods and services tax). The essay argues that the compromises made by not sweeping away inter-tax boundaries in totality, and permitting them to continue for an interim period, are well worth the benefit of bringing all states on board.

Finally, "On Budgetary Allocations and Finance Bills" is on the Finance Bill 2015 accompanying the Union Budget. The essay argues that the changes proposed in the Bill, to shift the function of public debt issuance out of the RBI to the Ministry of Finance, were poorly designed, and had potentially serious consequences for the conduct of monetary policy, and a number of other functions executed by the RBI. In the event, all these sections were deleted from the amended Finance Bill eventually passed.

Figure 1.0

Central Fiscal Deficits Achieved and Projected

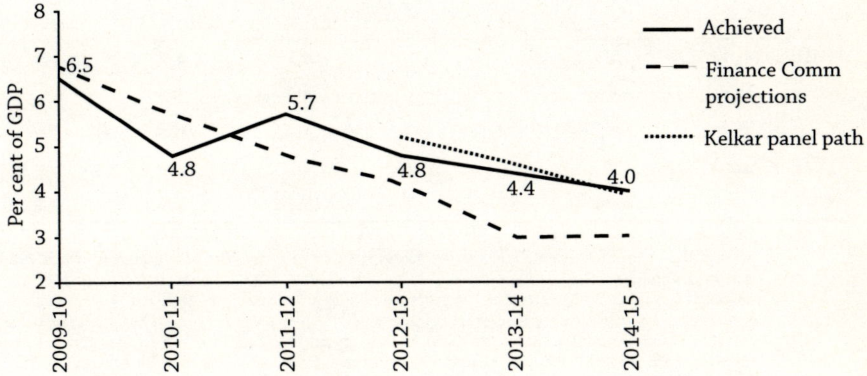

Notes: All percentages are with respect to the earlier GDP series, since the new series starts from 2011-12, and has not been extended back so far; the only exception is the achieved percentage for 2014-15, which shifts to the new series (current price nominal magnitudes by the new series converged to the old series by 2013-14, the last year for which both series are available; for prior years, the new series magnitudes were below the old series). The fiscal deficit targets in the amended FRBM act, as notified in May 2013, were 3 per cent of GDP in 2016-17, and an annual reduction by 0.5 per cent of GDP, implying a required 4 per cent of GDP in 2014-15 (actual achievement was on target). The FRBM was further amended through the Finance Bill 2015 accompanying the Union Budget, to push back the final deficit target of 3 percent by one year to 2017-18. The path targets were accordingly revised to 3.9 percent (2015-16) and 3.5 percent (2016-17).

Source: Achieved deficit percentages are calculated with absolute figures as supplied in Union Budget 2015-16, except for the 2014-15 provisional final percentage directly taken from the Ministry of Finance website. Finance Commission projections from its report; and the mid term Kelkar panel correction path from the Report of the Committee on Roadmap for Fiscal Consolidation, which can be accessed at: finmin.nic.in/reports/Kelkar_Committee_Report.pdf. Union Budget documents are available at the website *http://indiabudget.nic.in* starting from the latest year and going back to 1996-97.

Figure 2.0

Central Subsidies 2010-2015

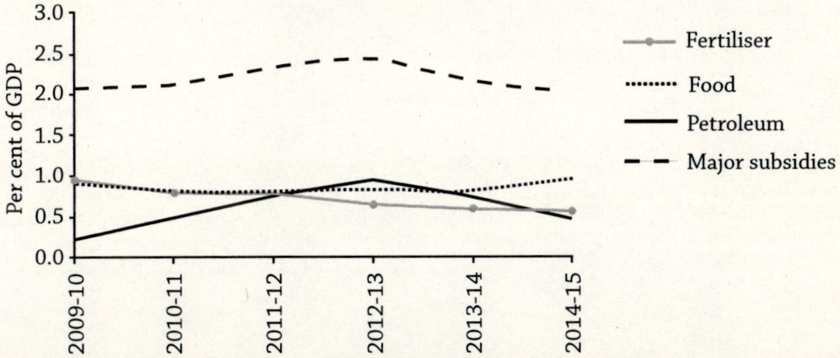

Note: All percentages are with respect to GDP by the old series except for 2014-15; see notes to Figure 1.0.

Source: Union Budget, assorted years going up to 2015-16.

Table 1.0

GDP Growth Rates for 2012-13 and 2013-14 by Old and New Series

		2012-13	*2013-14*	*2014-15*
GDP at fc	**old**	**4.5**	**4.7**	**-**
	new	4.9	6.6	-
GDP at bp	new	4.9	6.6	7.2
GDP at mp	old	4.7	5.0	-
	new	**5.1**	**6.9**	**7.3**

Notes: Factor cost, fc, is no longer to be estimated in the new series, but has been provided for the first two years of the new series to aid comparability across the shift in series. The new aggregate which will be routinely supplied is GDP at basic prices (bp), which adds on to the old factor cost some (net) taxes unrelated to quantum of production, like profession tax. But the basic price aggregate will not be used to generate real growth rates. For that, there is a shift to GDP at market prices (mp). The bold face estimates show the result of both the shift to a new series with its new databases and estimation procedures, and the shift in the aggregate used for estimating growth rates from factor cost to market prices.

Source: Press releases on the Ministry of Statistics and Programme Implementation website: *http://mospi.nic.in/Mospi_New/site/home.aspx.*

33 The Fiscal Middle Distance

The fiscal problem at the Centre has gradually been brought under control after 2012-13,[1] but looking beyond into the middle distance, there is a boulder up ahead which needs to be stopped from rolling down the hill.

So what is the boulder? I have to backtrack all the way to 1997-98, when the pay scales recommended by the 5th Pay Commission were given to Central civil servants retrospectively from calendar 1996. By 1999-2000, all state-level employees had won parity in pay scales and pensions with their Central counterparts; there were equivalent arrears payable; and the aggregate fiscal deficit of states had climbed to 4.5 per cent of GDP. The two major borrowing avenues for state government were securities; or alternatively small savings, which were at that time collected by the Centre and loaned back to states. Either way, interest rates shot up (small savings deposit rates were actually administered, but had to be raised in order to collect more). States found themselves saddled with a ballooning interest bill to go with their salary and pension bills.

That story is acutely relevant today because one of the last acts of the outgoing government in 2014 was to appoint a 7th Pay Commission, three years before it was due. So we have to go back to see how that earlier pay hike played out in the system.

In a commendable reform in 1999-2000, the Central government ceased its intermediary role in the small savings fund flow, and moved it to a separate fund in the public account. The separation made it transparently clear that if lending rates on loans to states were to be reduced, small savings deposit rates would have to come down too. In this way, state acquiescence was sought and (reluctantly) granted for a steady reduction in small savings deposit rates, which had always acted as a floor to bank deposit rates.

---

1. See Figure 1.0 in the preamble.

Over the three years from 2000 to 2003, with dwindling inflows into small savings, and the heavy backlog of interest dues on loans taken to cover the pay hike and arrears, states were forced to engage in strenuous primary fiscal correction. The payoff was that interest rates fell all round, private investment leapt up, growth hummed. The National Democratic Alliance (NDA) government went to the 2004 polls with their India Shining campaign. And they lost.

Many constructions have been placed upon that electoral defeat, but there is no question that state governments' unhappiness with the brutal fiscal correction forced upon them, played into it. The fiscal reform by itself was absolutely the right thing to have done. It set the groundwork for the high growth rates and tax revenue inflows enjoyed by the successor United Progressive Alliance (UPA) government right across their first term, surviving even the global crash of September 2008. The public policy error lay in the manner in which the 5th Pay Commission scales were accepted at Central level in 1997, with no thought to the fiscal implications for states.

Discrete ramp-ups of civil servant pay every 10 years or so are not a good way to go. No attempt is made at these decadal points to examine the structure of the civil service, using the term in the sense of government employees rather than in the Indian sense of an elite cadre sitting at the top of the governmental pyramid. (In international usage, a postman is as much as a civil servant as the Postmaster General).

The Indian civil service in that sense, aggregating across Central and state government employees, is not large by international standards. There is no consolidated database on public servants employed across Centre and states, but the last reported estimate places it at 1.2 per cent of the population (excluding military personnel), implying an absolute number today of around 14 million. The corresponding estimate for China is 2.4 per cent, the most appropriate large-population federal comparator country.

The problem in India is not the large size of the service but its structure. The elite layer, consisting of A and B level officers, accounts for 5 per cent of the total. Level C accounts for 70 per cent and level D for 25 per cent (these estimates are from a study that is now 12 years old,[2] but I suspect the percentages would not have changed substantially). Within each of these levels, there is a very wide range in terms of competence. Without highly skilled C-level employees, the budget documents at the Centre (and states), for example, simply could not be produced. There are highly skilled drivers and gardeners in level D too. But there are also large numbers with no apparent duties to perform, visible in the corridors of government offices.

The 6th Pay Commission scales were accommodated within the fiscal stimulus sanctioned after the global crash in 2008-09, but the difficulty of applying the brakes on that stimulus soon became apparent. The 13th Finance Commission recommended that Centre and states make annual contributions towards a fund to cover decadal pay scale revisions. There is still time. The 7th Pay Commission was not due to be appointed until 2016-17, and its report is not due until 2017-18. The Centre should make a start on a fund build-up. States will have to be brought in on the feasible increase in civil service pay, and the fiscal challenge it will pose.

---

2. Beschel Jr., Robert P. (2003). "Civil Service Reform in India", in Stephen Howes, A.K. Lahiri and N. Stern (eds.), *State Level Reform in India*. MacMillan.

34 Tax Policy

The global crash of 2008 was bad for most people, but like all disasters, it marked an upward turn in the fortunes of some. Prior to the crash, whole seminars were held on the irrelevance of the International Monetary Fund (IMF). Today the IMF has a new set of biceps after having presided over the rescue package for the Greek imbroglio,[1] and is prepared with rolled-up sleeves to take on more.

Prior to 2008, fiscal policy analysts had just about the lowest standing in the economics profession, a tad above accountants. After the crash, their status has not exactly risen, but they are being asked, if a bit tetchily, to design tax policy such that exit from the fiscal stimulus is enabled through enhanced revenue, without diminishing public and private spending.

A new draft Direct Tax Code (DTC) was circulated in August 2009, to replace the Income Tax Act of 1961. The DTC, incorporating some revisions issued in June 2010 was placed before Parliament, remained pending and therefore lapsed with the outgoing government in 2014. In the Union Budget presented in February 2015, the DTC itself was dropped, but its principal recommendation for a simultaneous cut in exemptions and in the base rate was adopted with a one-year lag.

Effective 2016-17, the corporate tax rate will be dropped from 30 per cent (excluding cesses and surcharges) to 25 per cent over four years. However, for the immediate financial year 2015-16, there was an increase in the surcharge on corporate entities, raising the effective tax rate inclusive of all add-ons from 32.445 to 33.063 per cent for taxable income of ₹1 to 10 crore; and from 33.99 to 34.60 per cent for taxable income above ₹10 crore. What will happen to exemptions is not clear.

1. The rescue package involved fiscal austerities that had devastating recessionary and job loss impacts, and was finally rejected by the Greek voter. A new package with European Central Bank (ECB) support of Greek debt was negotiated in early 2015, put to referumdum in July 2015 and again rejected. Yet another package was under negotiation at the time of writing.

Ideally, a quantitative estimate is needed of avoidance under the present regime, and how much of that can be eliminated. Avoidance, unlike evasion, can be estimated from filed returns.

Fortunately, budget documents in recent years provide estimates, based on electronically filed returns, of revenue foregone from both direct and indirect tax exemptions, disaggregated by the relevant section of the code in each case.

An exclusive focus on corporate taxation will help keep things simple, and is justified since corporate taxes yield nearly two-thirds of all direct tax revenues. Corporate tax returns electronically filed were 90 per cent of total returns in 2014-15.

The document does not generate avoidance percentages from the estimates of absolute revenue foregone. A simple enough step, one might imagine, but not that simple as it turns out.

Corporate returns filed in 2014-15 pertain to the PY (previous year) 2013-14. Reported taxes paid, inclusive of all cesses and surcharges for 2013-14 show an effective tax rate of 23.22 per cent of reported profit before taxes. This is 70 per cent of the statutory tax rate of 33.22 per cent (inclusive of add-ons),[2] thus yielding an avoidance rate of 30.0 per cent.

But if the absolute estimate of revenue foregone is applied to corporate tax revenue actually collected in 2013-14, we get a lower avoidance estimate of 22 per cent of potential revenue.[3] This is because total corporate tax collections that year were ₹3.94 lakh crore, higher than taxes reported paid by the universe of all tax-paying corporate entities for that year, by ₹1.36 lakh crore. Of this, ₹25,000 crore was from the Dividend Distribution Tax (DDT). That leaves an unexplained element of additional revenue amounting to nearly 1.0 per cent of the GDP.

If we accept mystification, and place avoidance at 22 per cent of potential revenue, it implies that corporate tax collections, amounting to 3.5 per cent of GDP in 2013-14, could have ramped up to 4.5 per

2. This is the reported average across a levy of 32.445 per cent on corporate income upto, and 33.99 per cent on income exceeding, ₹10 crore.

3. Potential revenue defined as the sum of actual collections, and foregone revenue obtained from the difference between the stautory and effective rates applied to profit before taxes.

cent with zero avoidance. Is that where the DTC would have got us to? Not quite. Exemptions accounting for around half of revenue presently foregone still remained, in the form of profits in specified sectors listed in the 13th schedule, and retention of enhanced capital allowances for accelerated depreciation and scientific research. So an avoidance rate of around 11.0 per cent would have remained, on average. That was with the now lapsed DTC. The avoidance rate that remains will be a function of how many of the present exemptions will get eliminated with the reduction in the corporate tax rate promised over the four years, 2016-2020.

Even if it had started out with zero avoidance, the tax code could not have stayed that way. Corporate tax history the world over shows that parsimonious exemptions get loosened over time because of the power of corporate lobbies. A Minimum Alternate Tax (MAT) acts as an avoidance cap. The purpose is achieved whether the MAT is based on assets or on book profits. But an asset-based MAT carries some additional advantages over a levy on book profits. It curbs tax evasion by bypassing reported income and going straight to the income-generating base, and carries the efficiency gain of incentivising better returns from assets (but this could be punitive without carry forward). The absence of carry forward in the draft DTC asset-based MAT was a design defect.

The initial draft of the DTC carried an asset-based MAT. The switch back to a book profits base in the June 2010 revision seems to have been because the 2 per cent rate of MAT levy, at a corporate tax rate of 25 per cent, placed the minimum expected return at 8 per cent of assets. This could have been addressed by a MAT rate reduction to 1.25 per cent, or lower. The principle was surrendered for a rate, which was unfortunate. And a sectorally varied MAT rate structure is always possible. The only good reason why an asset-based MAT in India may be a bit premature is that any levy which asks for efficiency in the use of assets, requires ease of exit for inefficient manufacturing units. And that is something we still do not have.

Union Budget 2015 promises a comprehensive Bankruptcy Code during 2015-16, conforming to global standards, with attention to the necessary judicial capacity. May be we could then introduce an asset based levy, at a nominal return, with carry forward. The efficiency incentive is contained in such a taxation structure, even at a low rate.

Finally, the eventual corporate tax rate proposed of 25 per cent is not aligned to the maximum marginal rate on individuals of 30 per cent. This is inequitable when dividends are not taxed in the hands of recipients. A dividend distribution tax at 15 per cent alters the incentive structure away from dividend payouts, in favour of deferred capital gains, which always receive lenient tax treatment. Alignment between the corporate and individual rate structures addresses the equity issue in a more non-distortionary way.

35 Tedious TDS

In the current discourse about black money, let us not lose sight of the honest taxpayer in India, whose good intentions are severely tested every year by procedural obstacles. Among the worst is getting certification for taxes already paid through deduction at source.

A total of 47 million income tax returns were filed in 2013-14,[1] by Report 3 of 2014-15 of the Comptroller and Auditor General (CAG). The number of PAN (permanent account number) card holders is estimated at 170 million as of 2013, although this number includes duplicate cards. Whatever, there clearly remains a huge distance between the number of filers, and the universe of those with taxable potential.

Tax withholding at source from income tax payable is universally endorsed as the key structural corrective for filing failure. TDS (tax deducted at source) signals to the tax authority the existence of an income recipient with taxable potential. It also achieves another very important purpose, which is to yield revenue to government as and when incomes are earned, thus evening out the revenue flow over the year.

TDS signalling can be achieved even through a system of final withholding, whereby tax is withheld at the lowest slab rate, and is not refundable. This system does not encourage the recipient to file for refunds due, if any, but a good information network will register the existence of a taxpayer with additional taxes potentially due, by virtue of the low rate of withholding, and give the tax authority a basis on which to follow up if no return is filed.

In India, we have provisional withholding, whereby refunds on TDS (along with other advance payments) can be claimed. This carries a greater incentive to file a return, and is fair to deductees whose income falls below the taxable threshold. TDS on salary is unlikely to be refundable, since the deduction is calibrated to the marginal rate

1. This is an update of an article orginally published in July 2011.

payable on each slab. So refundability arises largely in respect of non-salary payments like interest. And TDS on interest is where all the problems arise, for taxpayers and deductors alike.

Banks are expected to pay TDS on interest due every quarter. So if there is a fixed deposit (FD) with interest cumulated every quarter, TDS is deducted from gross interest, and the net amount cumulated to the next quarter. So far, the procedure is understandable, although deductees do not actually receive any income. They are only deemed to have received income by virtue of the quarterly cumulation of the FD. But let that pass.

There is further complexity. Suppose there is an FD maturing on 18 September, which is then renewed for a further period of, say, one year. Practices vary on whether the gross income payable on the new FD for the 12 remaining days in the quarter ending on 30 September, is assessed to TDS or carried forward into the next quarter. Either way, it adds to the workload of bank staff. If the bank overestimates TDS due by error, it cumulates its way into the gross interest payable in subsequent quarters.

Unlike a monthly salary statement from which salary earners receive full information on tax deducted each month, information on TDS from bank interest is not conveyed to FD holders every quarter. The TDS certificate is issued only after the conclusion of the financial year. Furthermore, the burden of extracting this certificate lies on the deductee. After much effort, the aspiring filer can expect to wave it triumphantly only by the middle of June. There is further harassment involved for those individuals wanting to file electronically, if TDS has been wrongly uploaded.

The TDS rate itself can change in the course of the year, without any information to deductees. For example, upto September 2009, TDS was deducted at 10.3 per cent, inclusive of cesses. Then it was changed to a flat 10.0 per cent. The Direct Tax Code (DTC) (now lapsed), prescribed TDS rates in its Third Schedule; hopefully stability in TDS rates will be adopted going forward, even if not necessarily codified in legislation.

TDS is relatively insignificant for corporate taxpayers, but accounts for over half of gross collections from non-corporates (mostly individuals).[2] Clearly, for individual taxpayers, taking credit for TDS paid is an important part of their tax filing exercise.

Category-wise details of TDS by source are not available, but interest income (for which tax is deducted at the lowest slab rate of 10 per cent) would have a lower share than salary (for which TDS is slabbed). A CAG report on direct taxes for an earlier year (No. 21 of 2009) which did give TDS by source, shows interest accounting for 20 per cent of gross TDS collections. Refunds are reported in aggregate for direct taxes, and amounted to 36 per cent of gross TDS. The numbers suggest that TDS from interest income prompts the deductee to file only when a refund is due.

If this is true, TDS is not playing its signalling role in the manner it is meant to, and the compliance costs at both the bank and taxpayers ends are not yielding commensurate revenue.

More simplification of TDS procedures is needed, along with greater follow-up of non-filing TDS deductees.

2. In 2013-14 for example, TDS accounted for 18 per cent of total corporate tax collected, but for 64 per cent of total non-corporate direct tax collected.

36 Fiscally Induced Investment

The present growth slowdown in the Indian economy, to an estimated 4.7 per cent for 2013-14 [the growth rate by the new series is 6.9 per cent; see Table 1.0], has gone hand in hand with investment remaining above 30 per cent of GDP (gross domestic product). This has been widely noticed and commented on. The ratio between the investment rate and the growth rate, called the ICOR (incremental capital-output ratio), is a handy if very rough measure, ignoring leads and lags, of the productivity of investment in the aggregate. When the ICOR goes up as it has, investment in the numerator is just not yielding enough growth juice in the denominator.

The ICOR is really a very blunt measure of the productivity of investment and has been quite volatile between years. All the same, we have to ask the question whether there is anything in the fabric of our taxation structure which actually encourages infructuous investment, and gives an upward policy-induced upward push to the ICOR. Any such push would of course be a structural feature, and would not explain the year-to-year variation in ICOR.

One such in our income tax law is AD (accelerated depreciation), by which investment in certain chosen sectors is allowed depreciation at higher than normal rates right upfront (section 32 of the income tax act, rule 5). There is a long list of types of investment eligible for AD. Some of it is equipment with a naturally short life, like rollers in sugar or flour mills. Others carry positive externalities, like air or water pollution control equipment, or solid waste treatment plants, or water supply and purification, or renewable energy.

Wind energy was withdrawn from the list at the end of March 2012 (the list still includes solar and other renewable sources). Until that date, against taxable profit in any other sector, you could write off depreciation at 80 per cent of the value of your renewable energy plant as expenditure, and immediately gain the one-third share of that expenditure which would have gone as taxes to government. It amounts to cash upfront right then and there, which would otherwise have been surrendered as taxes to government.

So what is wrong with tax incentives for investments that work to control industrial effluents, or generate clean energy? Surely we need more, not less, of those. The problem is that there is nothing in the incentive structure to ensure that the objective sought is actually achieved. The tax authorities cannot monitor equipment (effluent treatment, say), incentivised with a tax break, to ensure that it actually is in working condition. Effluent monitoring is the responsibility of local authorities and frequently degenerates into a rent-collection opportunity. The investor has no incentive to keep it in working order because his profits are unaffected (that was the whole point of why he was tax incentivised to install it in the first place).

A renewable energy plant, wind or solar, by contrast is an income-generating proposition, whether sold to the grid, or held for captive use. So these are bank-loan worthy, upto 70 per cent of the cost of the plant. This then means that, since the bank loan has to be serviced, the promoter cannot afford to let the plant lie idle. So argues the powerful lobby that is trying to restore wind energy to the AD list, buttressing their case with anecdotal evidence that there are no defaults on bank loans to wind energy plants.

There remain two problems with AD as an incentive mechanism even for income generating equipment. The plant may be kept functional enough to service the bank loan, but there is no incentive to maximise generation. And because the incentive calls for speed in installation, the investor typically gets a package deal which is likely to carry a higher cost than necessary. This padded investment is incentivised into the numerator of the ICOR, and although some output does go into the denominator, there is no push to maximise that.

A GBI (generation-based incentive) was introduced in 2009-10, to do precisely what its name intends, by offering 50 paise for every kilowatt-hour of wind energy generation. This was a Plan scheme, with a short life upto the end of March 2012. It excluded AD beneficiaries, so that the incremental investment effect under the scheme became neatly identifiable, and amounted to 1000 MW per year. Because AD was dropped at the same time that GBI came to an end, at the close of March 2012, there was a sharp fall after that date in investment in wind energy.

The reasons for the sudden cessation of AD for wind energy are not known. Perhaps it was the revenue loss, which cannot be discerned from the aggregate revenue loss from AD as reported in the Budget documents, but can be worked out at roughly ₹1.6 crore per MW of installed capacity. GBI meanwhile has been restored in November 2013, with retrospective effect. The GBI payout cap has been raised to ₹1 crore per MW over 10 years. Even at this higher cap it remains much cheaper than AD, in terms of capacity per rupee of (tax or subsidy) expenditure. Most of all, it is better structured to get us what we really want, which is renewable energy output, not just capacity installed.

The aggregate revenue loss from AD, across all sectors, is around one-third of one per cent of GDP. It is impossible to get a sectoral breakup of that revenue loss, because the sector box to be ticked in corporate tax returns does not indicate clearly whether it should be the major activity of the taxpayer, or the sector for which AD is being claimed. We need to get a better idea of what we are paying for so that, like GBI, we might devise a superior route to what we want to achieve in the end – more output from investment.

37 Financing Urban Infrastructure

Lifting the lid on the GDP (gross domestic product) growth rate will take strenuous effort on a number of fronts,[1] but a very key component has to be urban infrastructure. Easier movement of people and goods within cities, functioning sanitation and sewage systems, storm water drainage – all these are essential for the economic machine to function. The problem lies with the financing of it.

Public private partnerships (PPPs) are seen as the solution to the funding of urban infrastructure. It is thought that knocking the heads of municipal leaders and financial honchos together can bring about the right financial products to kickstart the process. The problem lies much deeper, and can only be set right by getting property taxes to work. And for that, state governments have to partner the process.

Without base support from property taxes there can quite simply be no progress on urban infrastructure, except of the Mumbai sea link or Delhi metro variety catering to identifiable usage, and therefore amenable to user fees. Private capital to fund general purpose urban infrastructure will only be forthcoming on a time stream of guaranteed payback unrelated to usage. Property taxes are especially suited for this because they do not carry downside risk. The value of housing and land does not typically decline in nominal value except in extreme situations (such as the 2008 mortgage crisis in the US), and property value is marked to market sufficiently infrequently to ride over temporary downside blips. This makes property taxes acceptable worldwide as a reliable basis for calculating the payback time-stream for urban infrastructure funded with private participation.

Property tax revenues can only improve when the taxation structure is designed by trained professionals. Ideally, a permanent

---

1. This was written in the June 2013 context of the depressed growth rate estimates by the old series of GDP. Although the new series shows higher growth rates, it cannot overwrite other indicators such as high capacity under-utilisation as measured by Reserve Bank of India (RBI) surveys.

core of personnel in a state-level property tax board could provide expertise to all municipalities in the state, big and small. The 13th Finance Commission took a first and much-needed step in this direction, by requiring the setting up of state-level property tax boards as a conditionality for a performance grant to ULBs (urban local bodies), over and above an unconditional basic grant.

Progress on this and other conditionalities is not yet displayed on any public website.[2] Information accessed from the National Institute of Urban Affairs shows that as of 31 March 2012, the latest available, 18 states had set up state-level property tax boards. But in many of these, the board is a mere shell, not functional in any sense because there is no budgetary provision for technical personnel.

The 13th Finance Commission performance grant flowed directly to ULBs, with no part going to state governments to fund the property tax board. The intent (not explicitly stated in the report) was to have these bodies function on a commission basis, getting a small part of the increment in property taxes as a result of their services, but clearly an initial budget line is needed for hiring qualified technical personnel in the first place, with a training provision if necessary. The incentive to states, of receiving the additional performance grant flow to municipalities from the Centre, should have sufficed just by itself. But apparently, states see the property tax board as an unfunded mandate, instead of as an opportunity to free municipal governments from continued financial dependence on state governments.

Property taxes are not popular. There have been state elections in which parties rode to power on a manifesto that included the promise to repeal property taxes. People see the income tax or sales tax as justifiable, but to be taxed for just living in a house strikes them as monstrous. For this reason, it is especially important that property taxation should be fair, and seen to be fair. Over time worldwide, property taxation practice has moved away from intrusive checking for internal opulence (marble floors, gold faucets), to more macro assessments of the taxable base, by differentiating between cities, and between zones within cities, by market value. But even such a

2. See footnote 1 in chapter 17 for details on the deficiency in terms of information on fund flow and conditionalities met.

seemingly simple exercise calls for assigning a rateable value per unit floor area based on location. Smaller municipalities have no way of getting such technical expertise by themselves.

The year 2010-11 was a gap year given to states to get their act together on the qualifying conditionalities for the urban performance grant. If they came up against a budget constraint for a new line item for the property tax board, this was an issue they could have brought to the nodal ministry. The amounts are so small that a solution could easily have been worked out.

Revenues presently collected through property taxation in the country are not known with any certainty. There is no annual issue of audited finance accounts for local bodies in aggregate, of the kind available for state governments. Data supplied by states to finance commissions are the only source of information on own revenue collected by municipalities, but these display such inconsistencies across commissions as to be not plausible. The 11th and 12th finance commissions incentivised own revenue collection by local government, but those very incentives introduced an upward reporting bias in later years. If the figures are taken just as they stand, own revenue of municipalities stood at 0.47 per cent of GDP in 1990-91 (the first year of the series collected by the Eleventh Commission), and remained at 0.47 per cent in 2007-08 (the last year of the series collected by the 13th Commission). The true figure for 2007-08 is likely to have been much lower.

These are for total own revenue, and cover cities located in states like Mumbai, but exclude Delhi and other Union Territory (UT) cities (for which audited figures are indeed available). They include revenue in earlier years from octroi, a levy on goods at the urban entry point. Octroi has since been dropped, so property tax collections do seem to have risen to some degree to cover the revenue loss from octroi.

There is room for a further huge leap in property tax collections with better coverage of the taxable base, given the increase in the housing stock over the last two decades. Once the funding for staffing and training of property tax boards is addressed, that potential can be realised, and provide the revenue base for private funding of general purpose infrastructure across urban India.

38 Partial Fiscal Exit

The Action Taken Report on the recommendations of the 13th Finance Commission (TFC), tabled the day before the Union Budget for 2010-11, gratifyingly accepts all its major provisions. A tradition has built up over the years whereby Finance Commission prescriptions on the core task assigned to them are accepted in totality by the government of the day. A good practice in general, this averts the kind of disastrous part acceptance, for example of Pay Commission reports, which has played havoc with fiscal discipline. There are downsides to the practice as well. Finance Commissions become excessively risk-averse about departing from the trodden path, in a bid not to go down in history as the first to have been partially rejected.

Only a few of the recommendations of TFC are set aside for further examination. These include the interest rate reset on National Social Security Fund (NSSF) loans to states, accounting and budget reforms, and disclosure requirements. Some disclosures, such as for example on state-local transfers, are actually built into the fabric of fully accepted recommendations, so it is those pertaining to the Centre that are set aside for consideration. Finance Commissions have no instruments in any case with which to enforce or incentivise their recommendations for the Centre. But in many ways, these are arguably of even greater importance for fiscal discipline in the system than incentives formally built into the transfer mechanism, which in the very nature of Finance Commissions, apply to subnational governments alone. For example, the Centre has to take the lead in removing structural shocks from Pay Commission arrears by making the pay award commence from the date of acceptance, not retrospectively for prior years. Pay Commission salary revisions apply to Central civil servants in the first instance, but within an interval of a few years work their way through all states.[1] Arrears from back-dated (6th) Pay Commission awards were a major

1. The cataclysmic impact of the Fifth Pay Commission is the subject of "The Fiscal Middle Distance".

fiscal overload on states during 2008-2010, as much or more than the revenue impact of the global slowdown.

TFC treated the first year 2010-11 of its five-year horizon as a gap year in which both Centre and states were given room to begin reversal of the fiscal loosening of the last two years.[2] The formal correction horizon for states actually begins only from 2011-12, with a year given to them in which to enact legislation carrying the state-specific time path prescribed in the report. For the Centre, the correction path prescribed by the FC does start right from 2010-11, but deficit targets for the first year are actually more lax than in the Centre's own MTFP (medium term fiscal plan) accompanying last year's fiscal policy statement in July 2009. The FC was driven by the objective of prescribing feasible targets in place of infeasible promises.

But the latest Union Budget [2010-11], while staying with its original MTFP fiscal deficit of 5.5, actually has a whopper of a revenue deficit of 4 per cent.[3] So we have fiscal exit, yes, but through capital expenditure containment, a bad idea in the midst of stark infrastructure deprivation. The state of water, sewerage, road and power infrastructure in India is no secret. We creak on in the midst of it all. Where Plan capital expenditure grew 25 per cent last year over 2008-09, growth is contained at 14 per cent in the year to come. Where Plan revenue expenditure grew last year at 13 per cent, it is budgeted to grow at 19 per cent next year.

An influential body of opinion holds that the revenue deficit does not matter. Capital markets, they will argue, care about the reach of the government into the supply of financial savings, not about the expenditure uses to which those borrowings are put. Keynes himself, the saviour in 1936 as in 2008, said of fiscal expansion during a

2. Part of the fiscal stimulus starting with the year 2008-09, as a result of a G20 agreement for co-ordinated action to prevent a slump following the global crisis.

3. The final deficit figures, at 4.8 per cent and 3.2 per cent respectively, were much lower, but the difference, i.e., capital expenditure, was about the same. Capital expenditure protection through fiscal legislation has conventionally stood at 3 per cent of GDP at the level of the Central government, by the twin targets of zero on the revenue deficit, and 3 per cent on the overall fiscal deficit (if there is disinvestment, capital expenditure will be higher than the protected floor). Other countries achieve similar objectives by prescribing a balanced budget for current expenditure alone, which corresponds to our zero revenue deficit, and by freeing government borrowing to match capital expenditure.

downturn that it could just as well be spent on digging holes and filling them up. And conversely, when the budgetary imbalance is being reversed, could it not be argued likewise that the kind of expenditure curtailed is of no importance?

Keynes in the 1930s was fighting a fire, and was rightly impatient with classical economists at the time, who worried about the longer term implications of deficits, when there was a short-term imperative to jump-start a stagnant system. We too are fighting a fire no less urgent – the demographic pressure on infrastructure that will be felt 5-10 years down the line. The capital expenditure to avert that has to happen now.

The problem with present budgetary practices is that Plan revenue expenditure, feeding into the revenue deficit, actually has capital expenditure components tucked away in it. Of total Plan revenue expenditure of ₹3.15 lakh crore budgeted for next year, some goes as assistance to state and Union Territory (UT) plans, leaving ₹2.3 lakh crore to be spent by the Centre. It is the Central component that has risen substantially, by ₹43,000 crore over the revised estimate of last year, a 23 per cent increase.

Of Central Plan revenue expenditure, 60 per cent is transferred out – most of it to a forest of autonomous implementing agencies. These include expenditure on rural roads for example, under the Pradhan Mantri Gram Sadak Yojana (PMGSY), on rural housing under the Indira Awaas Yojana (IAY), and of course on the rural employment guarantee scheme.[4] Disregarding asset quality issues, these transfers from the revenue account resulting in creation of capital assets do serve to muddy the distinction between revenue and fiscal deficits. The Finance Commission report specifically recommends that new accounting conventions be developed, such as capital grants, for example, to handle the problem.[5]

Transfers out account for only 20.5 per cent of the ₹43,000 crore increase in Central Plan revenue expenditure. Even adjusting for them

4. Starting with 2014-15, funds for all three schemes flowed directly to state governments rather than to autonomous agencies, although the capital content issue remained the same as before.

5. See epilogue.

does not bring down the projected revenue deficit. The issue remains that if an increase in current expenditure was thought necessary, at a time when the need for fiscal exit is acknowledged, the pattern and quantum of that hike have to be justified. Budget documents have to serve a clarificatory purpose for the tax-paying citizen.

Epilogue

Starting with the budget for the very next year 2011-12, an Effective Revenue Deficit, after subtracting out the capital expenditure content of revenue expenditure, was shown in the formal Budget documents. It showed the capital expenditure content, over the period 2010-15, at somewhere between 1.1 to 1.5 per cent of GDP.

But is the capital expenditure content in current grants really growth promoting? For the Mahatma Gandhi National Rural Employment Guarantee Scheme (MGNREGS), the capital content is estimated at the full budgetary provision for the programme. That surely is a bit of a stretch. MGNREGS is principally an income transfer scheme through workfare, where asset creation is incidental and does not correspond to a structured programme of public investment to expand the growth potential of the economy.

As opposed to that, the Pradhan Mantri Gram Sadak Yojna (PMGSY), also buried in the current account, goes entirely into well-defined road construction with permanent asset creation properties. But the capital content of this programme is shown at only four-fifths of the full amount budgeted for this scheme. The lower capital content must be because PMGSY funding is partially round-tripped through the Central Road Fund (CRF), where the CRF funds road upgradation and is therefore treated as current maintenance expenditure. But the figures from Demand 82 on the contribution from the CRF are not an exact match. I have a dream, that there will one day be a Union Budget which will be internally consistent in every particular.

39 Fiscal Policy 2012

Union Budget 2012 moves towards fiscal correction, but does not go far enough. The quality of fiscal consolidation is also in the right direction, but not far enough to address the massive public investment deficit. Other constraints holding down growth and holding up inflation are recognised, though not with enough granularity. The MTEF (medium term expenditure framework) prescribed by the Thirteenth Finance Commission (TFC) finally promised in the Fiscal Responsibility and Budget Management (FRBM) Amendment comes one year too late, but better late than never.

Fiscal correction at the Centre was an imperative, at a time when inflation was still at 7.6 per cent,[1] a depreciating rupee and slowing growth together point clearly to supply side constraints. Fiscal deficits of states are no longer a worry, because incentives designed by successive Finance Commissions have structured financial rewards into the system for states practising fiscal prudence. West Bengal remains an exception, but in all fairness, the interest bill they face today is a legacy from earlier failure to enact fiscal responsibility legislation in line with other states.

This is not to say that expenditures on social sector schemes at state-level are reaching targeted beneficiaries. Horror stories abound of state-level hijacking of food meant for the most vulnerable segments of the population. Fiscal discipline should rightly imply both restraint in aggregate expenditure, and well-monitored expenditure. The first is structurally in place at state level. The second eludes us still.

Back to the Centre, the fiscal consolidation in the MTFP (medium term fiscal programme), after the disastrous loss of control in 2011-12, is directionally correct, if not ambitious. The slow pace is justified on the grounds that the promise of sharper cuts would have lacked credibility. Incidentally, the final GDP numbers for 2011-12 will

1. This was by the Wholesale Price Index (WPI), the instrument of choice at the time for the measurement of inflation. The Consumer Price Index (CPI) for February and March 2012 averaged at 9.1 per cent.

probably be a bit higher, so the final fiscal deficit per cent may be a touch lower [it finally registered at 5.7%] than the revised estimate [5.9%].

Between a final estimate of the deficit for 2011-12 at 5.7 per cent, the budgeted deficit for 2012-13 of 5.1 per cent implies a headline fiscal correction of 0.6 per cent of GDP. One-off revenue receipts from spectrum sales and disinvestment, which are episodic and therefore not a predictable component of the revenue generation properties of the system, should ideally be removed from this so as to obtain the structural content of the fiscal correction. However, the budget papers do not permit a detailed breakdown of telecom receipts into recurrent and one-off receipts.

Some of the revenue moves are laudable, such as the doubling of import duty rates on gold. Smuggling networks have been largely dismantled over the last 20 years, and this hike is not large enough to motivate erstwhile smugglers to come out of retirement and put those networks together again.

The total expenditure correction is modest, but the capital expenditure component of it is budgeted to go up by 0.38 per cent of GDP including (0.26% of GDP excluding) disinvestment funded expenditure.

However, the content of what is called capital expenditure is a bit worrying. Starting last year, an effective revenue deficit was calculated, by removing from revenue (current) expenditure those grants going towards creation of public capital assets. As an idea, I support it, and indeed did it myself in 2006 when reviewing public expenditure at the level of states (I called it an adjusted, not an effective revenue deficit). The spirit of the adjustment however requires removal of only capital expenditure on major public asset creation programmes funded through current grants. A legitimate example is the Pradhan Mantri Gram Sadak Yojana (PMGSY), which indeed is one of the big ticket items. But getting capital asset creation mileage out of the entire expenditure on the Mahatma Gandhi National Rural Employment Guarantee (MGNREGS) is not defensible. This is a poverty alleviation scheme, only a small fraction of which, maybe 10 per cent, might result in enduring capital assets of any value.

Along with these two big schemes, the effective revenue deficit has been defined to exclude every scrap of capital content in revenue grants going to a large assortment of educational institutions. These may fund an auditorium or other such structure contributing nothing to the productive capacity of the economy. Plan transfers to states have also been bundled out, along with some statutory grants prescribed by the Finance Commission, but these certainly carry more justification. The justified elements add up to roughly half the total estimated capital expenditure content of revenue grants.

The exercise assumes importance in view of its hardwiring into the proposed[2] amendment to the FRBM, which targets elimination of the effective revenue deficit by 31 March 2015, and caps the (total) revenue deficit on that date at 2 per cent, an uncomfortably large margin for accommodation of possibly infructuous capital expenditure, of the auditorium variety.

The saving grace in the FRBM Amendment is the provision for review by the Comptroller and Auditor General (CAG) of compliance with the provision of the Act, a much-needed element of external review which was missing in the original Act. That leaves room for continued monitoring of the quality of capital assets brought into existence through the grant route.

More even than the quantum of public investment, there is need for focused attention on supply constraints in critical sectors of the economy. These include the dairy sector in the context of runaway inflation in milk;[3] thermal power generation; and expansion of public transportation networks for goods and passengers, including last mile connectivity, in light of the forthcoming correction of petroleum prices.

2. The amendment was a part of the Finance Bill of 2012, and was therefore passed with the Bill. Only the revenue deficit target was in the Bill itself and therefore stands enacted. The rules, notified as late as May 2013, carried the other targets, among them fiscal deficit reduction to 3 per cent by end-March 2017, further amended in 2015 to 3 per cent by end-March 2018.

3. Milk inflation by the CPI was running at an average of 15.5 per cent, in the first four months of 2012.

40 Make GST

The 122nd Constitution Amendment Bill to enable the GST (goods and services tax) introduced during the Winter Session of Parliament in 2014 is great news. Even though the intent to create a common market by eliminating tax barriers on inter-state sales was marred somewhat by the temporary retention of a reduced barrier, that is a small price to pay for passage of such a landmark bill. The tax on inter-state sales is to be levied and collected by the Centre, but with the revenue handed over to the selling state. Named an additional inter-state levy, it is essentially a replacement for the Central Sales Tax (CST), albeit at 1.0 per cent, lower than the present 2.0 per cent CST. It will be in place for two years, but is extendable by the GST Council, and could in principle be around for some years into the future.

That and the compensation provision for revenue losses right in the Constitutional Amendment itself are seen by many as deep flaws in the Bill. Compensation carries a sunset clause of five years, and was possibly the only way states could have been brought on board for such a major reform. The continued inter-state levy is essentially an adjunct to this provision, since the compensation payable will be reduced by the amount collected through the additional levy. Defenders of the need to insert compensation into the Constitutional Amendment see a need for statutory comfort to states, given the past history of broken compensation promises by the Centre, when the CST was reduced from 4.0 to 2.0 per cent. The sunset clause however makes it tolerable, and is an implicit recognition that there will be eventual revenue gain from GST to all parties, by virtue of the efficiency and compliance properties of the new levy. It also incentivises states to climb down to a zero CST while still within the compensation period.

Looking past its flaws, the bill carries two commendable features. The first is the long list of taxes broomed out. Among them is the purchase tax, legally leviable by any state on purchases within its boundaries but whose incidence, in the case of bulk purchase for nationwide sale, falls on buyers outside the state. The Punjab purchase tax on foodgrain has been paid regularly as part of the procurement price by the Food Corporation of India (FCI). Likewise, the Assam purchase tax on crude oil has been incorporated into the price at which oil refinery products from that state have been bought by the oil marketing companies. Purchase taxes on food and oil have ramped up the food and petroleum subsidies over the years. In both cases, the new additional levy of 1.0 per cent will reduce the burden on the food and petroleum subsidies. At the same time, of course, the revenue compensation ensures that over a period of five years, a compensation burden will continue on the Central exchequer in place of the subsidy burden.

The second commendable feature of the bill is that contentious issues surrounding rate structure, thresholds for taxability, and exempted goods, have been assigned to the GST Council, an inter-state body, whose formation and operating procedures have been clearly spelled out. It was extremely important to keep these issues outside the scope of the Constitutional amendment bill, so that any change in operating parameters did not have to require further amendments to the Constitution.

On balance, therefore, the amendment is an excellent beginning. The state GST will not be levied on exports from one state to other states, but the Central GST will (since to the Centre, an export happens only when the good or service goes to other countries). The revenue from the Central GST on inter-state sales is to be apportioned between states in a manner to be decided by the GST Council. This particular feature is regrettable, because it requires a revenue carve-out from the total revenue collected by the Centre from the GST. Calculational complexities of this kind are best avoided. The carve-out was unnecessary in view of the transitional compensation scheme, and could still be deleted before final passage of the Constitutional Amendment. Without that, there remains room for the eventual possibility of the Centre demarcating a portion of its overall GST collection for shoring up the revenues of municipalities, which are in terrible fiscal shape.

The battle lines between producer and consumer states over the GST, and earlier over the state VAT (value added tax) when it was introduced, result from an original sin – the CST. The right given to states to tax sales, in List II of the Seventh Schedule of the Constitution, did not permit taxation of sales across state borders. States that for locational or historical reasons had industrial belts, which sent goods across the country, demanded revenue compensation for the services they provided to enable production within their boundaries. In those days of administered prices, the claim was undoubtedly backed by underpriced inputs. To this day, states like Punjab levy a purchase tax on foodgrains instead of reducing the subsidies on inputs to agriculture like water and electricity.

The CST was therefore seen as a neat solution by which to levy a tax on inter-state sales, by naming it Central, but allowing states to collect and retain the revenue proceeds. It continued at (a maximum of) 4 per cent for so many decades that collecting states regarded it as a permanent revenue entitlement. At no point were states with CST revenue made to see that as production centres, they were already reaping the revenue advantage of high consumption from incomes earned by residents within their states. The present tax reform, which marks the culmination of what was begun with the state VAT on goods, rams home exactly that message. Exporting states reap revenues from the high consumption of the producers located within their boundaries.

Meanwhile, the 4 per cent CST which functioned essentially as an export tax, and therefore as a self-inflicted competitive disadvantage, did not actually result in importing states building up their own production centres behind this externally provided protection barrier. The cost disadvantage in most other states was simply too high to compensate for a tax barrier at a mere 4 per cent. In recent years however, increasing congestion has finally robbed first movers of their historical advantage, and there has been some spatial dispersal of activity, especially in production of intermediates after the introduction of the state VAT starting 2005. This activity is what has led to the new buzz in small town India.

When states agreed to come down in stages from a 4 per cent CST with imposition of the state VAT on goods starting 2005, they were promised compensation, which was variously not delivered. Thus began the mistrust of the Centre by states, which has to be very carefully bridged today. Even so, the process of reducing CST today has many takers. Even first mover states are able to see the cost advantage to producers within their boundaries of sourcing intermediates from outside the state at lower rates of CST levy, and that perceived advantage has to be built up slowly but surely to wean these states off CST altogether.

The Amendment Bill is just a beginning. The GST Council has to be constituted with membership as prescribed in the bill, and the vexed issue of the rate structure has to be resolved. Present-day Central levies on services and goods cascade onto the state VAT, resulting in tax rates in the 28.2-30.8 band (cascading makes the final incidence more than the simple sum of rates). Existing suggestions for GST rates going up to 27.0 per cent approach the current levels of taxation prevailing. That will make the GST not a reform, but just a slightly cleaned up replacement.

The search for revenue neutrality at present rates of levy is being done in a static way, not factoring in two improvements the GST is meant to bring in. There is first the compliance improvement expected, as a result of sellers being keen to collect from their buyers the tax from which they can claim a refund on taxes they paid on inputs. This revenue chain acts as an inducement to enter into the tax net.

Then there is the growth impact of the levy. Even if expectations that GST will raise the growth rate by anywhere from 1 to 2 per cent sound implausible, every reduction of the levy on inter-state sales clearly enhances the ability to source low-cost inputs (including services) from across state borders. The cost reduction and efficiency enhancement possibilities are immense. At a time when the Indian economy is suffering from depressed growth and elevated prices, the GST is a reform we cannot afford to lose through poor management of transition problems.

The staggered march through first initiating moves towards a VAT configuration by Centre and states within their independent taxation spheres, has given enough time for all parties to see the advantage to themselves of moving forward, together.

41 On Budgetary Allocations and Finance Bills

Every Union Budget makes choices on behalf of all of us, which will inevitably dissatisfy some of us.

On budgetary allocations Krishnadeva Raya, the fabled ruler in the years 1509-1529 of the Vijayanagar Empire, has this to say in the *raj-niti* section of "Amuktamalyada", a celebrated poem ascribed to him:

> Even if it is big, a quarter of the budget
> should go to the king's gifts and pleasures,
> half to maintain a powerful military
> and a fourth to the treasury vault.
>
> [AM IV.238: Translated by Srinivas Reddy, *Poems of Empire*]

Social sector expenditures were not routinely provided for, even by a fondly remembered monarch. What went into the vault was the fiscal surplus, a risk buffer presumably drawn down in years of agrarian distress. In the absence of a financial market, wise kings made sure they did not have to depend on money lenders.

Today we are lucky to have established financial markets, but we have to make sure that nothing disrupts their functioning. The changes in the Finance Bill 2015 accompanying the Union Budget for 2015-16, which impact those markets therefore merit very close attention. A major change is proposed in the issuance and management of public debt. These functions, hitherto performed by the Reserve Bank of India (RBI), will now be shifted out to a Public Debt Management Agency (PDMA), for Central government debt in the first instance. The proposal for an independent debt management office was announced by the Finance Ministry many years ago. It was endorsed for immediate implementation in a 2008 report by a committee to reform the financial system, headed by the present RBI Governor.

Subsequently there was further endorsement in the 2013 report of the Financial Sector Legislative Reforms Commission (FSLRC).

The reason for the shift is the potential conflict of interest between RBI as the monetary policy agent (with the ability to influence interest rates), and the function of public debt issuance, which carries discretionary powers over timing of issuance. Even so, I did not favour the shift then, and still think it is a bad idea. India is not a country with robust institutions. The RBI is one of our finest public institutions with a proven record of exemplary integrity in the execution of its functions. There has been alarm in the past about the size of the public debt, but never about the manner its issuance, which has been so seamless that the process itself has drawn no attention whatever (the 1992 Harshad Mehta scam preceded electronic trading). As the saying goes: 'If it ain't broke, don't fix it.'

But the decision has now been taken, and we have to run with it, and make sure that the shift is done with least disruption to financial markets. It is here that the Finance Bill has me seriously worried.

There are four sections in the Finance Bill bearing on the debt management role of the RBI. Chapter VII of the Bill enables the formation of a PDMA. Then there is Chapter IX, of which Part I amends the RBI Act, Part III amends the Securities and Contracts Regulation Act (SCRA), and Part XI repeals the Government Securities Act (GSA).

Starting with amendment of the RBI Act in Chapter IX Part I, clauses 156 and 157 remove RBI power to regulate the repo and reverse repo markets in government securities. Since these are instruments of monetary policy, removal of regulatory power over them has the potential to interfere with both the monetary policy and banking regulation functions of the RBI. Clauses 156 and 157 of the Finance Bill need to be deleted.

The principle justifying transfer of the issuance function extends to all government debt, Central as well as state, but the legal paths differ, and without due attention to these differences, there could be obstructions ahead to the fiscal functioning of state governments. Chapter VII enabling the formation of the PDMA, as presently worded, defines a government security in clause 119 as a security that is created and issued by the Central goverment. It is government securities, so defined, that the PDMA is vested with the issuance and management of in clause 124. The sub-clauses covering cash management and contingent liabilities also explicitly cover the Central government alone. Meanwhile, clauses 185 and 186 in Part XI, Chapter IX of the Finance Bill repeal the Government Securities Act (which covers all securities issued by both Centre and states), and transfer all functions performed under that Act from RBI to the newly created PDMA. RBI empowerment to issue state debt ceases after repeal of the GSA, and gets transferred to the PDMA, which is presently not legally empowered to perform that function.

The GSA was enacted in 2006 following legislative resolutions adopted by all states barring Jammu and Kashmir, ceding to Parliament (under Article 252, clause (1) of the Constitution) the right to enact laws with respect to state debt and the management thereof by the RBI. Clause (2) of Article 252 also reserves to Parliament the right to amend or repeal such laws, but since the underpinning state resolutions were predicated on management of the debt by RBI, it is not clear if transfer of that function can be legally done without fresh resolutions being passed by the states.

In this legal vacuum, with RBI disempowered with respect to state government debt issuance, and no institution empowered to assume that function, there will be fiscal uncertainty for state governments, and disruption in the market for state securities. The key need at this hour is for legal clarity.

The repeal of the GSA also ends the role of the RBI as the depository of government securities, and transfers it to the PDMA, which is empowered to outsource it. There has at the very least to be an insertion in the Finance Bill to cover the interim period between repeal of the GSA, which will happen with passage of the Finance Bill in its present form, and notification of the PDMA.

Nothing in the present Finance Bill prohibits the PDMA from choosing RBI as the depository. It would be best if the PDMA does appoint RBI as the depository. The RBI is the banker to the primary seller in these transactions, and holds accounts for all the buyers as well, since the vast majority of government securities, whether Central or state, are bought by banks and financial institutions. This may slowly change over time, as the SLR (statutory liquidity ratio) compulsion on banks to hold government securities is steadily reduced. Until then, the RBI is far and away the most efficient choice, offering instantaneous settlement since parties to all transactions hold both depository and fund accounts with it. The RBI does not charge a fee for the depository function, whereas others do.

There are a number of other frictions that will grow in the financial system if another depository is appointed. The Real Time Gross Settlements (RTGS) system, which enables instantaneous financial transfers across the country, allows intra-day borrowing for banks which fall temporarily short of liquidity, using securities in their depository account as collateral. At a time when the Indian payments and settlements system has been painstakingly winched up to higher levels of efficiency, introduction of avoidable friction is surely something we do not want. The RBI also offers temporary use of surplus cash in government accounts through an assortment of mechanisms enabled by the in-house depository. This carries efficiency benefits for the system, and yields fiscal revenue for governments.

Finally, clause 160 of the Finance Bill in Chapter IX, Part III, amends the SCRA to include repos in the category of derivatives under that Act. Since only exchange traded derivatives are legal under section 18A of the SCRA, this removes the legality of inter-bank over the counter trade in repos, presently performed through an efficient online platform under RBI supervision.

The Statement of Objects and Reasons at the end of the Finance Bill for clauses 156, 157, 160, 185 and 186 merely re-state amendment of the relevant legislative as the intent, without any further justification of the direction of amendment.

To summarise, there are four issues at stake. There are implications for both monetary policy and banking regulation of the cessation of RBI regulatory power over repos and reverse repos. There are the further implications of the classification of these as derivatives, which can legally only be traded through exchanges. Repeal of the GSA introduces uncertainty over who is legally authorised to manage the issue and servicing of state debt. And finally, ending the role of the RBI as the depository for government securities has multiple implications, including disruptions in the smooth functioning of the RTGS.[1]

1. In the event, all sections of the Finance Bill 2015 referred to in this article were dropped in the amended version presented for passage in Parliament, and the issue of transfer of debt issuance was deferred for further consideration.

Part V

INFLATION AND MONETARY POLICY

Inflation in India, whether as in the past by the WPI (wholesale price index), or as now by the CPI (consumer price index), is measured year-on-year, by the change in the index from its level a year previously. This is the way by which seasonal movements are sought to be removed from inflation rates over the year. The shift to the CPI has been enabled only since a single national CPI was issued starting January 2011, replacing what were earlier three CPIs, each specific to a particular socio-economic segment – middle class, industrial workers, and agricultural labourers.[1] National inflation rates year-on-year by the CPI are therefore available only starting January 2012.

That series was replaced by a new CPI, which has been issued starting January 2015. The new series has a slightly altered weighting pattern, involving reduced weights for food and fuel, and correspondingly higher weights for the residual – the core. It also uses a geometric mean to obtain the average, rather than the arithmetic mean as earlier. The new series has been generated from January 2014, so as to enable inflation rates by the new series from January 2015. However, because of the provision of an official linking factor linking the old to the earlier series, the integrity of the old series within itself stands. Correspondingly, all the figures shown in this section, dealing with price indices and inflation rates generated from the old series remain perfectly valid.

Figures 3.0 and 4.0 at the conclusion of this preamble, show CPI levels from January 2011 to December 2014, the total span of the old series, in terms of the major sub-groups – food, fuel and core – and in terms of the sub-groups within food – foodgrains, protein foodstuffs, and vegetables and fruits – respectively. They provide the database relevant for the essays that follow in this section. Figure

1. Which still exist and are issued independently by the Labour Bureau.

42.1, unbundles the elements in core inflation in the epilogue to the first essay, "Inflation Targeting", which comments on the Urjit Patel Committee report made public in January 2014. The piece dwells at length on core inflation and its components.

"Transparency as Cure" looks at the alarming worsening in asset quality of commercial banks over the period 2013-14, which was as much an outcome of slowing growth and tightening monetary policy at a time of high inflation, as it was an outcome of poor governance and delayed government approvals for infrastructure projects. It recommends that the time taken for project approvals be transparently displayed. A commendable new initiative, the Centralised Repository of Information on Large Credits (CRILC), is designed for early detection of stressed assets, but the information is for banks, not for public dissemination. Public display by lending banks on their respective websites, of project approval durations by class of project and location, is recommended as a useful information base for the banking system going forward.

"Wanted: New Financial Instruments" was written in May 2012, provoked by two developments at the time. One was Parliamentary consideration of a Land Acquisition Bill, the provisions of which introduced extraordinary delays in the process of conversion of agricultural land to non-agricultural uses, as part of a well-intentioned attempt to protect sellers of agricultural land from exploitation. The second was the alarming rise in gold imports, and with it the CAD (current account deficit), which mounted further to a record high in 2012-13 of 4.7 per cent of GDP (gross domestic product). On the land bill, the essay emphasises that delay and extended deliberation benefit neither seller nor buyer, and that what sellers need instead is a fair exchange to a financial annuity, that will effectively replace land as an income-generating asset. Likewise, the replacement of gold, which generates no income, with a well-designed financial annuity, should be possible (and indeed, exactly such an option is on offer in the Union Budget for 2015-16). Both themes are picked up in the piece that follows.

"Gold and the CAD", was written in July 2013, after a combination of de-facilitation of gold imports through commercial banks (not tantamount to import controls) and increases in import duty on gold had been introduced, in response to the disastrous CAD of 2012-13. Gold import facilitation through commercial banks had been introduced during the 1990s, as part of the then reform of the external account, to replace smuggled gold with formally permissible imports. But at the time of the widening CAD in 2013, there was a need to roll back that process temporarily. Needless to say, the reform process will be complete only when gold duties are normalised. By the end of 2014, gold duties remained at the levels to which they had been elevated, but facilitation of gold imports through commercial banks had been restored. A short epilogue to the essay spells out the twists and turns in policy towards gold imports in the 18-month period between the mid-2013 and the February statement of the Union Budget for 2015-16.

"Monetary Levers" deals with monetary transmission in India, and the painful lack of data on the basis of which alone it is possible to tell how rapidly monetary policy changes are transmitted to the final borrower. There have been some improvements since then, with commercial banks now required to submit information on rates at which incremental loans have been made, rather than just the weighted average on their outstanding stock of loans.

"Monetary Signals", the following piece, deals with the need for the monetary stance to be conveyed both through the policy repo rate, and through rates on markets where banks access short-term liquidity. Unless the monetary signal itself is clear, monetary transmission will not follow.

"Prices and Wages", "Political Governments" and "Stallflation" are on governmental failure to tackle the supply-side constraints that fuelled the inflationary process in India over the period 2010-2014.

The last essay, "Dismantling Food Inflation", ends on a hopeful note. The Union Budget of July 2014 introduced a number of micro measures that could, if well implemented, reduce the supply chain inefficiencies that had served to keep food and overall inflation unacceptably high.

Inflation rates are reported year-on-year, and therefore suffer from base effect issues. Therefore, two figures are provided below of the CPI in levels over the period January 2011 to December 2014. These will be a useful reference to the essays that follow. Figure 3.0 shows the three major strands – food, fuel and core – of overall inflation. Figure 4.0 charts the further three major strands within food – foodgrain, protein foodstuffs, and vegetables and fruits.

Figure 3.0

Major Groups of the Consumer Price Index: January 2011 to December 2014

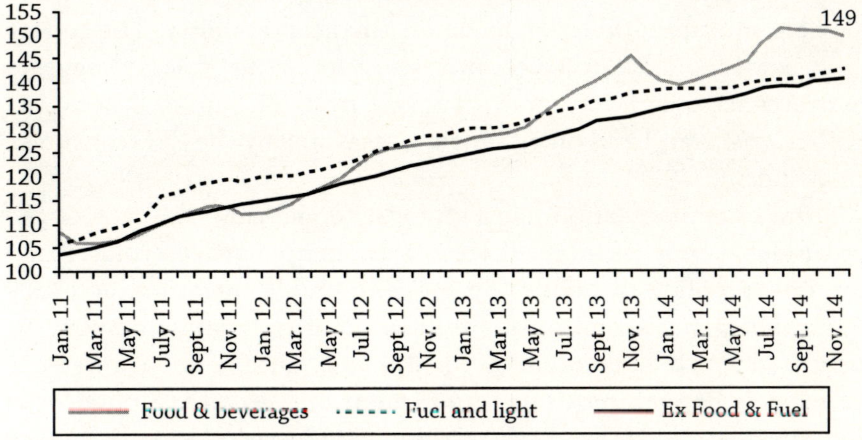

Notes: Both figures 3.0 and 4.0 are generated from the CPI index with base 2010. The new series with base 2012 can be spliced to the earlier series using an overall linking factor of 1.21.

Source: Website of Ministry of Statistics and Programme Implementation: *http://mospi.nic.in/Mospi_New/site/home.aspx*

Figure 4.0

Major Groups of the Consumer Price Index for Food and Beverages: January 2011 to December 2014

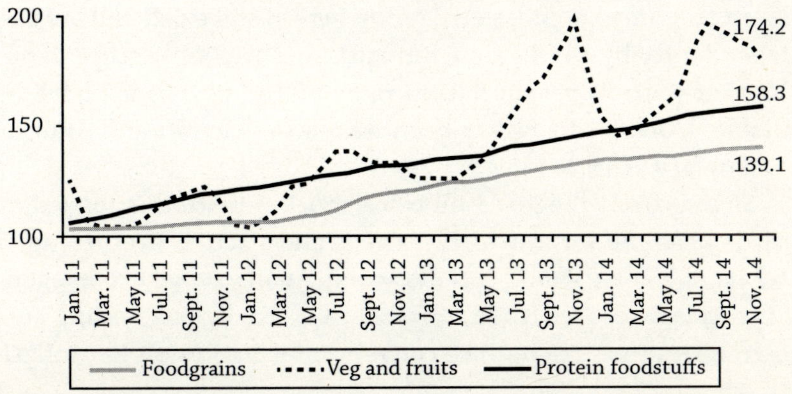

Source: Same as Figure 3.0.

42 Inflation Targeting

The January 2014 report of the RBI Expert Committee to Revise and Strengthen the Monetary Policy Framework (MPF)[1] recommends switching to inflation targeting, instead of a more flexible multiple indicator focus on financial stability. The report cites evidence from other countries to support its case. It suggests convergence over two years to a target inflation rate of 4 per cent, with a 2 per cent band on either side, measured by the CPI (consumer price index).

The recommendation has a strangely dated ring, this side of the great global crash of 2008. There is a difference between committing monetary policy to delivering low and stable inflation, as every Central bank must, and a prior declaration of an inflation number (or band), to which alone monetary policy will dance, without reference to what is happening to unemployment and growth. Single-focus inflation targeting is nowhere nearly as confidence inducing as a policy commitment to financial stability, of which stable, and hopefully low, inflation will be a component.

Since all prices do not rise in tandem, measuring inflation involves assigning weights by their relative importance to consumers. It is only since January 2011 that India has had a single nationwide CPI (split into rural and urban), to replace the earlier three indices, each relevant to a broad occupational group (which still exist, and are issued independently by the Labour Bureau). And it is only since January 2012 that year-on-year inflation rates by the new index have been available. [A revised CPI has been issued to generate inflation rates after January 2015.]

Starting from the 1973 oil price shock, inflation is looked at in both its headline form, which is the average across everything, and in terms of a core, which excludes components subject to exogenous shocks, from weather (food), or other externally originating supply uncertainties (fuels). The core conveys information on the inflation-

1. Known commonly by the name of its Chair as the Urjit Patel Committee report.

generating dynamic within the system. It could be influenced by non-core elements, as when wages are indexed to keep up with prices of fuel and food, or not so influenced. Core inflation then becomes the barometer of inflation as the endogenously generated disease, which, by common consensus, introduces uncertainty and reduces the incentive to invest. High core inflation is a growth-killer (although what really matters is uncertainty resulting from variability in the core over time and across components rather than the average core rate just by itself).

Food carried a weight of 47.6 per cent in the first national CPI (excluding intoxicants).[2] Fuel accounted for 9.5 per cent, leaving a core with a weight of 43 per cent. In the new index, intoxicants have been removed from the food and beverages group, which has a weight of 46. A food price index is reported along with the overall index, with an even lower weight of 39, but that is after subtraction of beverages and prepared meals from the food group. Greater comparability is ensured by staying with the total weight of 46 for food. The fuel and light group also carries a lower weight of 7 as compared to 9.5 earlier. The core in the new index thereby carries a higher weight of 47, higher by four percentage points.

Food inflation gyrated wildly in the 10-15 per cent range for much of calendar years 2012 and 2013, as a result of causes too widely known to warrant repetition. Because of the lower and more steady core, the headline rate settled to a sedate trot around the 10 per cent mark, finally dipping below 9 per cent in January 2014, below 8 percent from June 2014, and well below 6 per cent from October 2014.

The core came to rest after August 2012 at a steady and sticky 8 per cent, finally dipping decisively below 8 percent only in June 2014. It fell quite precipitously after that, to the 4-5 per cent range in mid-2015. Figure 42.1 unpacks the core. Housing, the single largest component of the core, with a weight of 10 per cent overall in both the old and the new index, held steady and high in the 10-11 per cent range, until the general pattern of decline starting mid-2014. Clothing

2. The weight of the food, beverage and intoxicants group in the CPI was 49.7 per cent, of which intoxicants was 2.1, yielding a weight of 47.6.

has climbed steadily down from 15 per cent in early 2012, but along with housing holds up the core rate. The remaining elements in core inflation, mostly an assortment of services, are either holding steady at, or have fallen to, levels in the 5-8 per cent range.

Housing dominates the core. Since housing has no weight at all in the rural index, this is because of its high weight in the urban index, at 23 per cent in the old index, 22 per cent in the new. Even that probably understates the impact of housing inflation in urban India, where housing rentals can equal the sum of household expenditure on everything else including food. Supply constraints drive housing inflation, due to the impossibly throttled market for land, in conjunction with transport constraints, which call for housing near the workplace. The GDP figures show that construction by the old series went into a deep dive, from 11 per cent growth in 2011-12, to between 1 and 2 per cent over 2012-14. By the new GDP series, construction showed negative growth of (-) 4.3 per cent in 2012-13, but picked up to 2.5 per cent in 2013-14, and 4.5 per cent in 2014-15. These are low rates of growth. Because of this, it is unlikely that housing inflation will climb down any time soon.

I am making three points here. First, reported inflation, whether headline or core, probably understates inflation as it is experienced today because the actual weight of housing is higher than the assigned weight even in the urban index. Second, although housing inflation rates crashed with the introduction of the new CPI index in January 2015, from well above 8 per cent to the 4-5 per cent range over a few months, this is a somewhat questionable fall in what is clearly a supply-constrained phenomenon. Luckily, there are some stroke-of-the-pen reforms that can relieve the housing constraint, such as re-zoning industrial estates as multiple use land, so as to permit low-cost housing for industrial labour within those areas.

The third point, given this supply-driven configuration of Indian inflation in its key drivers today – food and housing – is that there is little monetary policy can do to control inflation in more than the immediate sense of demand compression. In fact, a rise in policy rates could actually worsen housing inflation, since EMI (equal monthly instalment) payments are the first to transmit a rise in policy rates, and potential buyers on EMI instalments will fall back on rental housing with knock-on effects down the line.

At the end of the day, a Central bank derives credibility from the financial stability it is able to deliver by responding flexibly to the need of the hour, rather than from the fact of having strapped itself into a one-indicator straitjacket. There can even be downsides to formal inflation targeting, if it makes the Central bank feel compelled to wiggle the policy rate every time there is what may well be a short-term upward tick in the headline CPI, just to demonstrate alertness and vigilance. Policy rates take time to transmit through the system, and constant up-down changes in policy rates leads to directional confusion in monetary transmission.

Figure 42.1

Core Inflation and its Components January 2012 to June 2015

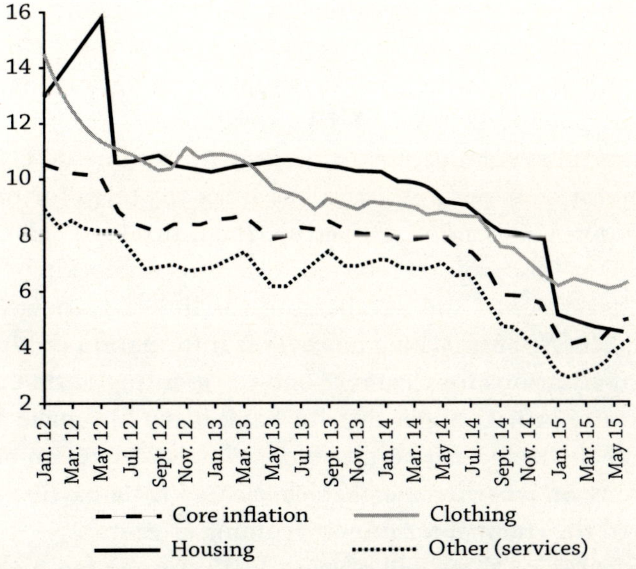

Note: These inflation rates upto December 2014 are based on the first nationwide Consumer Price Index starting January 2011; the rates are year-on-year, and therefore begin only from January 2012. From January 2015 the rates, year-on-year, are based on the new CPI starting January 2014. The new CPI series has an official linking factor to the level of the index in the old series, so that the integrity of inflation rates within the old series stands. Inflation rates from the new series, have been spliced to the earlier series directly in rates. There is a noticeable discontinuity going from December 2014 to January 2015, a function to some degree of the change in the weighting pattern, but also of discontinuities in particular components such as housing.

Source: Website of Ministry of Statistics and Programme Implementation *http://mospi.nic.in/Mospi_New/site/home.aspx*

43 Transparency as Cure

Banks are not in good shape. At the end-March 2015, gross NPAs (non-performing assets) stood at 4.6 per cent of gross loans and advances, as against 4.1 per cent at end-March 2014 and 3.4 per cent at end-March 2013. Stressed assets, summing across NPAs and restructured assets, crept up from 9.2 per cent at the outset of 2013-14 to 10 per cent at its close, and further to 11.1 per cent at the close of 2014-15.[1]

Bank loans have turned sour not just because of the slowing economy and high interest rates, but also because of slow government clearances to projects. The previous government at the Centre took cognisance of this and started an online project management system to clear obstacles blocking investments, under the Cabinet Secretariat. The website calls it a project management system of the Government of India and states, which is most gratifying because it offers to address obstacles at all levels of the government.

The central system accepts projects with a value of ₹1000 crore and above for consideration, and has links to states for projects of value between ₹100 and ₹1,000 crore. The central list claims to have cleared 272 of 662 projects referred to it, thus unblocking ₹9.45 lakh crore of investment.[2] The numbers on the linked state websites are much smaller. What is lacking however is information on the interval between applications for clearance and the granting of that clearance, so that future project applicants for bank loans can make a sensible estimate of the time such permissions will take. More importantly, it says nothing on whether the obstacle cleared for a particular project also cleared the channel for projects coming after it.

An investment threshold of even ₹100 crore is too high anyway. There is a need for a public listing of projects of any size which have received bank loans, with information on project clearances sought, and the time taken to receive them. There is now a Central Repository

1. Figures from *Financial Stability Report* No. 11, June 2015.

2. By July 2015.

of Information on Large Credits (CRILC), introduced by the Reserve Bank of India (RBI) from 1 April 2014, to which banks must report loan exposures of ₹5 crore and above. The intent behind this initiative was to help early detection of stressed assets, well before they turn into full-fledged NPAs. CRILC data will be aggregated every quarter, but will not be made public.

The CRILC is about loan servicing, but it can form the nucleus of a project-specific reporting mechanism on processes and approvals. Against a listing of project loans of ₹5 crore and above, a link can be provided for each project where promoters will list in a prescribed format all Central and state clearances needed. For each, the time at which the application is made needs to be entered, and the time at which it is granted.

In principle, there is no reason why this information could not be revealed on a public website by the lending bank. Nothing will be shown about the terms of the loan other than its amount. All that banks reveal will be the name of the project, its state of location, and its sectoral classification. This information is so public in nature that it could be obtained even through an RTI (Right to Information) application. The subsequent information on clearances required also falls squarely within the RTI domain.

What difference will this make? Well, in the first place, it will show up differences in approval intervals between applicants in the same state for the same type of approval, with the plain fact of public revelation serving to converge the distance between them. There may of course be perfectly justifiable differences, simply because all projects are not the same. But clearly having the numbers up for all to see pulls away the veil that enables facilitation payments.

Second, sizeable differences between states in mean intervals can emerge out of the data, which can then be taken up for examination, as part of a national governance initiative.

Third, the data will enable banks to make an objective judgement on whether a new project loan applicant has made a reasonable estimation of the distance to the DCCO (date of commencement of commercial operations), which is part of the commitment entered into with the borrower.

Environmental clearances should actually be required before rather than after financial closure. This is one area where information is required not merely on the speed of clearance, but on the content of the agreement with respect to the commitment by the project on impact and clean-up. Publicising this helps environmental activists monitor performance.

In an announcement in May 2013 of a policy to take effect from 1 April 2015, a bank loan will lose its classification as a standard asset (not an NPA), if it has been restructured once. However, the RBI granted an exception for delays in the DCCO, a clear accommodation to the governance delays to which projects are subjected.[3] And the acceptable delay in the DCCO was actually enhanced subsequently.[4]

All this would be fine as a reasonable regulatory response to bumbling governance – but there is increasing evidence that delays in the DCCO are not exogenous to the project, but may well be the endogenous outcome of a partnership between promoter and government in defrauding banks. The way it allegedly works, the longer the DCCO is postponed, the more the scope for the promoter to pull money out of his loan account to serve as equity on some other venture. After he navigates his Ponzi path through a few such zig-zags, the promoter emerges enriched, the politician who has cooperated by withholding approval gets his share, and the banks are left to pick up the pieces.

Transparent disclosure of loan clearances and delays will help cut this partnership. Transparency in process approvals is totally harmless, in the sense of not shaming any particular individual, and is therefore something banks can unilaterally provide. Its information content is critical for attacking the unholy nexus that holds banks, and their hapless depositors, to ransom.

---

3. The notification dated 30 May 2013 was intended to give banks and borrowers time to adjust to withdrawal of the regulatory forbearance previously in place, whereby a loan could continue to be classified as a standard asset if restructured once. However, delays in the DCCO will not be treated as restructuring upto 2 years (infrastructure); 1 year (non-infrastructure).

4. In a subsequent notification dated 26 June 2014, multiple revisions will be treated as a single event of restructuring within a total extension for infrastructure of 4 years for litigation, 3 for other reasons and 2 years for non-infrastructure. This policy shows evidence of accommodation not merely to delays in approvals, but to the reality of the delay not being known at any time with certainty.

44 Wanted: New Financial Instruments

Rating analysts look for evidence of official willingness to do something about the twin deficits that plague India: fiscal and external.[1] They are looking for removal of the immediate supply-side impediments to growth, principally the supply of coal for thermal generation, the multiple obstacles in the agriculture sector, and the shortage of skilled labour.

Most of all, they are looking for delivery on governance promises. An official initiative this year to address the coal availability issue with publicised deadlines fizzled out and came to naught. They are looking for a functioning Parliament, which will responsibly transact the business for which its members got elected in the first place. Long-pending financial legislation on the GST (goods and services tax) and a multiplicity of other issues is shelved in favour of footling debates. They would like to see firm handling of some rogue public sector behemoths.

But there is actually something the financial sector itself can do, in the way of designing new financial instruments to address two of the key structural problems confronting the Indian economy. One is the land acquisition issue. The other is the appetite for gold, which is fuelling the huge CAD (current account deficit).

The Land Acquisition Bill [eventually passed in 2013] does not give any attention to the form of compensation for displaced people. Cash compensation of the one-time variety, in place of a time-stream, is not suitable for sellers of land who are typically not adept at the management of large financial assets, in such a way as to generate a recurring income stream. The compensating land option is better in that sense, but it is hard to imagine where such land might be sourced which does not involve the displacement in turn of other people.

1. This was written in May 2012, at a time when India's sovereign credit rating was under imminent threat of being downgraded.

This is where we need innovative responses from the financial sector for formal, enforceable, compensation for displaced people in the form of financial instruments yielding a monthly return, akin in configuration to a reverse mortgage. Here finally is a situation where the mighty expenditure allocations for Aadhar might actually yield some return. If displaced people are given a UID (Unique Identification Authority) with which they can access this income wherever they go, we will finally give them a meaningful alternative against which they can weigh their choices.

Land acquisition for non-agricultural uses involves negotiation between parties unequal in education and financial literacy. Even a time-stream of income has to be explained in great detail, through the mediation of people trusted by the sellers, in order for fairness, and the appearance of fairness, in the deal. It should not be perceived as yet another elaborate confidence trick played by people hungry for land.

Given the difficulties of negotiating with individual property owners, acquisition of land for public purposes (like bus stands) in the past has tended to reach into common lands. There are even cases where irrigation tanks are drained, impoverishing the surrounding farmland and the farmers who once relied on it.[2]

Therefore, easing up the process of negotiating with individual landowners is no longer a luxury. It is an imperative, and the sooner it is facilitated with suitable financial instruments, the closer we will get to releasing the brakes on growth.[3]

On gold, the Indian appetite for it is well known. Gold imports in 2011-12 amounted to 72 per cent of the CAD [over the last decade, it has fallen below 60 per cent]. About a fifth of this is estimated to be re-exported as jewellery. The remainder is a net new flow that goes into domestic holdings as a store of value. If by some magical wand, we could reduce gold imports to zero, the CAD would diminish to

2. See "Stallflation" in this section for an account of one such case.

3. An amendment to the Land Acquisition Bill was proposed by the new government which took charge at the Centre in May 2014., but does not successfully resolve the contesting needs of fairness to land sellers, and speed of resolution. See epilogue to this essay.

insignificance. The fall of the rupee would have been stemmed without recourse to capital inflows.

We need a way by which to unlock existing stocks of gold in India so as to feed this incremental domestic demand. This calls for a financial instrument which will provide an alternative inflation-indexed cash return for surrendered gold [see epilogue to "Gold and the CAD" for a three-pronged gold monetisation strategy announced in the Union Budget for 2015-16, including the offer of exactly one such financial instrument].

Would Indians ever give up the gold they hold, which is handed down through the generations and embodies the inter-generational links of the Indian family? Well, things are changing. With urban life becoming more insecure, and without stay-at-home household members guarding the family residence, safe storage of gold has become increasingly burdensome.

Surrender of gold by individuals does happen, wholly voluntarily, to religious institutions, as a result of which institutional holdings of gold are stupendously large. These were the hoards that drew marauders like Mahmud of Ghazni. Many of these institutions today would like to convert gold contributed by devotees into financial resources with which they could set up health and education centres. An inflation-indexed monthly income financial instrument could be the very answer to their requirement.

The operational requirements of such a scheme are daunting, but not insurmountable. Gold varies in quality and has to be valued at a trusted counter. It may be surrendered as stone-encrusted jewellery, which will pose further valuation problems. But the payback to resolution of these issues is enormous. The fund from the sale of the surrendered gold gets released for financial investment, the income from which will service the indexed income instrument. We will finally have tackled the external deficit head on, without resort to the capital account. Import of gold will continue to be legal, but can in principle be reduced to zero by recycling the massive stock we already hold within the country. The sooner we do this, the better.

Epilogue

This Land Acquisition Bill of 2013, by trying to bring in transparency, introduces new rigidities. With its provision for overlapping layers of diligence by committee, it will markedly slow down the pace of land acquisition, and lead to further choking of supply and escalation in the price of land. Authority for driving the process is hugely vested in the District Collector. Any officer will be understandably risk-averse, far preferring delay to any hasty step that could bring on a vigilance inquiry. It would have been far better to entrust the process for all land acquisition to a state-level body, which is experienced in the matter of land valuation. The state-level property tax board, recommended by the 13th Finance Commission to standardise property valuation across the state, would have been a more appropriate authority. The social impact assessment called for in the bill would be better done by local *panchayats* than by a committee constituted by the District Collector.

The bill interestingly has a provision for preventing hoarding of land by requiring utilisation within five years (among its good features). But it says nothing about the vast hoards of land acquired by both public and private institutions in the pre-reform era. The Food Corporation of India (FCI), the defence establishment, Indian Railways, and an assortment of other enterprises both public and private sit on large stretches of real estate which are not in use.

Unutilised hoarded land will clearly have been targeted by squatters. Many of the most egregious disputes have arisen over the terms on which these occupants are to be compensated. The land bill sidesteps this issue. There are incentive problems here, because recognition of squatter rights will invite other claimants who did not have long residence on the site. This calls for inclusion boundaries in the rules accompanying a land bill, but the bill itself has to recognise the problem arising out of long decades of neglect of unoccupied land.

The 13th Finance Commission, in its report covering the period 2010-2015, recommended that all government budget documents at national and subnational levels list unused land holdings, including land holdings of parastatals, in physical and value terms. Needless to say, that recommendation has gone largely unheeded so far.

The compensation provisions in the Land Acquisition bill in the First Schedule (a ramp-up of the market value of land by ad hoc factors of four for rural and two for urban) and in the Second Schedule (for rehabilitation and resettlement) are a mixed bag of upfront and monthly financial payments, guaranteed employment, and housing. A simpler single-bundled financial option, preferably equity participation in the activity proposed on the converted land with a guaranteed floor, would have been far better. The complexity of the provisions in the bill will make the beneficiaries wholly dependent on intermediaries to explain to them what their entitlements are. The services of these intermediaries will not be free of charge.

The amended bill introduced in Parliament in May 2015 replaces an amendment ordinance introduced in December 2014, but did not pass before lapse of the ordinance in June 2014. The major changes proposed, which have become politically contentious, are the removal of consent of 70-80 per cent of landowners for land acquisition for five type of projects – defence; rural infrastructure; affordable housing; industrial corridors set up by government and infrastructure projects. The scope of the Act has also been extended to cover private entities, rather than just private companies as under the 2013 Act. No changes are proposed to the extent, or form, of compensation for displaced and resettled people, other than a requirement that employment be provided to at least one member of every family of farm labourers on any activity initiated on acquired land.

45 Gold and the CAD

The external CAD (current account deficit) in 2012-13 stood at 4.7 per cent of GDP.[1] That was much too large an asking number for capital account inflows to keep the rupee on an even keel. Gold imports alone stood at $54 billion, a whopping 61 per cent of the overall current deficit.

Without gold imports, the CAD in 2012-13 would have been a little under 2 per cent of GDP (gross domestic product), a well-behaved and totally tractable level. So our external problem reduces to the gold problem. I have written on the urgency of this issue before, when figures for the previous year, 2011-12, showed gold imports at over 70 per cent of the CAD for that year. And I am compelled to sound the gold gong yet again.[2]

The conversion of the import duty on gold to an *ad valorem* basis in 2012 was a long overdue structural corrective. Subsequently, the duty rate on gold has been steadily raised [to 10 per cent by the end of calendar year 2013]. There have also been recent reversals by the Reserve Bank of India (RBI) of the earlier facilitative role of commercial banks as authorised importers of gold. These measures over the months of April and May 2013 succeeded in dropping gold imports by June 2013 to 46 tonnes, down from a high monthly average of 150 tonnes in April and May. [See Epilogue.]

It was the EXIM Policy for the period 1997-2002, which permitted banks nominated by the RBI to import gold. Thirty-six banks were nominated, and in recent years their share had risen to more then half of gold imports. Like much of world trade in gold, bank imports were done on a consignment basis. The importing bank passed on the proceeds of domestic sales to the supplier, and incurred no risk on unsold inventory. Consignment trade calls for trust between the exporter and importer, and from the supplier's perspective, a reputed commercial bank was just about the best buyer to engage with. Banks

1. This was written in July 2013, at the time of a plunge in the external value of the rupee.

2. Gold remains a live issue in 2015; see epilogue.

also engaged in retail sale of gold coins to individual buyers (but that accounted for only 2-3 per cent of total imports).

Legitimising gold imports was a part of the reform package in 1991, since pre-reform hostility to gold imports had led to flourishing smuggling and *hawala* markets, and had kept remittance inflows from Indian workers in the Gulf out of official channels. The further step of letting banks import gold was a part of that push.

Subsequent to the April 2013 monetary policy restricting gold imports by banks on credit or consignment terms to gold jewellery exporters alone, there have been further restrictions to make the importing of gold procedurally more difficult. These short-term initiatives are needed at this juncture. However, in the long term, our appetite for gold has to be examined for what drives it, and we also need to see if it can be fed from a different source than fresh imports.

Jewellery exports are estimated to account for 16 per cent of imported gold, but that still leaves anywhere from 2-3 per cent of GDP worth of gold imports going into the domestic sector, steadily every year over the four years 2009-2013. What on earth has it gone into? The seasonal pattern of peaks during wedding and festival seasons does not tell us the underpinnings of why gold is gifted or hoarded.

It is well known that gold surges as a store of value, when financial instruments do not offer a return sufficiently above the rate of retail inflation. This is borne out by the poor rate of deposit growth at commercial banks today. Gold also seems to be replacing currency as a medium of exchange in real estate transactions. As everyone knows, any real estate transaction can only be closed with a supplementary dose of cash, over and above the recorded deal. Increasingly, the rise in value of real estate transactions seems to have led to the replacement of gold bars for currency in these deals. Gold bars are less bulky than currency notes to store, and less susceptible to damage than paper.

But there is also a very wide-based demand for gold among ordinary people far removed from real estate transactions, because of the ease with which it can be converted into cash at short notice. Gold is readily accepted as collateral at NBFC (non-bank finance company) lending windows, with minimal procedural delays. The increasing privatisation of health and post-school education confronts people with sharp and unpredictable payments spikes. Even for those with access to bank loans, gold can be pledged for a bridge loan while a bank application is being processed.

Gold essentially plays the role of a pre-paid credit card. In the long term, this role of gold can only be curbed if insurance companies develop an effective outreach business model, whereby event insurance is obtainable as easily as at an NBFC window. Even so, the role of gold as a friction reducer in the financial system may persist for a long time. At the end of the day, there is only one solution to the gold problem, and that is by offering financial instruments in exchange for the surrender of gold, from which the incremental demand for gold can be met.

The stocks of privately-held gold in India are estimated conservatively at 20,000 tonnes (it could be twice that number). We should aim to offer financial instruments sufficiently attractive that gold held privately or by institutions will be surrendered to the extent of some if not all of annual import demand. Already, scrap gold is recycled to the extent of 300 tonnes every year. If this could be nudged up to the point where it meets most of the annual quantum imported, which stood at 1,078 tonnes in 2011-12 and 1,014 tonnes in 2012-13 (the peak years), gold would need to be imported only for the purposes of re-export as gold jewellery, which is as it should be, and wholly sustainable.

Epilogue

In a set of notifications issued between 13 May and 27 June 2013, gold imports on consignment by banks and all authorised importers was restricted to jewellery exporters' requirements, and a 100 per cent cash margin imposed on imports through suppliers' or buyers' credit. Import of gold in the form of coins and medallions stood prohibited. The consignment restriction was soon (22 July) relaxed to a gold export requirement amounting to one-fifth of imports (popularly called the 80:20 scheme), and sale to domestic jewellery manufacturers became permissible on full upfront payment, but major trading houses (termed premium or star) continued to be restricted to imports exclusively for the purpose of exports. One year later, on

46 Monetary Levers

Big and Small

Monetary policy operates through the big levers, the repo and reverse repo rates, the CRR (cash reserve ratio), the SLR (statutory liquidity rate). These signal the intent of the central bank.

The transmission of these signals to the lending end of commercial banks requires a lot of little connections, nuts and bolts, to be in working order for the eventual intent to be realised. Sadly, unlike a Rube Goldberg cartoon, where the ultimate purpose is something laughably trivial, like activating a napkin to wipe someone's mouth after each spoonful of food, the intent of monetary policy is the deadly serious business of stabilising the economic environment. In the cartoon, we get to observe what the napkin does. In the case of monetary policy, the official data as reported until 2014 simply did not help to assess the speed and extent of transmission to borrowers from the banking system. [This changed starting February 2014, when the weighted average on incremental lending began to be reported quarterly on the Reserve Bank of India (RBI) website.]

Monetary transmission in India tends to be asymmetric, because deposits held by the public with commercial banks are locked in at fixed rates for long maturities of as much as five years. When the policy rate goes up, banks happily follow suit with lending rates. When the policy rate goes down, lending rates are sticky downwards, because deposit rates cannot be reduced immediately. In the present situation, where deposit inflow into banks has already slowed because interest rates are not sufficiently attractive relative to inflation, transmission is that much more obstructed.

Banks report something called a base rate to which lending rates are pegged, but what matters to a borrower is the margin fixed above the base rate. A downward base rate adjustment in response to a repo reduction does not mean that pre-existing borrowers automatically reap the advantage. They should, in principle, unless their credit rating changes in the opposite direction in the interim, but without data, we simply do not know what the banks actually do. And in all fairness, if borrowing rates are floated to a base rate, so should deposit rates.

Borrowers vary in their credit ratings, and consequently, the rate at which they can borrow. Even a weighted average across incremental loans will, by definition, weight the big, and hence highly creditworthy, loans more than the small. A fall in the weighted average on incremental loans can seem like a repo rate reduction is being transmitted, when in fact it is not being felt at all at the small end. And the small end is where it matters, for a spatially dispersed impact on the economy.

A median gets rid of that problem. And a median of medians across banks on incremental loans by class of loan will tell us what we really want to know: whether loans are becoming cheaper to the average borrower. Thus, for example, in order to assess the impact of a reduction in the repo rate of say 25 basis points, we need to know what the median impact was on new project loans, and at the other end, on small loans to priority sectors.[1]

Discretion and confidentiality in risk assessment and rates charged are absolutely essential if banks are to perform their intermediation task effectively. None of this is threatened by requiring more disclosure in the reporting system of commercial banks. We merely seek to know whether, and with how much of a lag, alterations in the monetary policy stance reach the borrower.

The borrower from the formal financial sector, that is. The *aam admi* has no truck with the formal banking system. No matter how frenetically direct bank transfer of benefits under various schemes might be promoted, the leap from that to actually being able to borrow from a bank in rural areas is impossible, except for landowning holders of Kisan Credit Cards.

As for the urban sector, despite the density of bank outlets, the reach of formal finance is pathetically limited. Delhi and many other urban centres have weekly markets in even the most upscale

1. The weighted average lending rate on fresh bank loans is still reported only as a weighted mean across all incremental loans.

residential areas, a kind of mobile supermarket which comes to the customer. On designated days of the week, a few roads in the locality are closed off and sprout pushcarts selling everything from vegetables to kitchen utensils and clothing.

The very mobility of these vendors means that they cannot deal with the documentary requirements of the formal banking system. The informal financial system reportedly charges an astronomical 10 per cent per day on working capital loans to these vendors. This creates a huge wedge between the retail price paid by consumers, and the price received by producers. If formal bank finance could bring overnight loans to small vendors through mobile units even at rates at the high end of the formal spectrum, this wedge will collapse. Group enforcement should ensure close to zero default.

A radical outreach of this kind by banks does of course require that they reconfigure their operating procedures so as to permit mobile lending and deposit collection operations. The need for them to do so is surely staringly obvious, in a country where exclusion from formal finance is not a marginal phenomenon, and at a time of stubbornly high retail food inflation.[2]

The larger structural constraints on the supply side of agriculture will remain. But there will be immediate rewards to worshipping at the shrine of small things.

2. By 2015, despite the enormous success of the Jan Dhan Yojana (see "The First Year") the reach of formal credit to mobile service providers still remains a distant dream.

47 Monetary Signals

Monetary policy in India entered an easing cycle on 15 January 2015, when the policy rate – the flat overnight rate on repurchase of securities (repos) through which the Reserve Bank of India (RBI) injects short-term liquidity into the system – was brought down by 25 basis points from 8.0 to 7.75 per cent. This was followed by two equivalent reductions, on 4 March and 2 June. Together, these have reduced the repo rate by 75 basis points in all, to 7.25 per cent currently. Cautious easing is the message sought to be conveyed.

Any policy rate, in our case the repo, seems to suggest that there is some kind of guarantee that the central bank will lend short-term at that rate with unlimited access, but that can never be the case. Banks are not supposed to be given the comfort that the central bank will bail them out endlessly if they need liquidity at short notice, so that they remain ever vigilant. In reality of course, as we saw at the time of the global crisis, banks do get bailed out by the taxpayer, but the policy rate itself never carries that unlimited attribute.

In September 2014, the RBI sharply cut access limits to the flat rate repo to one-quarter of its previous level. The residual access to the old level was made auctionable, for terms going beyond overnight, to 7 or 14 days. This marked a decisive shift towards market determination of access to short-term liquidity. Two possibilities open up with that. One is that at any time, the market rate or rates for overnight liquidity may lie on either side of the flat rate overnight repo, depending on the monetary stance. The second is that when the repo is reduced by, say, 25 basis points, what happens to the market rate for short-term liquidity (wherever it is in terms of levels) becomes a function of whether the central bank eases liquidity commensurately with the policy rate, or not.

The declared operating target of the RBI is the overnight call money rate. This is referred to as the weighted average call rate (WACR), since it has to be averaged across what can be quite wild swings even in the course of any single trading day.

Call money is uncollateralised borrowing, unlike the repo where the lender has in effect purchased the security for the brief duration of the loan. A domestic analogy to call money would be a loan of milk taken from a neighbour for an unexpected flood of guests demanding tea. The neighbour is left holding no assets to encash in case the milk loan is not returned in cash or kind. Default in call money borrowing is probably rare, because of the mutuality in relationships between players in the market, just like the milk loan which would normally be repaid to maintain good neighbourly relations. Nevertheless, to guard against rogue players, call money access is not unlimited either. It is hedged by a number of quite tedious capital adequacy and other qualifying conditions that the borrower must satisfy.

There is also collateralised borrowing in the money market. Exactly the same kind of agreement as the repo between a bank and the RBI can be entered into bilaterally between two banks, called a market repo. And if this market repo is entered into on a platform provided by the Clearing Corporation of India Limited (CCIL), it is called a Collateralised Borrowing and Lending Obligation (CBLO). Either of these can be entered into freely, limited only by whether the borrowing bank has the collateral necessary.

CBLO accounts for more than half of daily trading volumes on the money market, going up to two-third in some months. CBLO and market repos together account for 64-78 per cent of daily volumes. These figures are publicly available on the RBI website, which has had a makeover and wears a snappy new look. The section on Daily Money Market Operations (DMMO) provides figures on volumes of daily trading (on everything except term auctions, which instead of being included here are given in another table, but are not very large anyway). Call money, the tracking indicator for monetary policy, accounts for under 10 per cent of daily trading in most recent months. The flat overnight repo with the RBI also accounts for under 10 per cent of daily trading volumes. Both call money and the RBI repo window, it turns out, are minor players in terms of volumes on the overnight liquidity market.

If we want to track monetary easing through the first two step reductions in the repo rate on 15 January and 4 March, we need to know what happened to the WACR (the official operating target), and to the CBLO rate (the more relevant rate, by trading volume). To enable statistical testing, we need to take averages across periods with the same number of trading days before the first reduction, and after the second. For the period after the second rate cut, it is best if the rest of March is left out, because that is a year-end month marked by tight liquidity and high volatility. The periods taken here are therefore 1 December 2014 to 14 January 2015, 15 January to 3 March, and 1 April to 21 May. As for the 2 June step reduction, there are not enough trading days since then to average across.[1]

In all three periods, the CBLO rate in levels lies above the WACR on 69-86 per cent of trading days. This in itself is quite intriguing. Why should the CBLO money rate, which is collateralised, lie above the call rate, which is not (and therefore more risky)? The only answer I can think of is that the qualifying conditions for access to the call money rate are so onerous, that the CBLO window carries a compensating premium for lower transaction costs.

In an easing cycle, when the central bank's intent is to lower the cost of short-term funds to banks, enough liquidity should normally be released into the system so that the market rate being tracked as a liquidity indicator does not cross above the policy rate. That then creates the right conditions in which monetary transmission by banks to their borrowers could reasonably be expected.

Going with the WACR, the officially tracked indicator, what were its levels before and after the first repo rate reduction by 25 basis points in mid-January? The WACR stood at 7.75 per cent on average across the 38 trading days before mid-January, when the repo rate stood at 8.0 per cent. The WACR fell to an average 7.42 per cent in the 38 trading days after, also below the reduced repo rate of 7.75 per cent. But in this second period, the day-to-day volatility increased quite sharply, with the daily WACR exceeding the repo rate on 14 out of 38 trading days. As a result, the reduction in the average WACR

1. This essay was published on 3 July 2015.

from 7.75 to 7.42 per cent between the two periods, a fall of 33 basis points, barely passes the t-test for statistical difference from zero.

What of the CBLO platform, where most of the trading action is? The average CBLO rate stood at 8.07 per cent, above the then repo of 8.0 per cent. When the repo was cut to 7.75, it declined by a mere one basis point to 8.06 per cent. CBLO rate volatility also rose in the second period. Needless to say, the fall in the CBLO rate was not statistically greater than zero.

The CBLO rate finally fell from 8.06 to an average of 7.45 per cent over 1 April to 21 May, with markedly less volatility. But 7.45 was not a whole lot below the new repo rate of 7.5 per cent, so despite the lower volatility, the daily CBLO average rate rose above the repo on 22 out of the 38 trading days. The call money rate also experienced lower volatility in these months, with the daily WACR rising above the repo on only 9 out of 38 days. But going by trading volumes, the signal that mattered to borrowing banks would have been the CBLO rate, not the call money rate.

Repo rate cuts need to be accompanied by enough easing of liquidity in order for money market rates to move decisively and in tandem with the policy rate. If this is not done, the easing signal is not conveyed in the way it has to be – through rates on markets where banks access short-term liquidity. Unless the monetary signal itself is clear, monetary transmission will not follow.

Monetary transmission in India is hobbled by a variety of reasons especially in an easing cycle, on account of fixed rates on term deposits, and administered rates on small savings deposits. Clarity of policy signalling becomes doubly important therefore.

48 Prices and Wages

When the Union minister, for what was then a comprehensive portfolio covering both Food and Agriculture, said he was responsible for the prices of five stockpiled commodities, and not for "tomatoes, onions or lady finger", he put his finger on the central structural problem with the current inflation,[1] which is that no one really seems to know where responsibility lies.

It became necessary for the prime minister to convene meetings of concerned officials, when such a group should have been routinely wired into the system. A government cannot function if it requires the personal intervention of the prime minister to sort out problems ranging from unfinished sports venues for major international meets, to the price of onions.

There is the macro problem of the general price level, which at its core measures the inflation generating dynamic in the system, responsibility for which is shared between the Reserve Bank of India (RBI) and the Union Ministry of Finance. Superimposed on the core are the exogenous shocks that can come from a rise in world fuel prices, or from adverse weather events (like the unseasonal rains which destroyed the onion crop in Maharashtra). These non-core elements in the price rise can begin to feed into the core, if food prices rise sufficiently for labour to demand, and succeed in getting, higher wages to preserve some fraction of their earlier purchasing power (also happening).

Decisions with respect to fuel and food carry difficult trade-offs. Whether to let the rise in world fuel prices pass straight through the system, or protect the consumer with a subsidy buffer or reduced domestic fuel taxes, is basically a fiscal issue. There are also trade balance implications of a subsidy buffer, which prevents the consumption response to a price rise from restraining imports. Everything depends on how long the world fuel price rise is expected to

1. This was written in January 2011.

continue.[2] Then there are choices within fuels, of whether to subsidise diesel but not petrol, whether to phase in the price rise and at what rate, and what long-run structural changes in the transportation system are planned as an alternative if personal fuel-powered vehicles are ruled out as an option for most people.

The exogenous shocks in agriculture this time, it is true, came from the horticultural fringes rather than the main foodgrain crops. But it is this fringe that needs the closest monitoring. Crops in India are divided into those carrying minimum support prices (MSP) (effectively, not just nominally) and the rest. The situation is further confounded by the fact that effective support is operative only in selected regions. When the farmer is faced with a choice between price-protected and other crops, the choice is dictated wherever the land is capable of producing both. Horticultural crops carry the highest price volatility, as all consumers know, and from a purely risk perspective, would be the least attractive crop for a farmer to grow. These therefore need the closest watching for area sown, expected arrival on the major *mandis*, and contingency options for failure of arrival.

The onion crop failure this time should have been fully foreseen officially, but was not. The wholesale traders on the other hand did, and stepped in to hoard. There clearly was a key absence of the kind of official market intelligence which should have picked this up. The rain which destroyed the crop signaled the problem sufficiently in advance for imports to have been arranged well ahead of time.

Data feeds of this kind into price projections have to be routinely structured into the system, completely protected from the political coloration of whoever may hold the ministerial portfolio at the time. The information basis for inflation control must be technically driven, with no possibility for political interference. At the end of the day, inflation control is a political issue, where inflation tolerance and the willingness to test that tolerance are necessarily subordinate to the ideology of the government in power. But the technical information that feeds into it has to be clearly separable.

2. The sudden fall in the price of oil in June 2014 was totally unforeseen; see "The Volatile Price of Oil".

While it is true that foodgrain inflation has currently tapered off,[3] foodgrain price levels today, relative to five years ago, reflect stagnation in productivity, at a time when rural wages have risen. Whatever the nature of MGNREGA works in place, they have not had any discernible impact on agricultural productivity. The poor offtake of employment under the scheme in some states, like Goa and Punjab, is a reflection of the disparity in rural incomes over the country, and should have been a matter of pride to the states concerned. As initially conceived, the scheme was meant to redress inter-regional inequalities at a nationally uniform wage. Even though the original act of 2005 specified only a uniform nominal floor, and explicitly stated that the wage offered could differ by region, the implicit intent was to permit cross-state wage variation with reference to a spatial price index, such that there is price-adjusted real uniformity in the offered wage across the country. The cross-state pattern of new wage rates legislated in January 2011 adjusts for more than spatial variation in price levels.

Food has now very simply been priced beyond the reach of many people in terms of levels, even if food inflation has slowed relative to non-food. The boundaries of entitlement to food security have to be drawn in such a manner as to benefit those who cannot get food security through a workfare scheme like MGNREGA. Unless the direct food entitlement is directed to the residual poor, who are unable to access MGNREGA because of disability, or locational disadvantages, there will be a horrible divide between those with access to both, and those with access to neither. MGNREGA by its very design requires a clustering of claimants. If the Food Security Bill targets the scattered poor, it will be both fair and fiscally manageable.

---

3. The reference at the time was to foodgrain inflation by the WPI (wholesale price index). Foodgrain inflation roared back again. Measured by the new CPI (consumer price index), the year-on-year rate for foodgrains rose to 10 per cent in August 2012, and after rising to a peak of over 16 per cent in mid-2013, fell below 10 per cent in February 2014 and declined thereafter to a steady rate in the region of 5 per cent after November 2014.

49 Political Governments

For a long time, the economics literature on public policy assumed that (democratically elected) governments were benevolent maximisers of the collective welfare of the people who elected them. Although the seminal work of Kenneth Arrow and others pointed to the difficulty of defining a formal social welfare function which satisfies some basic internal consistency properties, the idea of benevolence was a useful construct, because it suggested that normative policy advice, on the best course of action in any particular situation, would immediately be acted upon by the benevolent government to which it was addressed.

Beginning in the 1970s, the policy literature increasingly questioned the assumption of benevolence, and posited political government, whose sole interest lies in getting re-elected, and whose gaze is fixed on the next election. Political governments in turn come in two colours. Partisan governments adhere to party ideology on economic issues like inflation and unemployment. Opportunistic governments on the other hand will do whatever serves the need of the hour regardless of party ideology. Clearly, the art of staying in power forever has not been mastered by any government no matter how opportunistic, since opposition parties do manage to seize the reins of power everywhere (even in West Bengal). Notwithstanding that, the overriding objective of securing electoral victory is a realistic representation of elected governments. Empirical work in a number of contexts has validated this.

Alberto Alesina and others found that governments in the developed world were more partisan than opportunistic, with predictable stances on macroeconomic issues dictated by party ideology. In work that I did on the Indian economy, on governments in power over the 55 years, 1950-2005, I found a clear spike in the (primary) fiscal deficit[1] in every year preceding a general election, across all parties in power and therefore opportunistic rather than

1. This was the consolidated deficit, across Centre and states.

partisan, amounting to an increase over the previous year of between 0.5-0.6 per cent of GDP (gross domestic product). The spike before the general election in 2004 was reduced by the Fiscal Responsibility Act of 2003, but the need for a fiscal stimulus in 2008-09 threw off that restraint before the general election of 2009.[2]

The next pre-election year for the Centre, by the formal electoral timetable, is 2013-14. Yet, the fiscal deficit in 2011-12 was 5.7 per cent and in 2012-13 it will be 6.1 per cent without urgent mid-year correctives [eventually reduced through course correction to 4.8 per cent of GDP, old series]. The current account deficit (CAD) on external payments, other things remaining the same, is the twin of the fiscal deficit (more correctly, the revenue deficit, and of the Centre and states taken together). The CAD stood at 4.2 per cent of GDP in 2011-12, and 4.7 per cent in 2012-13. The CAD is a measure of our dependence on capital inflows if we wish to hold the external value of the rupee on an even keel. Until the flurry of policy announcements in September 2012 reactivated capital inflows, the rupee was falling in value.

Faced with a macroeconomic situation out of control, the government appointed the Kelkar panel in mid-August to submit in two weeks a roadmap for fiscal consolidation and credibility. The government, in its initial reactions to the report of the panel, suggested that the needs of food security had not been factored in sufficiently. That was not the case at all. The report of the panel (of which I was a member) explicitly mentions specific demographic segments whose food needs must be protected, and supports continuance of the Mahatma Gandhi National Rural Employment Guarantee Scheme (MGNREGS). The panel pointed out the error in equating higher expenditure on the food subsidy through the PDS (public distribution system) with better food security for those who critically need it.

The food subsidy [in 2011-12] by the final estimate stood at 0.85 per cent of GDP. In part, this is because of the holding cost of large foodgrain stocks, which have outrun warehousing capacity and have

2. The paper under reference is Rajaraman, Indira (2008). "The Political Economy of the Indian Fiscal Federation", in Barry Bosworth, Suman Bery and Arvind Panagariya (eds.), *India Policy Forum 2007-08* 4: 1-35. Brookings and NCAER.

already rotted in the rain. A more Kafkaesque situation can scarcely be imagined, the coexistence of hunger and rotting foodgrain stocks. The panel therefore recommended that the usable remains of these stocks be immediately distributed. And it suggested that the whole issue of food security be examined afresh.

MGNREGS, started initially in selected districts and slowly extended to cover the whole country, was brilliant in design if not in execution. For the first time, poor households self-identified themselves by their willingness to do manual labour at a floor wage. With this, it became possible to do away with the terrible business of externally identifying which household is poor and which is not. By contrast, external identification of those not able to work on MGNREGS worksites is easily possible, and coverage of these groups will meaningfully supplement the employment scheme. Excluded from manual work are the disabled, the elderly, and pre-school children. A supplementary scheme must also extend to those who currently work on MGNREGS sites but should not, such as pregnant and lactating women.

This government was positioned, as no government before it, to ride on the MGNREGS to a new configuration of food security, which could have comprehensively covered the disadvantaged segments of the population by shaking resources out of the PDS as it presently stands, and directly targeting the disadvantaged groups mentioned above. There are Plan schemes for these groups, some like the Integrated Child Development Scheme (ICDS) of long standing, but seriously underfunded.

Corruption bedevils all these schemes, whether MGNREGS or PDS or ICDS. That is a separate issue. What is immediately needed is evidence that the government is able to distinguish between the requirements of food security, and fiscal profligacy in the name of food security. Fiscal laxity in the year immediately before elections is one matter, but when it goes on for many years, it merely entrenches inflation in the absence of any coherent strategy to push back supply constraints. Entrenched inflation is not an election-winning strategy.

50 Stallflation

The latest quarterly figures[1] show growth stalled in the 5.0-5.5 per cent range. The rest of the world, barring China, is not doing so great either, with perhaps worse to come. But then again, they do not have the stubborn inflation we have.

Looking back, could the seeds of the present growth slowdown and the persistent inflation be traced to design defects in the big reform package of 1991? The answer is yes.

There were three very serious defects in the design of the 1991 reforms. The process of correcting two of these was started over the period 1999-2001, but one remains uncorrected to this day.[2]

Trade was liberalised in 1991, and inward capital flows facilitated, to resolve the external payments crisis. The current account was further liberalised over time to enable discovery of the true external price of the rupee. With abolition of licensing for industrial entry, the product market reform required to reap the rewards of trade liberalisation was thought to have been completed.

Astonishingly, no attempt was made to reform the markets for labour and land – two key inputs without which no production is possible. Economists call these inputs factors of production. Just as industrial licensing was a policy wedge in product markets, restricting and hindering entry, there were a host of policy wedges in place in the markets for labour and land, which obstructed the free movement of labour and land between alternative uses. This was a fundamental defect of the 1991 package, since the word reform, as economists understand the term, is about freeing factors of production to flow into their most efficient uses. Only thus does the economic engine

1. Written in Decembet 2012, this refers to the figures for the second quarter of 2012-13.

2. This article deals with the uncorrected design defect. The other two, which were corrected starting 1999-2000 and therefore not dealt with at all here, were the process by which small savings collections at the Centre were on-lent to states (creating pressure from states for high deposit rates on small savings, and thus holding up the interest rate structure); and the revenue decline consequent upon trade liberalisation, following from failure to anticipate the need for compensating revenue from other taxes.

become reformed, in the sense of using its factor endowment to the greatest advantage.

Why was no attention directed towards reforming factor markets? The reason of course was that labour and land are on either the concurrent or state lists of functions in the Constitution. And the principal feature of the 1991 package was that it was done at the national level without any attempt to involve state governments as partners in the reform process. In part this may have been because of the powerful opposition to reform from many quarters at the time, who saw the decline in the external price of the rupee as a sell-out to foreign interests. The response to this, instead of taking states on board, was that reform was done by stealth, so that issues like factor market reform which required state co-operation remained unaddressed.

The constrictions imposed by labour laws in India are well known, and have been dealt with repeatedly by many economists. Although some states have on their own moved part-way towards making the labour market more flexible, and therefore more labour friendly, we continue to have corporate enterprises shying away from formal hiring, and relying on contract labour which falls outside the purview of labour regulation. The net result has been to make labour far worse off than if contractual hiring were made permissible, with equal pay for equal work, and health and retirement benefits. Periodic episodes of violence against factory managers indicate the pent-up rage on the shop floor. Industrial workers, far from being happy with unreformed labour markets, are extremely angry.

Still worse was the failure to do anything to reform the market for land. Transfer of agricultural land to non-agricultural uses is on the state list of the Constitution. Some states have done more to facilitate this than others, in such a way as not to harm the interests of people selling land. In states which did not, there have been episodes of violence. I have written earlier on how land sale should be structured ("Wanted New Financial Instruments"), so I will focus here on why we need facilitation of transfer, even of fertile land, to other uses.

A case will illustrate the point. In a fertile agricultural stretch on the Karnataka-Andhra border, irrigated by a rainfed tank, the switch several decades ago to horticultural crops for the urban market made the area so prosperous that demand grew for a bus depot to facilitate transport of produce. Because of the absence of any template for valuation and sale of privately owned agricultural land, the tank was drained to make way for the bus depot. Production continued for a while with pumped up groundwater, the water table fell, and now the area is a wasteland. The youth in the area who could have been prosperous farmers are embittered casual labourers in nearby factories.

Failure to reform the land market, and the resulting concealment of land transactions actually taking place, causally underpins today's food price inflation, stalled growth, and land scams.

Trade theory in economics is predicated on the assumption of perfect factor markets. The intellectual fathers of reform in India failed to see the disconnect between that assumption and Indian markets for labour and land, which are beyond Byzantine in their complexity. Even reputed Indian institutions desirous of complying with labour laws find them so complex and intrusive that they know themselves to be in violation of one or other of the laws prevalent in the states in which they operate.

Going forward, states need to be brought on board to unlock the India growth story. State (and Central) laws inhibiting the free and fair functioning of land and labour markets have to be reformed, if we want to release supply-side brakes on growth and bring down inflation.

51 Dismantling Food Inflation

Of all the measures in the first Union Budget and Rail Budget of the new government at the Centre for 2014-15, the micro-interventions that address food inflation by dismantling supply-side barriers are the most important. They carry added significance in a year when the monsoon has been deficient in a wide swathe of the western and northern parts of the country.

The promise to bring down the hold of wholesale warlords in the Agricultural Produce Marketing Committee (APMC) designated market yards is the most significant. The Central government "will work closely with state governments" to amend their respective APMC Acts, and provide for alternative private market yards. The new market spaces are expected to be privately funded, but even so, the state government will have to provide approach roads, and much else besides, extending possibly to developing competing networks of aggregators. This is largely a political battle, which can only be won by an adroit mix of persuasion and funding for states.

There is no direct budgetary provision towards this, which is perhaps wise, because that would pose the problem of having to define state shares within it. The rural last-mile road connectivity scheme (PMGSY) gets nearly ₹15,000 crore, and goes as a grant to states, but it cannot fund upgradation of access to market centres. The Rural Infrastructure Development Fund (RIDF) which merely on-lends, to state governments, commercial bank funding earmarked for the priority sector, is not a concessional scheme.

A new borrowing avenue for states is the resurrected Kisan Vikas Patra (KVP), but what it will do for state finances depends on how it is configured. This instrument will feed into the National Small Savings Fund (NSSF) in the Public Account, from which states are presently compelled to borrow at least one-half of collections from their respective jurisdictions. The currently prevailing NSSF lending rate to states is reported in the budget documents at 9.5 per cent, higher than yields on state government securities on financial markets. KVP was closed some years ago for enabling laundering of undeclared income – it can be bought with cash, and cumulates until it doubles in value to cash-out at maturity. If the past is any guide, collections through the KVP should prove quite buoyant.

The overall borrowing of states across all avenues is capped in their Fiscal Responsibility legislation as a per cent of state domestic product. If KVP accretions to the NSSF are added to what the states must borrow half of, and at 9.5 per cent, it will displace cheaper market borrowing and could actually worsen their fiscal situation. So presumably, the KVP will be a carve-out, and notified as a back-to-back instrument, passed on to states with the commitment to pay double the face value to the holder at the time of maturity. Even so, the implicit interest defined by the period over which it doubles has to be lower than the prevailing yield on government securities, for the states to actually get some benefit from displacement of market borrowings by the KVP. Therefore, the maturity period and configuration of the new KVP will have to be carefully weighed.

Two supporting budgetary provisions are ₹5,000 crore towards the Warehouse Infrastructure Fund, and ₹500 crore for a Price Stabilisation Fund. The price stabilisation fund will call for processing capacity for perishables. Perhaps the new agri-tech infrastructure fund (₹100 crore) is intended for this. The expectation seems to be that private entrepreneurs will respond to a small reduction in excise duty on specified food processing and packaging machinery from 10 to 6 per cent. The duty drop could have gone all the way to zero with no significant revenue loss. The Rail Budget also provides for temperature controlled warehousing of fruits and vegetables by the Central Railside Warehousing Corporation, at 10 locations – a small beginning to serve a vast unmet need.

Then there is a set of measures to address physical inputs into agriculture, which can yield productivity returns only in the medium term: a new Sinchai Yojana for irrigation (₹1,000 crore), and promise of a new urea policy, hopefully soon. The damage done by unbalanced urea application does not have to wait for the diagnostics that will emerge out of the soil health assessments.

The greatest budgetary importance has been accorded to enhancing credit availability to farmers. There is a massive ₹50,000 crore contribution towards refinance for short-term cooperative rural credit (STCRC), a fund set up in 2008-09. Another pre-existing interest subvention scheme for short-term crop loans has been continued. There are two new provisions, one for long-term rural credit (₹5,000 crore for refinance support through the National Bank for Agriculture and Rural Development, NABARD), and one for building 2000 producers organisations across the country over two years (₹200 crore). There is also an unfunded initiative to provide access to credit for 5 lakh joint groups of landless farmers through NABARD, which will benefit many landless women farmers.

The Rail Budget draws attention to the problem of empty wagons on the return journey in as many as one-third of freight trains. In effect, this means that for a freight train carrying goods only one way, the freight revenue realisation by the railway is half the freight rate levied. Trial on a pilot basis of automated freight rate reduction for goods carried on the return journey is proposed. The huge delay in covering any given distance compared to road transportation is another deterrent to rail haulage. The practice of loading wagons with multiple destinations on a single train is what causes the delay, as trains are shunted aside for wagons to be detached and re-attached. A number of solutions are possible, such as for instance, homogenisation of trains by type of good carried and nodes served, on designated days of the week. Rail transport of goods is more cost-effective than road haulage, but has steadily lost market share for a number of reasons that are amenable to correction.

If all the several budgetary initiatives to bring down food and overall inflation are well implemented, the *praja* would be happy. The great sage Kautilya would approve.[1]

1. The inflation rates from the new officially reported Consumer Food Price Index, show that food inflation declined from 8.85 per cent in July 2014 to 2.15 per cent in July 2015.

Part VI

REFORMS, INEQUALITY AND GROWTH

"Remembering Gandhiji" appeared on the birth anniversary of the Mahatma. His wish to eradicate the indignity of poverty was not realised in his lifetime. The essay addresses an Organisation for Economic Co-operation and Development (OECD) publication in 2010, which evaluated poverty eradication elasticities across the developing world. It makes the important point that if GDP growth is volatile, because of rainfall or export dependence, a high growth elasticity of poverty imparts high volatility to the poverty headcount, and that therefore stability in the GDP growth path is needed for steady poverty reductions, at whatever elasticity.

"Caste and the Census" was a live issue before the 2011 population census, when collecting information on caste was thought of, initially rejected as provocative and brought in through a second round. The need remains for accurate demographic data in order that caste-based quotas function evenly across the groups for whom they are intended.

"The Entitlement State" is on the path taken by the then administration through enactment of rights to doles as the route more likely to secure electoral payback, than addressing more fundamental rights – such as the right to public goods like sanitation and access to clean drinking water – which only governments can provide. This piece sounds a basic theme of the essays in this collection – the flotation of new social sector schemes with provision only for the primary fiscal cost, not for the secondary cost necessary to ensure improved delivery and enhanced monitoring.

The next two essays are "Jobs, Jobs, Jobs" and "Skills and Growth". As the titles suggest, they are on the failure to provide jobs and to embed skills and employability in the favourable youth demographics in India. The structural reform and heavy lifting required was what the then political dispensation sought to evade by the enactment of rights.

"Schools and Peace" follows, on the particular obstacles confronting access for girl children to literacy.

"Search and Match" continues with the theme of matching skills to vacancies in the labour market, and was written on the occasion of the Nobel award to Peter Diamond in October 2010. Most gratifyingly, the recommendations in that essay for enabling apprenticeship was finally realised in November 2014 with amendment of the sclerotic Indian Apprentice Act of 1961. An excellent piece of legislation, it even mandates a test for certifiable skills acquired at the end of the apprenticeship.

"Coherent Food Security", "Food Security Channels" and "The Sen-Bhagwati Debate" are on the urgent issue of food security. According to the most recent National Family Health Survey (NFHS-3, 2005-06),[1] half of all children are undernourished, and 80 per cent of the women anaemic. These essays take issue with the two favoured features of public policy to eradicate hunger. First, the household as the focus of enacted entitlements ignores inequality in the distribution of food within the household, and neglects also the naturally greater entitlement of pregnant and lactating women relative to other adults within the household, and in particular the foundational contribution this can make to the nutrition status of children. Although there is a carve-out for direct food provision to women and children in the final Food Security Act, its budgetary share is not specified.[2] The second feature is the identification of those households entitled to food support with reference to poverty lines, when universality is the only approach consistent with a tax-supported programme. Universality is entirely consistent with confinement of entitlement to children and pregnant women, who carry the advantage of immediate physical identifiability.

1. NFHS-4 is under way in 2014-15, with extended coverage to include all six union territories (UTs) for the first time, in addition to all 29 states. It will provide estimates of most indicators at the district level for all 640 districts in the country as per the 2011 census.

2. It is not reasonable to expect a budgetary share to be specified in a Bill of that nature. However, what is not clear is the manner in which the individual entitlements will be provided for, or monitored. And there is the more fundamental issue of how a justiceable right as enacted can be subordinated to annual voting, as a voted rather than as a charged item, in the annual budget presented before Parliament.

"Confronting *Kharif* 2015" is on an important alternative to traditional paddy cultivation practices, the System of Rice Intensification (SRI). For a alternative offering enhanced productivity with a halving of water intake, it has faced surprising resistance in a country with low crop productivity, food cost inflation, and perennial water scarcity.

"Social Sector Expenditure in India 1991-2014" is an updated version of a piece contributed in 2010 to a policy website. Although a repeated theme is that outcomes matter rather than expenditure itself, knowledge of how that expenditure has behaved over time is clearly necessary, if not sufficient, for our expectations regarding the trajectory of outcomes over time.

"Inequality Within States" uses the village directory from the census to look at inequality within states in the distribution of publicly provided education and health facilities.

"Financial Inclusion" examines the Nachiket Mor committee report on financial inclusion. Credit is a prominent example of something whose price is inversely related to the socio-economic status of the borrower and the size of the loan. Small loans to poor people carry the highest rates of interest because of both the higher perceived risk of default, and the larger burden of transactions costs in handling large numbers of applications for small loans, as compared to a single loan decision covering the entire amount. This essay looks at how that rate differential can be reduced through group formation, and what is most important, it looks at how access can be facilitated.

Finally, "The First Year" identifies the bid to reduce financial risk in the lives of the poor as the clearest new economic initiative of the government that took over at the Centre in May 2014, in the first year of its tenure.

52 Remembering Gandhiji[1]

On the birth anniversary of Gandhiji, it is useful to recall that he wanted to evict many things from India. One of those did happen a few months before his death. The others were deprivation, and societal disharmony. These still remain with us.

India currently has a high rank on the post-crisis growth league tables.[2] For a country once known for acute poverty, the issue that should engage us is how fast this growth is pulling us out of that reputation.

There is a recent study on shifting patterns of global wealth by the Development Centre of the Organisation for Economic Co-operation and Development (OECD), which estimates the growth elasticity of poverty reduction in 24 countries, India among them. Incidentally, India is one of the non-OECD members of the Development Centre.

These exercises are difficult to do, and easy to criticise. Clearly there are going to be severe data difficulties. Even something as standard as GDP growth can be under or overestimated, notwithstanding the worldwide standardisation of methodology under the auspices of the United Nations Statistical Office (UNSO; one of the useful functions performed by the UN system). As for poverty, annualised changes in the dollar-a-day headcount index necessarily have to be estimated from the discrete points in time at which survey data are available for each country. Poverty surveys with a large enough sample for statistical robustness are typically not conducted annually. So we do

1. This was an expanded version of my remarks at a panel discussion at New Delhi on 23 September 2010, on the OECD's 2010 report titled *Perspectives on Global Development: Shifting Wealth*.

2. There were still two years left of a nine-year growth run, over 2003-2012, at an average annual rate of 8.3 per cent. After that, a dramatic slump followed, of what by the earlier GDP (gross domestic product) series were two successive years at sub-five per cent, before a slow recovery starting in the first quarter of fiscal year 2014-15. The new series shows a growth rate of 5.1 per cent for 2012-13, followed by a dramatic recovery to 6.9 per cent in 2013-14, and further to 7.3 per cent by the provisional estimates for 2014-15.

not know the most critical thing about poverty, namely how much it fluctuates from year to year. Venezuela is a rare example of a country where annual income surveys are done. These show high volatility in growth and poverty from year to year, in response to fluctuations in the price of oil, the key commodity underpinning the Venezuelan economy.

For a family that graduates out of poverty in a particular year, the satisfaction of doing so will be tempered by the probability of slipping back into poverty the next year. If the graduation push came entirely from good rainfall, or some other such exogenous element, clearly there is no structural change in their situation, and a high probability of slippage. For the graduation to be more sustainable, there has to have been a positive structural change, such as drought-proofing from better watershed conservation, or a relatively stable source of non-farm income.

A survey conducted after say a lapse of five years, will show the net change relative to the previous year of survey, but will not by itself tell us anything about whether the improvement recorded is structural, or simply a reflection of fortunate timing.

Notwithstanding these limitations, the growth elasticities of poverty reduction estimated in the OECD report for 24 countries, over the 10 years, 1995-2005, invite our attention. They are obtained from average annual changes in poverty headcounts imputed from survey points, divided by average annual real growth rates of GDP per capita over those 10 years. Eight of the 24 countries actually had positive elasticities, implying headcounts and growth moving in the same direction. Of the remaining 18 with the required (negative) sign, India has the lowest rank, at 0.3 per cent of annual reduction in the poverty headcount for every 1 per cent of GDP growth (tied with Peru). China did much better, at a 1.2 per cent poverty reduction for every 1 per cent of GDP growth.

The stability of the denominator matters a great deal, when evaluating these elasticities. If GDP growth is itself volatile, either because of rainfall or export dependence – the latter exacerbated where there is high export concentration by product and/or destination, a high growth elasticity of poverty would imply wide year-to-year swings in the poverty headcount. Stable GDP growth imparts stability and permanence to poverty reduction, at whatever elasticity.

India, with stable GDP growth, offers the hope that the poverty reduction observed, slow as it is, marks a permanent shift in the economic status of some, if not all, of those graduating out. China, with a high and stable GDP growth, and a (negative) elasticity of 1.2 per cent, is clearly far ahead.

The OECD study prescribes a path going forward for more rapid growth rates in the developing South, based on a global model of trade flows. The simulations show that the gains to the South from reducing North-South trade tariffs to North-North levels, is nowhere nearly as great as the gains from reducing South-South trade tariffs to those same levels. These results in essence place the burden of further acceleration in Southern growth on the South. The North is absolved of all responsibility.

This conclusion is contestable on several grounds. The average tariff in the South on manufactured imports from the South is 7.8 per cent; on imports from the North, it is 2.4 per cent.[3] The reason is that Southern manufactured imports compete with domestic production, where manufactures from the North do not (on average). South-South tariff liberalisation simply cannot overcome domestic political opposition, unless at a very minimum, there is widespread confidence that the damage from closure of outcompeted production units can be contained. This in turn requires unobstructed, low-friction factor markets that are still a pipe dream in most countries of the South. It calls for a robust social safety net for those thrown out of work. Not many countries of the South can boast of such pre-conditions.

The distance between tariffs imposed by the North on imports originating in the South, and those originating in the North, is far wider than the equivalent distance in tariffs imposed by the South, for both primary and manufactured imports. This violation of the spirit, if not the letter, of the MFN (most-favoured nation) principle calls in

3. These tariff rates are as reported in the OECD report under reference.

the first instance for the North to lead the way by reducing the huge disparity in average tariffs by point of origin.

That still leaves a lot to do in the South so as to insulate those graduating out of poverty from slipping back in.

53 Caste and the Census

Even countries with good recording systems for births and deaths conduct a population census once in 10 years. These snapshot counts capture population movements in a more elegant way than having a police state that monitors movements within a country. And several countries go beyond the minimalist census to record information about all manner of things, including household income.

In developing countries, the census is the only source of data on demographics. The 2011 Indian census, for the first time since Independence, considered a collection of caste data. This generated some heat, as might be expected. In the event, this was dropped as a feature of the 2011 population census, and was relegated to a second round collection in conjunction with the first version of the Food Security Bill, which proposed a priority group within the set of designated beneficiaries of food aid, who would be identified by socio-economic class and caste. The Socio-economic and Caste Census (SECC), was begun in June 2011 but conducted at a slow pace by the Ministry for Housing and Urban Poverty Alleviation in urban areas, and by the Ministry for Rural Development in rural areas. Some preliminary estimates were released in July 2015 for rural India, but not pertaining to caste, so that as things presently stand, caste-based entitlements in access to education and jobs remain unrelated to underlying population demographics.

Had there not been a resurgence of caste-based quotas after 2006, there would have been no need whatever for introducing it into the census. But after 2006, accurate knowledge of caste shares in the total population is critical for equitable fixation of quotas. Even countries practising merely equal opportunity, with no preferential affirmative action, let alone quotas which are the last step up the positive discrimination ladder, conduct a baseline count along the relevant boundaries. The United States census, currently under way, routinely includes a question on race. The information is collected as self-declared, and is treated purely as an identity issue entirely independent of visual markers or fractional ancestry.

No quota can operate in a data vacuum. Indeed, constitutional equality is violated if a caste-based quota is mandated in the absence of a uniform nationwide database, of the kind only a census can provide. No country can put in place job and education quotas for an underprivileged segment of the population, and then bury its head in the sand about the boundaries along which those entitlements are drawn.

Among the urban elite, caste is seen as private information, of the kind people may choose to reveal in certain contexts like matrimonial advertisements, but which they should not be compelled to reveal to a census enumerator. This can be easily accommodated. There will clearly be a box for unknown or undeclared caste. Indeed, this freedom should be extended to questions on religion and sex. A third box for the last, in particular, would establish that the sum of males and females need not equal the total population, and so recognise the rights of the minority that is of indeterminate gender.

The majority of residents know their caste identity more clearly and unambiguously than they know their own age. I have marvelled at the ability of census enumerators to ferret out the age of individuals, by piecing together answers, often mutually conflicting, related to religious cycles like the *kumbh*, or by probing personal memories of major events. Between age and caste, age is unquestionably the more intrusive query. Even names in India are ambiguous, with public and private variants, and with the first names of women radically altered after marriage among certain groups, in accordance with custom. Caste by contrast is uniquely assigned, and is public information in any rural settlement. Although caste consciousness is decidedly lower in urban India, caste identity of households is publicly known in all but a small minority of urban residential neighbourhoods. Clearly, caste is neither relevant, nor sought to be known, in anonymous urban spaces like worksites or commercial areas. But it is known in places of residence, which is where the census is conducted.

The stand that caste consciousness, with its associative aspects of exclusion and entitlement, is best obliterated over time by neglect would have been tenable, but for the resurgence of quota consciousness. People are already familiar with classification, into categories like scheduled, backward and general, in contexts like college admissions or employment registration. The new question will just be a more factual version of information they are accustomed to providing.

Aside from yielding the database for defining caste-based quotas, knowing caste shares in the population will enable a more fair operation of the reservation among the beneficiaries, who are a mutually unconnected set of castes. The same network exclusion effects which led to the introduction of quotas in the first place operates also within the quota. Scheduled and backward reservation can be dominated by a few well-networked groups. The purpose of the quota will only be served if there is a database on representation of the stipulated groups in the population, and their representation in the quotas designed to give them privileged access.

The best analogy is the Generalised System of Preferences (GSP), a trade preference scheme operated under what was formerly GATT (now the WTO), whereby importing countries in the developed world were permitted to offer positive discrimination towards developing country exporters in the form of reduced tariffs, usually set at zero. Because the general MFN (most-favoured nation) tariff extended without discrimination had been lowered through successive rounds of trade negotiation, the differential advantage of a zero tariff GSP came down to somewhere between 1 and 4 per cent, varying by product. Only a few developing countries were close enough to compete effectively at such a narrow price advantage, so that GSP imports came to be dominated by them. A graduation provision was therefore introduced, usually set at half of total imports under the GSP. Even where Indian exporters were among those graduated out, they had to concede the fairness of the provision.

Quotas are designed to give forcible entry for underprivileged groups in a system which poses multiple obstacles to their advancement. If access to the quota is uneven across those groups for whom it is intended, clearly it only replicates the injustices of the larger system. But unevenness of access itself is impossible to assess without a census of population shares of beneficiary groups. If caste information is not collected, we will have denied ourselves an opportunity to make the quota function in an equitable manner.

54 The Entitlement State

In budget season[1] the emphasis always, and most especially at this juncture with our dependence on external capital being what it is, is on the numbers. Will the subsidy bill be appreciably lower than the 2.6 per cent of GDP (gross domestic product) at which it was pegged by the Kelkar Panel in September 2012, before the first diesel price correction?[2] The removal of the subsidy on bulk users like railways at the start of 2013 comes too late in the current fiscal year to make much of an impact, but it is an excellent move, and will hopefully lead to improvements in use efficiency.

The worry over the Food Security bill[3] is not the fiscal impact of the bill, so much as the absence of any plausible mechanism to improve the reach of subsidised grain to targeted beneficiaries.

With one in two children malnourished, and inter-generational transmission of malnourishment through the weak and anaemic bodies of pregnant mothers, the need for a basic entitlement to foodgrain for the poorer two-thirds of the population cannot possibly be a bad thing. The problem is, it comes on top of long-standing anti-poverty schemes, targeting both households and vulnerable demographic segments directly, which have had very poor outcomes. At the household level, in addition to the PDS (public distribution system), there is the Mahatma Gandhi National Rural Employment Guarantee Scheme (MGNREGS). Then, there are schemes directly targeting specified demographic groups, such as the Integrated Child Development Scheme (ICDS), for pregnant mothers and children under six. These directly targeted schemes are what we really need,

---

1. This was written in February 2013.
2. The subsidy bill finally stood at 2.5 per cent for the year 2012-13, one-tenth of a point lower than what it was estimated at by the Kelkar panel without corrective action. The Kelkar panel corrections were designed to bring down the subsidy bill to 2.2 per cent for 2013-14, and to 1.5 per cent by 2014-15. The corresponding figures were 2.2 and 2.0 (See Figure 2.0).
3. It was finally signed into law on 10 September 2013.

but they are not underwritten in the new bill, undoubtedly because of the difficult monitoring problems they pose.[4]

The corruption that renders these schemes ineffective is not a fringe phenomenon. What we have is heavy-duty diversion, so entrenched that the diverting channels have come to regard themselves rather than the intended beneficiaries as having the rightful entitlement. Shops in small town India openly display foodgrain packets for sale prominently marked 'ICDS'.

For schemes like these, our error lay in providing only for the primary fiscal cost, which is the direct expenditure on the scheme. We do not provide for the secondary cost, which is the expansion of governance capability required to ensure that the transfers reach where they should. Yet we pile more and more hard-won tax revenues onto the primary fiscal cost of food security, without providing for the secondary cost needed to ensure outcomes.

Supporters of the bill see no fiscal problem at all. They see a tax system marked by low compliance, estimates of vast flight capital parked in foreign banks, and every year budget papers that report tax revenues foregone from tax concessions of various kinds well in excess of the cost of the food security bill. Right. Bringing home flight capital will help finance both the external and fiscal deficits, but there is no flick of the wrist that will pry it loose at all easily.[5] Even settling domestic tax arrears locked up in disputes, the resolution of which does not involve other countries, cannot happen any time soon. As for tax concessions, the revenue lost from SEZs (special economic zones) and other such provisions is supported by legislation.

Now about tax compliance. Voluntary compliance in an entitlement environment is possible only when every taxpayer who funds the system knows that the entitlement will work for him or her, either because of unpredictable bad luck, or because of predictable dependence, as in old age. Europe ran with cradle-to-grave security, but accordingly ramped up tax-to-GDP to among the highest levels in

4. The final version of the Bill as enacted does carry a carve-out, which however is not given a defined fiscal share of the total cost, rendering it uncertain in terms of budgetary allocations from year to year.

5. This remains a current issue in 2015.

the world. And taxpayers complied because they knew they would be beneficiaries at some point. The fiscal problem in Europe today arises because entitlements have been locked in, and are either stable or actually growing (for unemployment compensation), at a time when tax revenues, calibrated to GDP, are stagnant or declining.

The entitlement state in Europe came well after governments had delivered on their core role as providers of public goods. Their roads are paved and lit, they have internal security, and they have sanitation. That is the usual sequence, with taxpayers voluntarily complying initially for the public goods they are getting, and at the next stage, for entitlements that embrace the entire population. In India, we are introducing an entitlement state, imperfectly at that, before any of the core public services have been provided. The sequence is wrong. Even before the brutal reminder in December 2012, no citizen saw government as having played its key role as a provider of essential public goods like internal security, which the government alone can do. So when the taxpayer remains underserved with public goods, and entitlements are not the kind the taxpayer will access, the pillars on which voluntary compliance rests are missing.

The entitlement blanket jostles for fiscal room with other expenditures that are far more meaningful for the poor. The Pradhan Mantri Gram Sadak Yojana (PMGSY), begun in 2000 for last-mile all-weather road connectivity for rural habitats, has led to a structural transformation, enabling the spatial spread of productive livelihood options and access to health and education facilities. Yet, it struggles for fiscal allocations. The 13th Finance Commission ensured that the road maintenance grant given to states covered these roads as well. But that is just a maintenance grant. New links call for capital expenditures by the Centre.

The poor need livelihoods, not charity handouts. We need to protect programmes like PMGSY which deliver poverty eradication, rather than the poverty alleviation we attempt, but deliver only feebly, through leaky channels.

55 Jobs, Jobs, Jobs

Faced with the task of controlling the fiscal deficit, Union Budget 2013 shows a marked retreat from public expenditure on capital formation, and issues a corresponding invitation to the private sector to step up investment and saving. The Budget proposes a number of excellent measures in this direction.

These have to be evaluated against the government's own assessment of the needs of the economy going forward, as set out in the draft Twelfth Five Year Plan (TFYP) document, for the period 2012-2017. The first fiscal year of that period is already over.

The impressive growth record of this government in its first term in office was not matched by a corresponding growth in employment. The National Sample Survey (NSS) employment surveys, held once every five years, are the only source of nationwide information on that front. By coincidence, the years covered in the two most recent employment surveys, in the 61st and 66th rounds, were 2004-05 and 2009-10, the beginning and end years of the first term of this government. The NSS data are extensively cited in the TFYP document and therefore carry the imprimatur of official acceptance.

The total number of people absorbed into what might broadly be termed an employed state, either full-time or part-time, increased by a mere 2.76 million over the entire five years from 2004-05 to 2009-10. By contrast, the corresponding increase in the preceding five-year period 1999-2000 to 2004-05, was 60.7 million. What made for such a fantastic difference between these two periods?

The sectoral breakdown shows that construction is the major employment spinner. The 1999-2004 period saw a rapid rate of highway construction, and last mile connectivity for previously marooned rural habitats. Even in the five years after 2004, with much slower highway development, construction added 18 million employed in terms of its direct impact alone, not counting its upstream impact through the demand for steel, cement and other materials. The positive (direct) contribution of construction actually outweighed the negative growth in employment in manufacturing and other sectors in the second period, and tipped the overall change in employment into a small positive number.

Accordingly, the budget for 2013-14 carries a large number of incentives for new construction. An initiative to facilitate rural housing, started last year through a refinance window at the National Housing Bank, is said to have received a good response, and has been given additional funding. A similar fund for urban housing is to be started this year. Stalled projects for 3,000 kilometres of highway are announced to have been released for implementation within the first half of the year. There is a much needed provision for funding of godowns to stock agricultural produce. A number of infrastructure financing initiatives will carry a construction component. And some of the work on industrial corridors linking major cities may also begin during the year.[1]

Employment provision has to be juxtaposed against the numbers entering the labour force. The NSS surveys show stagnation in the absolute labour force over 2004-2009, so that despite the poor employment increment, unemployment actually came down from 2.3 to 2 per cent. The decline in labour force participation was a puzzle, and there remains a question mark over the plausibility of it.

The important issue is the required employment absorption, going forward. The TFYP document, based on further projected declines in the labour force participation rate in the age group 15 and above, estimates the increase in people looking for work at around 4.5 million annually, a roughly 1 per cent increase in the labour force per year. The Economic Survey however estimates the annual increase at a little over 8 million. [The Economic Survey figure is the more plausible, and indeed is exceeded by other estimates placing the annual increase at 12 million.]

Going with the TFYP figures, absorbing 1 per cent increase in the labour force should not be very difficult at all. Even with the present GDP (gross domestic product) growth rate of 5 per cent, that is only

1. The report card on actual progress made in respect of these promises is not known. It was unrealistic to expect such an assessment in the following Union Budget for 2014-15, which fell due just before the term of the government ended.

an asking employment elasticity of 0.2. [An annual increase of 12 million translates into a percentage increase of 2.4 per cent in the labour force, and an asking elasticity of 0.48 with respect to a growth rate of 5 per cent.] The achieved employment elasticity between 1999-2000 and 2004-05 was 0.44, but it fell to 0.01 between 2004-05 and 2009-10. I have written earlier about the central failure of Indian reform – the total lack of attention to reforming the markets for land and labour ("Stallflation"). This neglect has fed into poor employment generation, and has to be reversed.

In a recent statement on the Land Acquisition Bill, a minister of the government declared that any resulting delays are needed to serve the needs of the perspirational masses, as distinct from the aspirational classes. Delays serve no purpose at all, least of all the needs of the poor. What does serve the interests of the poor is justice, quickly dispensed. As I have argued earlier ("Wanted: New Financial Instruments"), a well-structured financial annuity in payment for acquired land, rather than a lumpsum payment, is what sellers of land really need. This, together with a credible framework for rehabilitation of displaced people, once in place, will pose no delays in the case of any specific project. But to delay the development of these frameworks, and to justify it in the name of the poor, does no one any good. The important thing is to monitor delivery of the promised compensation, whatever it might be, so that the trust of people is not broken, as has repeatedly happened in the past.

The NSS surveys show that unemployment rates rise with the level of education. The highest rates are experienced among post-school diploma and certificate holders, which presumably reflects their poor employability. The budget speech rightly stresses the need for skill development, and sets aside ₹1,000 crore for authorised certification procedures. All excellent steps, needed and timely. But the Finance Ministry can only provide policy design and finance. It is left to the other Ministries and agencies of government to deliver.

56 Skills and Growth

The global market is in disarray. India can survive on the strength of its domestic market, but this calls for attention to the spatial spread of economic activity. The infrastructure for this in turn requires skilled personnel in volumes that are not even close to being met.

Engineering colleges are being set up at a frenetic pace all over India. But the mix of skills they produce is not tailored to the mix needed. Industrial training institutes (ITIs) are what we really need in much larger numbers, but funding seems to be going their way hardly at all. And they suffer from the lack of links to institutions higher up in the skills chain.

It might be instructive to go back to a time when the setting up of educational institutions in the country was more closely related to its manpower needs.

India has one of the oldest engineering colleges in the world. What in 2001 morphed into IIT Roorkee was first started in 1847 as Roorkee College, soon renamed Thomason College after its visionary founder. What made the college unique for its time was that it was established to train civil engineers, when the term civil distinguished it from institutions for training military engineers. The skills imparted were the same, but the few formal engineering institutions in the world then existing were mostly under the rubric of the military (today, the term civil denotes a particular branch of engineering). Non-military engineers were taught through apprenticeship at the workplace. Professional education was functional, driven by need.

In a fascinating history of the new civil engineering college in Roorkee by K.V. Mittal, who taught there for many years, there are lessons for today. Education, particularly at the tertiary level, succeeds best when it is tailored to the skill requirements of the economy.

Roorkee College was a response by the colonial administration to the urgent need for restoration of pre-existing irrigation works, which had fallen into disuse with the political anarchy after the arrival of the British. Traditional management structures had collapsed, and the British administration needed to replace what had died. New works like the famous Solani aqueduct on the Ganga were started in 1842, to boost agricultural productivity in a fertile region, for a regime critically dependent on land revenue for its fiscal survival. The British engineers overseeing the new work were from the military. But they needed supplementary civil personnel with engineering skills. Roorkee, in close proximity to Solani, was chosen as a suitable location for a college to train non-military civil engineers.

Right from the start, the college had three streams: for engineers, overseers and suboverseers. Today, there is a very rigid distinction between degree granting colleges, and diploma granting institutions which impart training of a more hands-on variety. Thomason College made no such distinction. It was a residential college for all three streams.

Thomason College faced choppy waters, with a competing civilian institution chargeable to the Government of India being forcibly set up in England in 1869, whose graduates had prior claims on engineering jobs in India. What is relevant is that Thomason College survived. Its strength lay in the very wide range of skill levels on offer. Its initial core of broad spectrum education in all branches of engineering continued on multiple levels, to the point where its output of prized overseers and technicians threatened to dominate its reputation. But it continued to produce outstanding engineers like Sir Ganga Ram, famous for his canal irrigation network in the part of Punjab now in Pakistan, and Sir William Willcocks, who built the Aswan dam in Egypt.

The institution was renamed Roorkee University in 1949. In 1958, its famed two-year training course for technicians was upgraded to three years, funding came from the United Nations for training of students from other countries in Asia, and a new Diploma Polytechnic was created within the University to house it.

Then all of a sudden in 1964, the Diploma Polytechnic was closed, and its staff either absorbed into other departments of the University or scattered to the four winds. The ostensible reason was that there was another competing polytechnic in the town of Roorkee. The real reason was that a slew of Indian Institutes of Technology (IITs) had come up in the 1950s, with integrated science and engineering departments, and an academic aspiration that was wrongly thought to demand an appropriate distance from training in manual engineering skills. Roorkee University was pushed into shedding the very features that had made it closely integrated into the skill requirements of the Indian economy.

Another engineering institution which provided education at several levels of skill, originated in the Jamalpur workshop of the East Indian Railway, established in 1862. The final and most academic stream, introduced in 1927, has produced mechanical engineers valued for their hands-on engineering capabilities.

The IITs have achieved world renown. Aspirants for the IIT entrance examination have created a private industry in coaching centres, which may account for as much as a tenth of a per cent of GDP. But aside from software, where famous practitioners like N.R. Narayanamurthy and Nandan Nilekani were trained in the IIT system, the alumni of these institutions are as likely to be found adorning academic departments of finance, management and science, as in departments of engineering.

Meanwhile, Indian infrastructure suffers from a severe shortage of well-trained technicians in manual engineering skills. The configuration of IITs cannot now be altered, but what is certainly possible is the fostering of close links between these, and ITIs falling within a reasonable radius. ITI trainees fortunate enough to benefit from these links can then impart remedial training in the workplaces which will compete to hire them. Meanwhile, our infrastructure plans can forge ahead only if we admit Chinese and Korean technicians to come and train our people.

57 Schools and Peace

The Nobel peace prize to be jointly awarded next week to Malala Yousufzai and Kailash Satyarthi carries a powerful message. Gender-neutral access to school education, unobstructed by early induction into the labour force, will undoubtedly make the world a more equal and peaceful place. But there remain difficult issues to resolve.

Although opposition to schooling for girl children is not usually expressed as viciously as it was against Malala Yousufzai, it is far more widespread than we imagine it to be. There are gradations to that opposition. There are those who oppose any schooling for girl children at all; those who will permit it only until puberty; and those who will support it beyond puberty but see a need to truncate it at some point.

Much of this opposition is not voiced, but swims close to the surface every time there is yet another criminal assault on a girl child in school, or on the way between school and home. As incidents of this kind become alarmingly commonplace in all parts of India, not enough attention gets focused on the kinds of regulation that would prevent them from happening, while those who would protect girl children by preventing them from going to school get increasingly convinced that they were right all along.

Literacy transmission to girls did happen before schools, within households so inclined and equipped. The business of outsourcing literacy transmission to schools open to all, with or without a fee barrier, is a fairly recent historical development. What moved the process was economies of scale. It was quite simply more cost effective to have the cost of a teacher be defrayed over a larger number of children.

As recently as 200 years ago in England, for instance, public schools open to all were far fewer in number than private schools operating within homes, with outside children boarded in to the extent space permitted. (The term 'public schools' in the Indian context today more commonly denotes government funded, but is also used in that earlier sense of admissions open to all fee-paying students.) For example, as we learn from biographies of Jane Austen, her family ran a private school at home for boys. Room for boarders from outside was created by turfing out the girl children of the house, Jane among them, to other families which ran private schools for girls. Fees for boys' schools were higher than that charged by girls' schools, and this difference contributed towards the Austen family income. Schools for girls charged lower fees because the teaching and facilities were inferior to what the boys got. Schooling for girls simply did not matter as much.

That gets us back to the question of why schooling for girls happened in India at all, when the benefits of doing so were by no means clear. Perhaps historians will document the process, but oral history from people who were young a century ago provides sketchy evidence of what might have happened. To hear them tell it, in the days before school provided a disciplined channelling of the energies of children first beginning to flex the functions of speech and movement, the task of controlling male children was a nightmare until they reached an age when they could be inducted into the performance of adult tasks. In rural India where there were large cohorts of boy children who ran wild in packs, horrific violence was exercised to keep them at heel.

School was the answer to this parental nightmare. It offered an enclosed space where children were incarcerated, and where their herd instinct to do the same thing was used to make them all accept a common template of alphabets and numerals, and the sound that went with each curlicue. They emerged tamed and tractable.

Girl children did not pose as much of a discipline problem, and therefore were not seen as needing school quite as much. But the few sent experimentally to the same institutions, seated apart or in the back of the classroom, displayed a similar impact. They became more accepting of convention, since literacy itself calls for acceptance of conformity to convention. In the marriage market, a premium developed for girls who had been given some (but limited) exposure to school education, because they were expected to become more manageable wives.

In time, the benefits of keeping male children in school for longer than the few initial years needed to discipline them began to be visible. There were job openings for literate boys, and part-time earnings from writing letters on behalf of non-literate people. These benefits did not accrue to girls, except where girl child attendance had grown sufficiently to create a demand for female teachers in girls' schools. There even developed openings for girls to become medical doctors with a specialisation in gynaecology, to preside over childbirth in royal and aristocratic homes.

Teachers and doctors – these were the avenues initially open to girl children lucky enough to receive the long years of education and training required. Today, this has expanded into a very wide set of opportunities. Indeed, Malala has spoken of how she rejected the notion of teaching and medicine being the only acceptable jobs for women. Even so, these rewards do not usually accrue to the natal family since, by the mainstream convention, the girls get married and go away.

The appetite for educating the girl child thus was (and remains) inherently limited, because her natal family undergoes all the sacrifice, and gets no commensurate gain. What has become today a demand for gender parity in school access, moved powerfully by global institutions like the United Nations (UN), derives its justification from the social gains of educating girls, but even with free uniforms and mid-day meals and school texts, the incentive for the family which sends a girl child to school is very limited. When to this is added the possibility of the child being assaulted in the school premises, or in transit between school and home, the burden becomes unbearable.

This disjunction between a socially imposed demand to send girl children to school for a long period of 10 years at a minimum, and the lack of any commensurate social assurance of her safety in those very premises, has to be urgently addressed. The toilet issue is closely related, because sequestered institutional spaces are precisely where the probability of assault is highest.

Female foeticide is a way by which families seek to wriggle out of the impossible demands placed upon them, to educate a girl child where that process is fraught with daily anxiety and yields no certain financial reward. Female foeticide rates are lowest among tribal groups where girl children stay on in the natal home after marriage, or among other groups where school education, if given to girls at all, is truncated fairly early. There are of course many other factors driving female foeticide.

If we want peace in a world where families who do not particularly wish to send their girl children to school are compelled to do so, the school itself has to be a peaceful place which provides a guarantee of freedom from assault, functioning toilets and safe drinking water. Free mid-day meals and free tuition are clearly welcome, but cannot replace the need for safety and toilets. School inspections, on a random roster like the new labour inspection system that has just been introduced; and compulsory display of inspection certificates signed by public officials who may be called to account by parents of school-going children – these are necessary for peace to co-exist with schooling for girl children, going forward.

When a child is switched from child labour servitude to (hopefully) school by the heroic efforts of Kailash Satyarthi and other activists like him, they certainly enter an environment that is far better for them in the long run. But it may not necessarily be more benign. Without remedial preparation, school could be a humiliating experience. If there is a family knowingly sending the child to work, and dependent on the child's earnings, they will support the move only if compensated fully for their income loss. Continued monitoring will be necessary to ensure that the child is not sent back to work, particularly where the child himself may prefer to go back to a known environment from one that is new and threatening.

As for the girl child, schools in many regions of the world are characterised by fundamental deprivations of rights like physical safety and access to functioning toilets, unlike the school Malala was fortunate enough to attend. The social compulsion to send girls to school in the face of such dangers may make families decide not to have that girl child at all.

58 Search and Match

The 2010 Nobel (Memorial) Prize for Economics speaks to the need of the hour. Even if double dip recession does not seem an immediate prospect for the major economic zones of the world, the nagging problem of high unemployment remains.[1]

'Search and match', the 1982 formulation of friction in the labour market by Peter Diamond in a paper in the *Journal of Political Economy*, is a pressing problem today.

Frictional unemployment has been known for years, as the unmatched need for jobs, even at an unobstructed market-determined wage. There was a Beveridge curve, proposed a long time ago by William Beveridge, a British economist (with an India connection; born in what is now Bangladesh, son of an ICS officer sympathetic to the country where he served). What Peter Diamond did was to construct a formal model incorporating information asymmetries between the two sides of the labour market, where these asymmetries could be a function of policies in place. In collaboration with Olivier Blanchard in later work published in 1990, and independently by his co-winners Pissarides and Mortensen, at varying points, we have matching functions on the joint behaviour of unemployment, employment, and vacancies, which opened up a large empirical literature inferring the sources and the dynamic effects of labour market shocks, and the impact of policies bearing on the labour market.

Peter Diamond is actually more widely known for his work on fiscal issues, most recently on the optimal design of the US Social Security system, which deducts savings at source for post-retirement benefits, akin to provident fund and pension schemes in India. Those ideas may well be implemented soon, since reform of Social Security is one of the critical areas targeted for bringing the path of public debt in the US onto a sustainable track.

---

1. At the time, both the US and the Eurozone seemed to be out of double dip danger, with only Japan having actually dipped. Subsequently, the US in early 2011 experienced a brief one quarter dip, and the Eurozone followed later with an extended dip over six quarters spanning 2011-12.

But Diamond is best-known for a two-part paper published in 1971, jointly with James Mirrlees, who got the Nobel award in 1996, on optimal taxation of goods. The paper formally showed the inefficiency in taxing intermediate goods, like steel going into cars, and thus the efficiency properties of a tax like the VAT (value added tax), which offsets the tax paid on steel against the tax payable on the final car. However, that paper did not give birth to the VAT, as economists are sometimes wont to claim. The VAT originated in 1954 in France, from tax practitioners, not from economists. The Diamond-Mirrlees paper merely offered a formal demonstration of the efficiency properties of allowing a tax credit on inputs.

The second, and greater, achievement of that paper was that it brought an end to an embarrassing phase starting with a paper by Frank Ramsey in 1927, when economists could only recommend differentiated tax rates on goods, with the highest taxes on items of mass consumption carrying a low price elasticity of demand, whose consumption would not be reduced greatly in response to the tax. That was a regressive message, and unacceptable to tax practitioners who found it impossible to calibrate tax rates to price elasticity, and in any case found taxes easiest to administer when the rate structure was uniform. Diamond-Mirrlees, by bringing in the possibility of higher weights for the welfare loss of taxation at lower income levels, paved the way by which, through some nimble-footed algebra, equity considerations could exactly counterbalance the regressivity of pure efficiency-based taxation, and point to a uniform rate structure on goods.

Those tax issues are now solved problems for policy purposes, but unemployment and jobless growth remain major challenges of the day everywhere. We have low unemployment rates in India, in the sense of involuntary idleness, because people must engage in, or migrate in search of, some activity in order to survive. But unmatched aspirations are high.

The launch in July 2015 of a National Career Service Portal connects the 959 employment exchanges in the country with information on non-government job opportunities in addition to Government vacancies (the traditional remit of employment exchanges). At the time of its launch, there were 4.48 crore registered job seekers across the country.

Labour policy in India targets job security, and therefore the difficulty of termination is loaded onto procedural delays and wariness at the point of hiring in the organised sector. Recognising this, Team Lease, a private sector entrant in 2003, offers a new model for the matching of aspirants to vacancies in the high friction Indian labour market.[2] Their model reduces the burden of filling a vacancy through offer of a lease in the first instance, without the commitment implicit in even a contractual hire directly entered into by the ultimate employer. If the vacancy has been effectively matched, the lease gets converted to a permanent placement very soon.

Team Lease does more than just perform a matching function to supplement employment exchanges. The skill deficit among the 95 per cent of applicants that are rejected is addressed by offering training in accounting, sales, retail, and other such soft skills. There are several remedial education agencies in the private sector today supplementing the formal school system, but this one matches the skill taught to vacancy requirements.

Germany and Japan have effective apprentice systems which combine remedial education, training on the job, and induction into the organisational culture, in hiring environments characterised by a lifetime employment preference similar to that of India. But the Indian Apprentice Act of 1961 ties us into knots by capping apprenticeships, and posing innumerable procedural hurdles in the way of organisations wishing to take on apprentices. Here is another stroke-of-the-pen reform waiting for its moment.

[The 1961 Act was finally amended in November 2014. The amendment introduces two important changes. It facilitates the induction of apprentices, subject to a ratio to workers as determined on a trade-specific basis by a Central Apprenticeship Council to be appointed under the Act, and ensures that apprentices are actually taught a skill to be tested through a proficiency test at the end of their period of training.]

---

2. The website *www.teamlease.com* provides free access to jobseekers.

59 Coherent Food Security

The Food Security Bill has been extensively debated on the issue of where the boundaries of entitlement to food security should be drawn.[1] There are minimalists, driven by fiscal concerns, and universalists, who would exclude no one, and rely upon the non-poor voluntary opting out to limit the fiscal bill. Then there is the issue of whether the transfer should be in the form of foodgrain, or a cash equivalent.

Except for universal access to foodgrains in kind, to which there will be voluntary opt-outs, all other approaches require exogenous identification of the poor, through some variant of BPL (below poverty line) identification. This is needed even for a universal cash transfer, since very few would choose not to self-select into cash. The universalist case for access to foodgrain in kind rather than cash is predicated precisely on the high transaction costs of externally identifying the poor, and monitoring the movement of households into and out of poverty over time.

The surprising feature of all sides to the debate is their exclusive focus on what is called the food subsidy, without embedding that subsidy in the larger set of Central schemes for subsidised or direct provision of food. It is only when all these schemes are pieced together that we can understand the present budgetary pattern for redressing hunger and nutritional deprivation, and judge its adequacy.

Going with the budget numbers for the current year 2011-12,[2] regardless of their plausibility, the food subsidy is budgeted at ₹60,573 crore. This merely covers foodgrain. There are other price subsidy

---

1. The reference here is to the boundaries drawn in the first bill presented to Parliament in 2011. That bill was replaced by the final enactment signed into law in September 2013. These issues are further discussed in the essay that follows, "Food Security Channels".

2. The figures that follow are for 2011-12 and are designed to demonstrate relative budgetary allocations that remained broadly valid in subsequent years. Later budgets are available in full at *http://indiabudget.nic.in*

schemes, for sugar, pulses and edible oil, which add up to nearly ₹800 crore, but let us ignore those, since they are general subsidies not targeting the poor specifically.

There are four other major food security schemes for the poor, not involving price subsidy. Three of these involve direct transfer of foodgrain, along with other foodstuffs and medicines, but to designated groups, not to households. The Integrated Child Development Scheme (ICDS) of the Central Plan, for pre-school children and pregnant and lactating mothers, has a budgetary provision of ₹10,000 crore, with foodgrain and nutritional supplements at its core, but covering much else besides, including salaries at its Anganwadi centres.

The mid-day meal (MDM) scheme of the Central Plan, now covering school children upto class 8, involves transfer of foodgrain, with a supplementary fund flow to state governments for meal preparation costs, budgeted at ₹10,380 crore. The National Social Assistance Programme (NSAP) for the elderly, a scheme in the State Plan sector, has an Annapurna food component, and gets ₹6,107 crore from the Centre.

These three food security schemes for targeted groups together get ₹26,487 crore.

The fourth food security scheme is operated through rural households. The Mahatma Gandhi National Rural Employment Guarantee Scheme (MGNREGS) is a wage and 100-workday guarantee on public works. It is an income transfer to those willing to self-select into manual work on public projects, budgeted at ₹39,974 crore.

The food subsidy and MGNREGS, the two tracks on which food security is run through household-based entitlements, together add up to more than ₹1,00,000 crore. Food security schemes through targeted groups get only a quarter of that.

Clearly, the present budgetary pattern overwhelmingly favours household-based food security over group-based security. The fundamental issue is whether this resource allocation pattern is the best response to the incidence of food deprivation. The most recent National Family Health Survey (NFHS) for 2005-06 shows the percentage of stunted children under age three at 45 per cent. Is this best addressed through a household-based entitlement, or through enhanced allocations and reform of the ICDS, which directly targets children of this age, along with the health of pregnant and lactating mothers?

These are the questions that need to be most urgently posed rather than just the configuration of the food subsidy by itself. The ICDS, as it is presently structured, probably leans too heavily in favour of Anganwadi centres already in existence. We do not unfortunately place any of our schemes on a Geographical Information Systems (GIS) platform. A GIS database would show us the present spatial pattern of the ICDS, and point to how its reach might be enhanced.

If household-based food security is to continue in the immediate future, the basic question that needs to be answered is whether or not household targeting should continue to run on the present two-track system. The MGNREGs has the advantage of its self-selection mechanism. At the first stage, only households with members willing or able to engage in manual labour on public works opt for a job card. Then from year to year, the number of days sought within the limit of 100 days is inversely related to the food status of the household.

MGNREGS has had its share of scams, from ghost muster rolls, wages underpaid or deferred, to wholesale hijacking of funds. The issue is whether, with a self-selecting scheme like MGNREGS in place, there remains a case for continuation of the food subsidy in its present form in the rural sector. MGNREGS carries the additional advantage that the rural works chosen could potentially enhance water conservation and agricultural productivity. If workfare schemes are chosen as the preferred form of household targeting, the rural food subsidy budgetary provision can be re-directed towards an enhanced ICDS. The household-based food subsidy can be retained in the urban sector, which does not have the public works option.

MGNREGS will need to be supplemented in the rural sector for those who cannot self-select into it. The scattered poor without sufficient numbers to justify a worksite have a provision for compensation within MGNREGS itself. The disabled and elderly can be covered through NSAP, administered through *panchayats*. With that, and with better monitoring, we will finally have a food security net that carries coherence, and the promise of better outcomes.

60 Food Security Channels

Poverty lines have been in the news again.[1] This round started when a Planning Commission affidavit to the Supreme Court placing the poverty line at ₹26 per capita per day (rural), ₹32 (urban), raised a furore over the use of these to set a cap on the percentage of the population covered by the Food Security Bill.

Since then, the pendulum has swung to the other extreme. The revisions presently under consideration propose coverage of an ambitious 75 per cent of the population (rural) and 50 per cent (urban). [A priority set, stipulated at 46 per cent (rural), and 28 per cent (urban), with a deeper subsidy margin and larger entitlement was eventually not retained.]

The population targeted for coverage will be reached through households as an access channel. There will also be channels accessible by individuals, such as community kitchens for destitutes. Another channel targeting individuals provides for meals for pregnant and lactating women and children upto six years. The bill will also carry supplementary funding for added nutritional content to the basic school mid-day meal, for children below 14 years of age.

The fiscal cost of all this will extend well beyond the Centre to the states. The present food security system has over time evolved (rightly) towards a more flexible accommodation of State preferences. Within their stipulated shares of the Central foodgrain allotment, states have over the years fought free to devise their own coverage patterns, and with that to enhance the subsidy margin under the PDS (public distribution system) should they so choose.

The Centre's food supplement could have been loaded onto MGNREGS, a national safety net based on self-selection into manual work on public projects. States would then remain free to devise their own food subsidy schemes. Self-selection through workfare is in any

1. Written in November 2011

case the best kind of safety net in a country where households move in and out of food sufficiency, as a function of a number of factors.

The chief defect in the present design of the bill is that the poor are identified through households rather than as a demographic segment cutting across households. The National Family Health Survey (NFHS), in its third round in 2005-06, revealed that 45 per cent of children under the age of three were physically stunted for lack of food, averaged across rural and urban India. The Integrated Child Development Scheme (ICDS) directly addresses this segment at present, regardless of the economic status of the household from where they originate. Luckily, ICDS centres have been retained in the latest version of the bill as a food distribution point, in place of the large one-time cash receipt proposed as a replacement for ICDS in some quarters. Cash payments will instantly be loaned out on informal credit markets, and will not be sequestered for food purchases.

How effective is the ICDS as an access channel for the most vulnerable segment of the Indian population, children under three? Luckily, the NFHS itself collected data on access to the ICDS, and these data for rural India have now been analysed in an excellent recent paper by Monica Jain. The ICDS works in two channels. Children in the 0-2 age group get a daily food grain entitlement for the mother to take home, and they do not have to walk very far to get it because 91.5 per cent of rural villages are reported in the paper to have an ICDS centre. Older children in the 2-5 age group get cooked food at the ICDS centre *in situ*.

The paper reports that the physical stature of girl children in the 0-2 age group whose mothers accessed the facility daily was higher, relative to other girl children of the same age. For boys, the difference was not statistically significant. These results are encouraging and plausible. Female infants are better fed when the cost of feeding them (and the lactating mother) goes down. Male infants are fed the same even when food is not free. For children in the 2-5 age group fed daily on site, ICDS children were no better off than other children in the age group.

However, the NFHS data reveal that only 6 per cent of the potential catchment of children of age 0-2 actually accessed the take home food ration on a daily basis. In the higher age group, only 14.5 per cent accessed the free food at the centre daily. If this is supply constrained, it suggests that the food bill will work on the ground only with better inventory monitoring at ICDS nodes.

The ICDS is the only scheme which directly targets the most vulnerable segment of the Indian population – children under three and their mothers. The retention of this channel is the best feature of the final version of the Food Security Bill.[2]

2. However, in the absence of a specified carve-out share, its fiscal support is not underwritten.

61 Confronting *Kharif* 2015

The prospect of a sub-normal monsoon is never good news, but [in 2015] it comes on top of a *rabi* harvest destroyed by being rained on at the wrong time, and a spate of farmer suicides. The only option remaining is to turn monsoon adversity into an opportunity for closer inspection of water usage in agriculture. We need to look at cultivation pathways that generate more output per unit input of water. We also need to release farmers from the clutches of the corporate seed mafia.

It is here that a miracle solution, which has been on offer in this country for at least 15 years, needs to be pressed into speedy action. No, this is not genetically modified seed. It is just a system of intensive cultivation that cuts water requirement in half, uses less seed, less fertiliser and less pesticide, and delivers higher output per acre by anywhere from 20 to 100 per cent. Initially developed for rice alone, it now extends to other crops such as wheat and sugarcane as well.

Called the System of Rice Intensification (SRI), it is an altered method of planting and cultivation rather than an altered seed, and thus holds promise for preserving the rich crop diversity of India from being drowned by the corporate seed mafia. In the context of other crops, SRI changes to System of Crop Intensification (SCI), replacing the word rice by crop. It offers the best hope for insulating the country's crop production from the fall in rain predicted by climate change scientists. The coming monsoon-deficient *kharif* season offers a great opportunity to test its promise.

Too good to be true? Data on relevant parameters of SRI are available on the website of the Cornell College of Agriculture and Life Sciences (*sri.cals.cornell.edu*). Cornell University is at the forefront of popularising SRI, through the untiring efforts of Norman Uphoff, a political science professor oddly enough, who works on rural development and happened upon SRI in Madagascar, where it originated.

Tripura leads Indian states, with 40 per cent of rice cultivation now practising SRI. Clearly, the rate of adoption in any state will be driven by the commitment of the state agriculture department, and here there are a number of political obstacles to overcome. First, the agricultural scientist fraternity sees SRI as scientifically unsupported, since it originated not in a laboratory but in the field. Second, there is powerful opposition stemming from the weight of rice planting practices over the centuries. Surely, so the argument goes, farming practices embodying the distilled wisdom of the ages could not be wrong, or improved upon?

In traditional rice transplanting, women wade their way down a row in a flooded field with a clutch of seedlings held in one hand, from which small clumps are detached and pushed into the soil at regular intervals. Rice originated in water abundant regions of the world, and this received practice, involving flooding of the field during transplanting and early growth of the plant, has been used in states like Punjab where poor drainage and high use of chemical fertiliser have had a devastating impact on soil quality. Punjab is said to be contemplating a ban on rice cultivation. What it could do instead is to switch to SRI.

The unique feature of SRI is that in place of a clump of seedlings, a single seedling is planted in slots at measured distances supplied with water, in a field otherwise kept unflooded. The source of the enhanced crop yield is said to be this very change, because the single seedling does not lose strength from having to battle its competitors for nutrients. The single seedling consequently is more sturdy, develops more tillers, and puts down deeper roots. SRI yields do well without chemical fertiliser, and pest infestation is reduced because of the wider spacing of plants.

SRI thus radically departs from tradition, with methods of planting and nurturing which are more artisanal. That also makes SRI more labour intensive. And there lies the catch today in rural India, where real rural wages have spurted up over the last 10 years. An embedded solution is however possible right there. The list of activities covered by Mahatma Gandhi National Rural Employment Guarantee Act (MGNREGA) can be extended to SRI cultivation. No better use of a public make-work scheme could surely be devised than one which directly increases agricultural productivity, instead of the indirect effects of building roads and other infrastructure, which are well known to be of poor quality because of materials to wages limits in the programme. There is a National Consortium on SRI which actually suggested this in a formal submission as far back as January 2012.

Based on that, a detailed suggestion was sent from the Planning Commission to the Ministry of Rural Development, justifying inclusion of SRI cultivation in the list of approved works for MGNREGA, on the grounds of the saving in water usage. However, like all such government documents, it specifies qualifying conditions that are impossible to monitor. Inclusion of SRI in the qualifying list was to be confined to blocks that declare themselves SRI blocks, and that too for a maximum of five years; and there were detailed prescriptions of how many person-days would be allowed for transplanting and weeding, which is quite impossible to monitor. These were further hedged by the overall eligibility conditions for MGNREGA labour on private land, the boundaries of which are defined in an unwieldy way. In the event, SRI did not get included in the MGNREGA list. Going forward, it would be best to include it as permissible, and leave it to the block *panchayat* to secure local consent.

In addition to higher labour requirements, SRI also calls for a hand-held mechanical weeder that turns over the weeds growing around the rice plant into the soil to enrich it. This holds the key to the reduced requirement of chemical fertiliser. The traditional flooding of rice plots tends to kill off weeds that do not thrive in excess water, unlike the rice plant. With SRI, these weeds grow unchecked. The weeder calls for an additional fixed expenditure of roughly ₹1,000 for a farmer switching to SRI cultivation. A subsidy on this device would be far below present subsidies on irrigation water, electricity for pumping up ground water, fertiliser and pesticide.

The global spread of SRI is impressive. SRI cultivation is now estimated to be practised in over 50 countries (essentially all countries which grow rice), with empirical evidence of enhanced yield ranging from 20-100 per cent, 90 per cent reduction of seed, and upto 50 per cent water savings. It is unquestionably the climate-smart way to go. In terms of cost of cultivation to the farmer, SRI saves massively on seed, water, fertiliser and pesticide, but adds to labour cost, and there is of course the one-time fixed cost of the weeder.

The International Rice Research Institute (IRRI) in Manila has only recently granted its imprimatur to SRI, with space on its website. You have to search for it though, under the tab "news", and within that, under "hot topics". The description of SRI falls short of total endorsement, describing it as a flexible package of crop practices which renders it a "challenge for evaluation and assessment", as against a menu of practices that is science-based, with "a solid track record of performance". IRRI explicitly states that it will refrain from research comparing SRI to other cropping practices, and will stay with its policies of disseminating only scientifically proven improvements. At the same time, IRRI declares its willingness to work with farmers practising SRI. By this, and links to the Cornell website, IRRI has finally conceded that SRI is worth mentioning, even though it did not jump out of a lab.

The reasons impelling adoption by farmers of SRI, even with its present lack of scientific endorsement, is that it scores in cost over the best management practices recommended by IRRI and other pillars of the establishment, predicated as those are on expensive hybrid seed bought from multinationals, and intensive application of water, chemical fertiliser and pesticide.

Paddy cultivation is the single biggest consumer of water in India. Even if the incremental yield is zero, the saving in water usage alone makes SRI the climate-smart way to go. Leading states like Tripura could be entrusted with the task of disseminating SRI methods to other paddy cultivating states. It is not too late to start with an SRI push for *kharif* 2015.

The timing of the news of a possibly sub-normal monsoon could not be worse. We have just had a parade of welcome price data. March 2015, the last month of the concluded fiscal year, showed wholesale prices as having fallen year-on-year for the fifth straight month. Retail consumer prices did rise in March year-on-year but, at 5.17 per cent as against 5.37 per cent in February, was the lowest in three months. We wanted the monsoon to rain on this parade. [1]

1. The prospects for the monsoon of 2015 remained uncertain even into mid-July. June saw above normal precipitation, which held out hope for the remaining monsoon months to follow. The case in this essay for SRI cultivation remains robust, even with the prospect of a good monsoon.

62 The Sen-Bhagwati Debate

The provocation for the latest face-off between Sen and Bhagwati was the book by Jean Dreze and Amartya Sen published in June 2013, titled *An Uncertain Glory: India and its Contradictions*. Books take production time of six months or so, and a minimum of a year for manuscript writing and editing. This book therefore would have been conceived no later than the end of calendar year 2011, at a time when India seemed confidently set on high growth. After a brief downward blip with the global crash to a (still respectable) growth rate of 6.7 per cent in 2008-09, the economy sprang back to an annual growth average of 8.75 per cent over the two years 2009-2011. In that context, the book's message was that high growth carries no glory when commensurate benefits do not flow to the population, in the most basic terms of eliminating food deprivation.

Two years down the line, we have tottered off that high growth path. What seemed a low point in 2008-09 was way above average growth achieved recently. [GDP growth in 2013-14 was estimated by the old series at 4.7 per cent, well below the 6.7 per cent reached in 2008-09. By the new series, the real growth in 2013-14 was 6.9 per cent.] Indians who can access a book costing 20 pounds sterling in the (depreciating) rupee equivalent are not feeling the glory of anything, least of all high growth [people do not experience the buoyancy suggested by the revised growth rates estimates in the new GDP series].

Dreze and Sen in their public pronouncements heavily support the Food Security Bill (FSB), whose major focus in terms of expansion, as distinct from mere incorporation of pre-existing schemes, is an increase in the number of targeted households under the PDS (public distribution system). The Integrated Child Development Scheme (ICDS), which targets pregnant women and pre-school children directly, and the mid-day meal scheme which operates through schools, are included within the ambit of the FSB as they stand, but the expansion in coverage of the Bill is focused on the PDS.

The malnutrition situation among women and children in India today is catastrophic. Household targeting is in general a risky way by which to reach these most vulnerable and deserving demographic groups. Within-household disparities in the distribution of food are hardwired into the culture, and will not change just because the ration card is issued in the name of the senior-most female in the household. Since the ICDS already has an infrastructure in place covering 90 per cent of all villages, if the data from the National Family Health Survey (NFHS) of 2005 are to be believed, this was the scheme which should have been clearly prioritised and deepened, with two meals a day in place of one. With this, the PDS could have been gradually phased out except for the Antyodaya scheme for the very poorest households.

The FSB also carries an additional cash component for pregnant women. If this is effected through the household entitlement, women as individuals cannot carry it with them when they move, in accordance with widespread (if not universal) custom, away from their marital to their natal home for the period before and after the birth. With the ICDS, they can. The ICDS does however suffer from high leakage. Dreze and Sen could have examined why existing outcomes of these schemes are so pitiable, instead of admonishing the country for indifference to poor outcomes.

The FSB will undoubtedly expand the ambit of subsidised grain, through the fractured and fractional pathways of the PDS, but the income equivalent to the recipients cannot possibly counter the continuing rise in the prices of non-grain protein foodstuffs. As any Indian mother can verify, a child does not consume a lot of grain, but it does need milk and other protein supplements. Any rise in milk consumption by the young who need it will only drive up prices even further unless something is done on the supply side, and soon. At present, one dollar per day in purchasing power parity terms buys less than a half litre of milk.

Structural moves to raise dairy productivity will be too slow to yield immediate dividends, but there are immediate actions possible, like subsidising farm equipment that helps preserve crop residue for use as livestock fodder. Mechanical harvesters, whose use is spreading rapidly, leave standing crop residue. This residue is actually being burned today in the grain-bowl states of Punjab and Haryana. Fodder has shot up in price also because it is being exported to the Middle East, and has been a major driver of milk inflation. Clearly the fodder price rise has not been sufficient to provide a market-led incentive for preserving crop residue, but by then milk would have been driven out of reach for most of the Indian population.

Removing supply side constraints in food production will call for messy and multiple interventions, in consultation with the nationwide network of agricultural universities. Three among the four protagonists in the big debate are non-resident Indians looking for elegant single-point solutions from afar. We have within the country whole institutes, with resident experts in agricultural and food technology, including post-harvest preservation, equipped to advise us on what needs to be done on the supply side. The best feature of the FSB is actually section 39, in conjunction with Schedule III, which does mention supply side bottlenecks in the production of food, but with a limited focus on foodgrain.

Jagdish Bhagwati and Arvind Panagariya also have a recent book with a self-explanatory title: *Why Growth Matters*. They argue for public investment in infrastructure, but with too much reliance on market cues for comfort. They do however highlight the need for reform of labour laws, a key and continuing deficiency in the policy configuration.

Because factories cannot fire labour on the formal payroll, they get flexibility under the radar through labour contractors. The service tax payable on the contract is deducted from the wage payable, several times over if there is a sub-contractor chain. A more regressive tax system can scarcely be imagined. Formal hiring flexibility, with factory labour getting pay parity and all benefits due for the duration of their hire, would surely be far better.

63 Social Sector Expenditure in India 1991-2014[1]

Public expenditure in India is classified under two major heads, developmental and non-developmental. Social sector expenditure has been obtained here from the developmental sub-heads 'Social and Community Services', which includes core components of social expenditure like education and health, and 'Rural Development' (principally rural employment schemes). To these have been added some from the non-developmental head, such as calamity relief, social security and welfare, transfers to the third tier of local government (for delivery of local public goods), and the food subsidy.

The share of social expenditure so defined, in aggregate expenditure consolidated across Central and state governments for the latest year (2013-14), and aggregated across current and capital accounts, has risen over the 10 years 1991-2014 (see Figure 63.1), and crossed the 30 per cent mark in 2007-08. Although local expenditure is not explicitly added onto aggregate expenditure, it is almost exclusively funded through transfers from above, and is therefore implicitly included in the aggregate obtained here.

In the latest year, 2011-12, for which confirmed actual expenditure estimates are available, the share of social expenditure stood at 33 per cent of the aggregate, and at 8.6 per cent of GDP. The estimates for later years are subject to revision, but provisionally had gone up to 9.5 per cent of GDP in 2013-14. In absolute terms, social expenditure amounted to nearly ₹18 per capita per day in 2011-12; by 2013-14 the budgeted figure had gone up to nearly ₹25, or about PPP (purchasing power parity) $1.5.[2] This is total departmental expenditure under the

1. This is an updated version of a blog titled "Fiscal Federalism, Social Expenditure and Equity - India's Approach" posted in June 2010 on *http://www.indiapolicyforum.org*.
2. Using the IMF October 2014 issue of the PPP equivalent for the 2013 US dollar, at ₹16.8.

various heads, and therefore includes salaries of public officials in the relevant departments, but excludes pensions for retired personnel.

Figure 63.1

Share of Social Expenditure in Consolidated Expenditure of Government (Per cent)

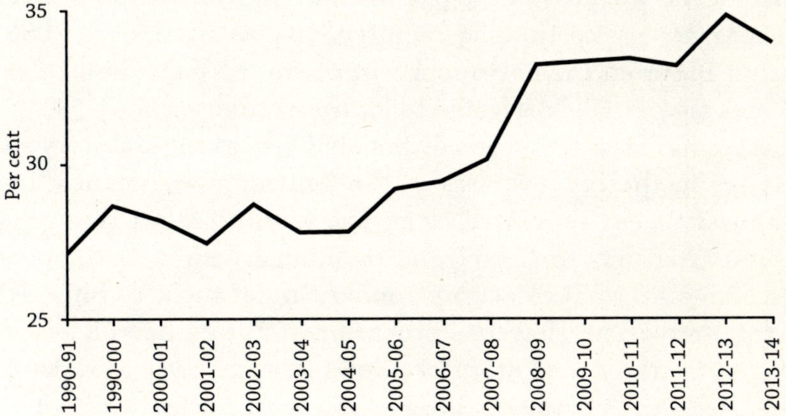

Notes: Consolidated expenditure sums across Centre and all states, taken here in aggregate across capital and current expenditure. Social sector expenditure is taken here as the sum of the developmental sub-heads 'Social and Community Services' (which includes education and health) and 'Rural Development' (principally rural employment schemes), with some elements of non-development expenditure added on (calamity relief, social security and welfare, transfers to the third tier of local government, and the food subsidy). Expenditure on scientific research was deducted from the total for Social and Community Services.

Source: All data are sourced from Indian Public Finance Statistics, an annual publication of the Ministry of Finance. The latest issue, dated August 2014, carries budget estimates for 2013-14, pre-final estimates for 2012-13, and finalised accounts for all preceding years.

The constitution assigns responsibility for social functions largely to subnational states,[3] but states' share in social expenditure has actually fallen to 73 per cent, from 79 per cent 10 years previously. Large national (Central government) schemes for education, health, and the rural employment guarantee have moved into the social space, motivated in part by impatience with social outcomes, but resulting in blurring of responsibility.

The drop in the relative share of states is because of the Centre having initiated large social expenditure schemes for rural employment

3. Social expenditure, under the Indian constitution, is functionally assigned largely to subnational state governments, who in turn are required after the constitutional amendments of 1993 to devolve responsibility over time to the third tier of local government. A few functions like education are listed in the constitution as concurrent functions, to be shared between the Central government, and states.

(the National Rural Employment Guarantee of 2005),[4] school education, and health. These programmes are designed by the Central government and executed through deconcentrated (locationally decentralised but reporting to the Centre) implementation agencies at field level, with co-funding at the margin by states in prescribed percentages. The co-funding requirement has risen since 2008-09, as is visible from the bottoming out of states' share. Some Central schemes are partially delegated to local government.

There has also been a steady but slow rise in the statutory shares of states in the tax revenues of the Central government. Finance Commissions are appointed every five years to re-set these shares. Statutory transfers are (largely) unconditional, with those components prescribing sectoral directions amounting at most to one-fifth of the total provision. However, other non-statutory flows have clearly adjusted for the rise in statutory flows in such a way as to keep the share of state governments in aggregate expenditure within a 50-55 per cent band (see Figure 63.2).

Aggregate social expenditure as measured here includes transfers to local government. These incorporate both transfers from states and the rising statutory flow prescribed by Finance Commissions from the Centre for local government, which are routed through states as required under the Constitution. In 2013-14, these together amounted to 1.5 per cent of aggregate expenditure across all categories, and 4.5 per cent of aggregate social expenditure.

But that is only the unconditional flow to local government. There are also function-specific transfers from states to local government, which vary widely across states (but are not very large in any case). A more substantial flow is from expenditure under some Central schemes, such as the MGNREGS, where a minimum of 50 per cent must be devolved to rural local government, with a fair degree of discretionary latitude.

4. Later renamed as the Mahatama Gandhi National Rural Employment Guarantee Scheme, MGNREGS.

Figure 63.2

Share of States in Aggregate Social and Total Expenditure (Per cent)

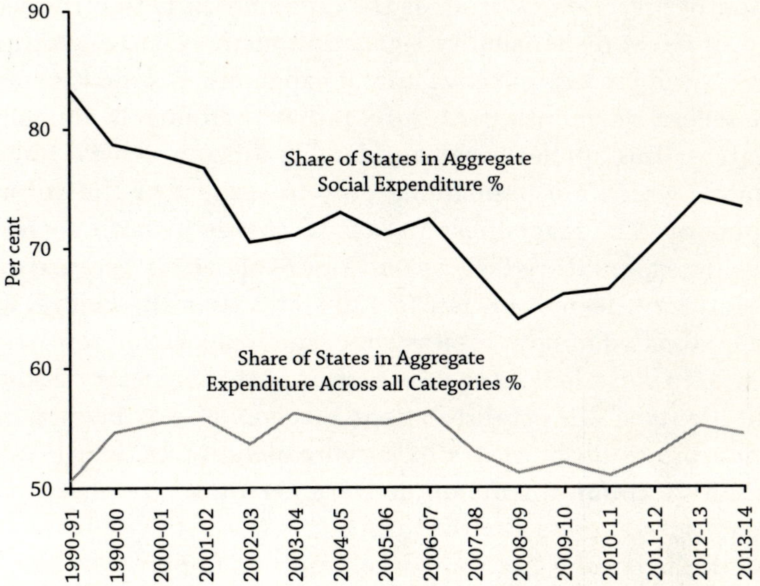

Source: See Figure 63.1.

The difficulty is that there is a data vacuum on receipts and expenditures of local government. This is addressed by the Thirteenth Finance Commission which, in its report for the horizon 2010-2015 tabled in Parliament in February 2010, substantially enhanced the statutory transfers from the Centre to local government, subject to conditionalities designed to improve fiscal reporting of flows to local government, and accounting and audit at local level. By the end of the next quinquennium, these institutional improvements should enable a better picture of the extent to which social expenditure is devolved to the third tier.

The Commission also attempted, for the very first time, to incentivise improved social outcomes by pegging one of the absolute grants for states to improvements during the grant horizon 2010-2015 in the IMR (infant mortality rate). These kinds of forward incentives were not possible earlier because of lack of reliable real-time data on critical social indicators.

Another recommendation of the Commission is that the second round of fiscal responsibility legislation at the Centre, starting in 2010-11, will be fully effective only if expenditure commitments are made several years into the future, rather than merely annually, as at present. This applies with considerable force to Central transfers to states, which are predictable only in respect of the statutory component. The jaggedness in states' shares in both social and aggregate expenditure (see second figure above) is because of the non-statutory element in transfers to states from the Centre, which are subordinated in both total volume, and in allocation to particular schemes, to variations from year to year at the budgetary discretion of the Centre.[5] Uncertainty about receivables has been a factor in underprovision by states of social expenditures, which call for expenditure commitments on delivery personnel (teachers, health workers) several years into the future.

With the current fiscal pressure, resulting in part from the fiscal stimulus sanctioned after the global crash of 2008, there is heightened awareness of the need to improve outcomes so that social expenditure effectively translates into better social equity.

Starting with fiscal year 2014-15, some of the larger schemes, such as the MGNREGS, flow to state government exchequers directly. This will show up in fiscal accounts as state government expenditure, and as a discontinuous upward shift in the share of state governments in social expenditure.

The shift to direct flow to state governments after a period of decline in state shares marks a decisive recognition of the need to decentralise expenditure downwards, for better alignment with spatially varying priorities and preferences.

5. In a paper in *India Policy Forum 2007-08* (cited in footnote 2, chapter 49), I demonstrate that the year-to-year changes in the statutory share of aggregate flows to states responds with a two-year lag to political fractionalisation in the Indian federation.

64 Inequality Within States

The hoopla surrounding election results in India is reminiscent of nothing so much as a horse race (...and X romps home the winner!). The difference is that for the horse and its handlers, the work is done when the race is over. For the winners in the recent round of state elections,[1] the work is yet to begin, or in the case of incumbent victories, the work continues.

Elected governments have to meet the expectations of a population alerted as never before to their unfilled needs from government. Disease, lack of sanitation, illiteracy and lack of access to transportation crowds into their lives like smog, and they want it waved away. The magnitude of what needs to be done on multiple fronts is huge, and the intensity with which the voter demands action is commensurate with the deprivation to which they have long been subjected.

Because of fiscal constraints, no state government can provide its entire population with any particular service all at once. Since universal coverage can only be an eventual target, what matters is the spatial manner in which that target is approached. This is because the public goods that lie at the core of what governments are supposed to provide are limited in their spatial reach. A functioning public toilet in one slum area is not accessible to residents of another. So while moving towards a target, when coverage is nowhere near universal, it is important to ensure equality of access in all areas of the state, at whatever fractional level it might be.

Although there has been some prominence lately in national discourse on inequalities between states, drummed up principally by Bihar, the issue of fair allocation of fiscal resources flowing from Centre to states is largely resolved (which is not to deny that there

1. This essay was written in early 2014, and refers to the same round of state elections in late 2013 referred to in chapter 17.

remains immense scope for improvement). But what has not attracted as much attention is the very considerable inequality existing within states. This issue arises if at all in the context of states with a Maoist problem, or in the current Andhra partitioning, but no one actually questions budgetary allocations between districts within states for the very simple reason that these are not known.

Most public services in states have not been functionally transferred to local bodies, and are still done by line departments of state governments. The allocation of funds between districts would of course be subordinated to some kind of administrative guidelines, if not very tight formulae, but these are not hung out in the courtyard for all to see. They lie buried in files and could only perhaps be uncovered by an application under the Right to Information.

But that is not necessary, as it turns out. There is a Census Directory that comes out separately for villages and towns in all states some years after the Census. The 2011 Census Directory is not yet out,[2] but that for 2001 was out in 2007, and even though the data pertain to 2001, they yield a lot of information on the cross-district patterns of allocation at less than universal levels of provision.

The great problem in all states in India is that districts are very uneven in size. In a sense, this mirrors the problem at national level as well, where the government has to divide fiscal flows equitably between states varying massively by population and area. But because of the formulaic and very public way in which it is done at the Centre, the allocation is known.

At state level, likewise, districts vary enormously in size by population, and even more by number of village habitations. In an exercise I did for 20 large states using the 2001 Village Directory, I found that the per cent of villages that had a primary school or medical facility within the village was not lower in districts with a larger population (except in two states). Clearly, budgetary allocations do accommodate variations in district population for the most part. But in 18 of the 20 states, the per cent of villages covered was systematically lower in districts where the population was splintered

2. The 2011 directory was eventually placed on the website in mid-2015.

into larger numbers of villages. Gujarat and Tamil Nadu were the two exceptions, where there was no fiscal penalty for village splintering.

In 9 of the 18 states, more splintered districts had a higher percentage of tribal population; in four states, they had a higher percentage of scheduled castes. There you have it – what a formula failure can do for systematic deprivation of a demographic group, even while avowed policy at both state and Central levels is to have special budgetary provisions for disadvantaged castes and tribes. These supplementary budget provisions for scheduled castes and tribes can do nothing to correct a fundamental defect in the formula used for mainstream budgetary allocations.

Budgetary allocation formulae are the kind of deep structural underpinning that very few state governments bother about particularly. Not surprisingly, in the recent round of state elections, a large minority among voters in tribal constituencies rejected all the candidates on offer.

Fortunately, this error can be very easily corrected by states adopting adjustment for number of villages rather than population in budgetary allocations between districts. Even better would be a reorganisation of districts in all states into jurisdictions of roughly even size by number of villages. District boundaries are not as sacrosanct as state boundaries and should in principle pose fewer obstacles to re-sizing. The only objections to this might come from economists, for whom geographical redefinition introduces an unwanted discontinuity in time-series data at district-level.

But how important are public services anyway for the re-election prospects of a party in power? Is the alternative of giving out subsidised foodgrain a better alternative? From the recent poll results, the best inference would seem to be that subsidised foodgrain does work in favour of the party in power, if it is effectively delivered, as in Chhattisgarh, but not if it is promised but not delivered, as in Delhi and Rajasthan.

65 Financial Inclusion

The Committee on Comprehensive Financial Services for Small Businesses and Low Income Households (the Nachiket Mor Committee on financial inclusion) has delivered a detailed report in a very short time. The architecture it envisions for a more inclusive financial structure recommends, in essence, moving away from the current structure of several overlapping full-service banks offering a comprehensive array of services over the entire country, towards functionally differentiated and regionally segmented banks.

The report recognises that the poor save; that they need a safe, interest-earning formal repository that is easily accessible in the face of income and event risk; and that the mobile phone network, supplemented by business correspondents, is the best way by which to reach vast swathes of the hinterland. It recommends that the present network of pre-paid instruments and e-wallets, provided in a limited way by a few authorised mobile phone service companies, be allowed to grow into payments banks which will allow cash withdrawals.[1]

But these payments banks will not engage in the task of providing local credit. They will be required to invest the entirety of their funds in government securities of the kind that satisfy the SLR (statutory liquidity ratio) of commercial banks today. With this, the report envisions that the SLR of commercial banks can be brought down, since there will be a much wider base of banks sharing the burden, thus setting the stage for corresponding release of commercial bank funds for other lending. In fact, it is envisioned that the SLR of commercial banks can eventually be reduced to zero.

If all savings going into payments banks are channelled into government securities in this manner, the architecture would work like a giant suction pump putting new catchment savings to work for

---

1. This recommendation preceded the Jan Dhan Yojana, announced on 15 August 2014, which by June 2015 had achieved 15 crore new bank accounts of the previously unbanked within the network of full-service public sector banks. These new accounts are expected to set the foundation for direct bank transfers of benefits under a number of welfare schemes.

government, but disregarding the credit needs of the savers. In the structure we have at present, provincial branches of national banks have tried to grapple with the problem of deploying local deposits towards local credit, but not very effectively. RRBs (regional rural banks) and co-operative banks were set up for exactly that purpose, but were beset by capture and mismanagement. SHGs (self-help groups) were devised to channel the savings of groups of the poor into meeting their credit needs. They have been effective in some regions but not in others.[2]

But the new payments banks offering the facility of banking through mobile telephones will successfully compete away the deposit base of local banks and branches, and credit will become that much harder to access in the hinterland. If another of the report's recommendations is implemented – that payments banks must offer at least one type of deposit at a nominal rate of interest exceeding the rate of consumer price inflation – other deposit collecting institutions will either have to follow suit, or risk losing their deposits altogether. Even without that, the payments banks will sweep up hinterland savings, so that it is vital that some of their deposits go into meeting local credit needs. The first correction necessary therefore is that payments banks must invest to some extent in the wholesale banks which, the report visualises, will fund the banks assigned the task of providing retail credit.

The idea of wholesale banks funding retail credit providers is a good idea in itself, because it helps to pool risk, but unless payments banks are required to place a mandated minimum with wholesale banks, the architecture will defeat rather than promote better access to credit, surely a key dimension of financial inclusion.

The report retains the task of retail credit provision in the rural hinterland with the present structure of local branches of national banks, RRBs and cooperative banks. These networks in their present

2. The credit needs of small borrowers has been addressed in the Union Budget for 2015-16, which envisions the setting up of a Micro Units Development Refinance Agency (MUDRA) with a corpus of ₹20,000 crore, and a credit guarantee corpus of ₹3,000 crore. The risk-sharing model and provision for recourse have to be carefully designed so that there is no perverse incentive for reduction of due diligence by the primary lender.

state do not inspire much confidence, least of all in their ability to engage in arm's length diligence in assessing lending risk. But the report has very little to say on how their functioning could be improved. Nor does it survey what by now is a fairly large literature on SHGs, to identify why it works in some regions and not in others.

A further deficiency is that credit access is dealt with as a spatial issue, which it is to some degree, but not entirely. In urban India, where physical access is near total, transactional access to credit is close to zero, especially for service providers, who are typically nomadic between and within cities, and may have no urban address at all. These groups require credit outreach of the kind the report does not discuss at all. The nomadic status of these groups calls for credit that is shaped to their needs, in both quantum (small) and duration (short), in the way moneylenders do, but at hopefully lower rates through better risk management than what moneylenders charge.

The structure envisioned retains the received framework of priority sector lending targets, adjusted (APSL) to give higher weightage to under-served sectors – agriculture and services. These are then interacted with higher weights for under-served districts to yield APSL multiples by district and sector, which will be revised every three years.

The APSL is too complex to work in practice. The report claims that these APSL weights will free banks to specialise in a sector in which they have expertise, but for that there is no need for weights. Weights would actually push banks without the necessary expertise to go into high weight sectors. All that is needed is that sub-targets within the PSL be done away with.

Larger APSL multiples of four are prescribed for lending to private companies installing and operating weather stations. This will move even such credit as presently flows to the poor into uses very far away from them.

There are no easy answers to the problem of meeting the needs of the poor for small loans in a default proof manner. What is certain is that APSL weights will not do the job.

66 The First Year

In the first year of the new government at the Centre,[1] the clearest new economic initiative has been the decisive shift towards financial inclusion as the pathway out of poverty – away from the exclusive reliance on household income supplements which had marked the approach of the previous 10 years.

The Jan Dhan scheme, targeting a savings bank account for every unbanked household, took off on 28 August 2014 in mission mode, and has been phenomenally successful in terms of sheer numbers. The 150 million new accounts have mostly gone to unbanked households, if not entirely – previously banked households may well have opened an account under the scheme for the insurance (life and accident) benefits carried. Banks have delivered commendably on a task for which they had very little lead time.

The scheme has ambitions extending beyond plugging subsidy leaks. It aims to pull a wider pool of savings into the formal banking system, and through an overdraft provision, to meet unforeseen liquidity needs at far lower rates than through the informal finance network that the poor presently access.

The poor save but on an unpredictable timeline, with upward spikes when there is a windfall income of some kind. Their borrowing needs are similarly unpredictable, driven by imperatives like medical expenditure. The informal financial world has successfully mediated between these saving and borrowing spikes, triumphing through ease of access, but at a high cost. The risk premium is built into both deposit and lending rates in that system. These informal systems operate well below the regulatory radar, because they are not large enough to even be called non-bank financial institutions. They are just individuals acting as saving aggregators, networked with other aggregators. The incidence of scams is high.

My personal efforts over the years to get a bank account for unbanked domestic workers failed repeatedly because formal deposit

1. Which took office on 26 May 2014.

rates were simply not high enough to pull them into the banking system, even when branch expansion had enabled ease of access. For a deposit of ₹100, even today a large sum for a poor family to save, a return of ₹1 or less per month was typically rejected as an absurdly low reward for the denial of present consumption that went into that saving. They operated at a different point on the risk-return trade-off.

Against that background, the success of the Jan Dhan scheme is most impressive. As of the latest figures on its website for mid-April 2015, the average deposit in the 150 million new accounts stands at a little over ₹1,000, although the burden of a non-zero deposit is actually carried by only one-third of the total number of accounts (by figures as of 31 January). The Rupay debit card that comes with the account has to be operated at least once every 45 days in order to keep its validity, which in turn is necessary for the insurance benefits going with the scheme. In this way, account holders are incentivised to engage continually with the bank.

Continual operation of the debit card will be something of a challenge in rural areas where the BC (banking correspondent) network has not become quite the effective last-mile link hoped for. An annual survey of BCs by the Reserve Bank of India (RBI) shows a high attrition rate, arising from the low volume of business to which their compensation structure is necessarily tied. The BC was part of an earlier financial inclusion thrust driven by RBI, which in its first phase over 2010-2013 covered nearly 75,000 previously unbanked villages with a population over 2,000, with either BCs or brick and mortar branches. Fortunately, the imminent licensing of India Post as a payment bank will add to the last mile reach of the banking network.

Urban India should pose much less of a zero deposit problem. The avidity with which the urban unbanked responded to Jan Dhan was not even the prospect of insurance or overdrafts so much as subsidised access to cylinders of LPG (liquefied petroleum gas) for cooking fuel, which became possible for the first time with evidence of a bank account into which the subsidy could directly be transferred. The scheme named PAHAL started 1 January 2015. PAHAL carries expenditure saving extending far beyond the subsidy itself, since there is an initial price advantage just from switching to a regulated gas supplier. Previously, access to LPG cylinders had to be hedged by severe user and residence identification, so as to protect against commercial profit making when the subsidy went to the oil company directly. That did not prevent the cylinders from circulating in the unregulated market anyway, at exorbitant prices. All but the very poor in urban India bought cooking gas at those prices because of the impossibility of buying or gathering enough firewood.

PAHAL is working. There are many triumphant recipients, reported to have reached 128.7 million (some of whom may be seriously non-poor), with every receipt spreading word that this is a promise that has been kept. And 40 million ghost customers have been weeded out. As time goes on, timely supply of gas cylinders will be threatened by obstruction from those previously making money off diverting those ghost sales into the unregulated market. So the protection of Jan Dhan as a promise goes beyond mere functioning of the scheme at the bank end. There has to be strict oversight on whether the ancillary benefits of the new account are being duly delivered as promised. And that is the key to whether Jan Dhan as an anti-poverty scheme succeeds or fails. If lower risk is what formal finance offers against informal finance, that prospectus has to be scrupulously respected.

The official world in India is very good at doing things in mission mode. We run the Kumbh Mela every 12 years with a flow of millions of pilgrims, doing sanitation and solid waste for that massive gathering without disease and disaster. But we are unable to adequately manage everyday sanitation and solid waste removal where people live. Routine everyday systems call for regulatory protocols, and reporting formats and templates. As a people, we seem to have a cultural aversion to this kind of procedural regimentation. Paradoxically, the person best known in the world for tirelessly preaching the benefits of checklists is an American doctor of Indian origin, Atul Gawande.

Two additional insurance schemes have now been made available to all those with a bank account, for both accident and term life insurance, with a provision for auto deduction of the premia from the account to which the scheme is linked. The scheme for accident insurance carries a very modest premium of ₹12 per year, and covers both accidental disability and accidental death.

Together, these initiatives demonstrate a coherent and most commendable thrust towards reducing financial risk in the lives of the poor. The other major disability from which the poor suffer, the high price of credit, has been addressed (for consumption loans) through the overdraft facility attached to the Jan Dhan Account. The overdraft facility will accrue only after 'satisfactory' operation of the account for six months. The manner in which that clause is interpreted holds the key to reducing the number of zero accounts, and to ensuring that another default window does not open up for banks already under stress from loans gone sour.

For larger production loans, the Micro Units Development and Refinance Agency (MUDRA) has been launched, presently as a division of the Small Industries Development Bank (SIDBI). Whether MUDRA succeeds where National Bank for Agriculture and Rural Development (NABARD) and other such refinance channels have failed depends on how it is structured. Production loans for the poor typically ask for ₹25,000 or less, based on a business model which is no more than a hunch. Protection against default can only be secured through formation of groups who will mutually underwrite each other. MUDRA refinance has to be so structured that it will not reduce due diligence at the primary lending end.

It may be a good idea to involve *gram panchayats*, for registration of borrowing groups if nothing else. Cynics may argue that involving *panchayats* will be the surest way to disastrous capture by local elites. Perhaps. The key is to have group formation at town hall meetings of the *gram sabha*, rather than to delegate it to the *panchayat* council.

If there is a downside to the financial inclusion initiative, it is that the burden of carrying financial inclusion to the poor falls on banks at a time when they are already under very severe stress. The hope however is that with a larger universe of bank connections to the poor, priority sector lending can be better directed towards meaningful production loans, rather than disbursed regardless of the quality of the loan application just to meet a disbursement target. With more effort towards formation of mutual guarantee groups, the default rates on priority sector lending should hopefully come down.

Index